Between the Lines

IMAGINING THE AMERICAS
Caroline F. Levander and Anthony B. Pinn, Series Editors

Imagining the Americas is a new interdisciplinary series that explores the cross-fertilization among cultures and forms in the American hemisphere. The series targets the intersections between literary, religious, and cultural studies that materialize once the idea of nation is understood as fluid and multiform. Extending from the northernmost regions of Canada to Cape Horn, books in this series move beyond a simple extension of U.S.-based American studies approaches and engage the American hemisphere directly.

Millennial Literatures of the Americas, 1492–2002
Thomas O. Beebee

The Plantation in the Postslavery Imagination
Elizabeth Christine Russ

The Interethnic Imagination
Caroline Rody

Between the Lines
Monique-Adelle Callahan

Religious Liberties
Elizabeth Fenton

Between the Lines

Literary Transnationalism and African American Poetics

by
Monique-Adelle Callahan

UNIVERSITY PRESS

OXFORD
UNIVERSITY PRESS

Oxford University Press, Inc., publishes works that further
Oxford University's objective of excellence
in research, scholarship, and education.

Oxford   New York
Auckland   Cape Town   Dar es Salaam   Hong Kong   Karachi
Kuala Lumpur   Madrid   Melbourne   Mexico City   Nairobi
New Delhi   Shanghai   Taipei   Toronto

With offices in
Argentina   Austria   Brazil   Chile   Czech Republic   France   Greece
Guatemala   Hungary   Italy   Japan   Poland   Portugal   Singapore
South Korea   Switzerland   Thailand   Turkey   Ukraine   Vietnam

Copyright © 2011 by Oxford University Press, Inc.

Published by Oxford University Press, Inc.
198 Madison Avenue, New York, New York 10016

www.oup.com

Oxford is a registered trademark of Oxford University Press

All rights reserved. No part of this publication may be reproduced,
stored in a retrieval system, or transmitted, in any form or by any means,
electronic, mechanical, photocopying, recording, or otherwise,
without the prior permission of Oxford University Press.
Library of Congress Cataloging-in-Publication Data
Callahan, Monique-Adelle.
Between the lines : literary transnationalism and African American poetics / Monique-Adelle Callahan.
    p. cm.—(Imagining the Americas)
Includes bibliographical references.
ISBN 978-0-19-974306-3 (cloth : acid-free paper) 1. Poetry—Black authors. 2. America—Literatures—19th Century—History and criticism. 3. Transnationalism in literature. 4. Poetics—History. 5. Slavery in literature. 6. Postcolonialism in literature. 7. Harper, Frances Ellen Watkins, 1825–1911—Criticism and interpretation. 8. Ayala, Cristina, b. 1856—Criticism and interpretation. 9. Souza, Auta de, 1876–1901—Criticism and interpretation. I. Title.
PN841.C35 2011
809.1′989607—dc22
2010028197

1 3 5 7 9 8 6 4 2
Printed in the United States of America
on acid-free paper

CONTENTS

Introduction
3

Chapter 1
Translations of Transnational Black Icons
in the Poetics of Frances Harper
42

Chapter 2
Signs of Blood: Redemption Songs and "American"
Poetry beyond Borders
59

Chapter 3
Write the Vision: Gender and Nation beyond Emancipation
74

Chapter 4
Prison Breaks: Modes of Escape in Auta de Souza's
Poetics of Freedom
96

Conclusion: Where Do We Go from Here? The Implications of Textual Migrations
114

Epilogue: *Afrodescendente* History As/And Transnational Poetics
123

Notes
149

Bibliography
165

Index
175

PREFACE

For the ancient Greeks, a poet was a *maker*. At its very root, the word *poet* meant someone who made, created, and authored through the act of writing. For centuries, at moments highly charged by political and social change, poets have walked what many have alleged to be a line between art and politics. One such period of change was the abolition eras spanning the second half of the nineteenth century. With slavery and women's rights at the forefront of national and transnational debate, men and women alike wrestled for political influence, social freedoms, and economic opportunity.

Women, however, were often also called on to be symbols of certain ideas and ideals: the idea(l) of a nation, the idea(l) of racial "purity," the idea(l) of moral clarity, and so on. To wear these hats, women were often either politely asked or legally required to be silent co-conspirators of a predominantly male public imagination.

But this is not a book about the sins of patriarchy. Nor is it a rallying cry for a brand of feminist revisionism. Instead, I want to take us back to language itself at one of its most concentrated forms: the poetic line. *Between the Lines* is a rigorous exercise in the reading of poetic texts in an effort to call attention to (and to call to attention) a group of voices whose individual and collective sound—produced by the clanging together of words against the rhetorical walls of racial slavery, abolition, and nationalism in the Western Hemisphere—called for a reinterpretation of history. At once within and between the boundary lines written for them, these writers used language poetically to recompose history and imagine new possibilities for their individual and collective lives. By engaging memory poetically they were the makers of new histories.

For students of nineteenth-century history there is a glaring truth: in the beginning the century, legal slavery existed; by the end of the century, it did not. This book examines how poets of African descent in the Americas, through the poetic use of language, endeavored to define and redefine freedom through the lens of slavery. I ask: how do we understand the ubiquitous specter of the slave in the poetic imagining of freedom in the New World during "abolition eras?" (By "abolition eras" I mean the second half of the nineteenth century, during which time the legally sanctioned system of slavery was officially wiped out of Western Hemisphere). I ask: how has the poetic use of language influenced and been influenced by a hemispheric vision of the Americas? How have poetic texts worked as instruments to redefine freedom and rewrite versions of a hemispheric American history? As the landscape of American cultures and languages evolves and our day-to-day experience of the world becomes increasingly global, how might the poetic use of language today shift us to yet another place in our social imagination?

An increasingly global culture, economy, and politics urges us to revisit the ways we read and interpret the stories we tell about our histories. Poetry is a particularly important entry point for this kind of inquiry. It challenges us to think about *how* language is functioning, not just *what* is being said. Furthermore, the poem, as a verbal performance, invites us to think about the speech act as a literary and political gesture. It is true that poems can use metaphor and metonymy in didactic ways and prose can express uncertainty and vacillation. Nevertheless, couched in a tradition of music and speech, poetry weds sound, rhythm, and form in a way that opens up even the most prosaic or didactic of poems to a different level of analytical scrutiny. This book features poems by North American poet Frances Harper (1825–1911), Cuban poet Cristina Ayala (1856–1936), and Brazilian poet Auta de Souza (1876–1901) as they showcase an existential and semiological tug-of-war—a dialectic—between slavery and freedom. These poetic texts serve as a surface on which to explore the intricacies of the power and presence of this dialectic in the modern history of the "American" imagination.

Race has loomed in the social and political imagination of the United States for generations. We tell stories about it to understand it, and we understand it through the stories we tell. The particular way in which race has been configured *literarily* has made the difference in the history of the Americas. Recent deliberations about the "mixed" racial ancestry of the first African American president of the United States, Barack Obama, remind us of the fact that the workings of race in the United States have much more to do with discourse than with DNA. The term *race* has been articulated through, by, and on the bodies of African descendants for centuries. But not just in the United States. Alongside the United States, two other countries sustained the practice of racial slavery well into the second half of the nineteenth century: Brazil and Cuba. If we look at rapidly developing Brazil, racial politics there also cast a shadow on the history of the Western Hemisphere. The popular myth of a "racial democracy" remains a cultural legacy, while the reality of glaring social disparities tells a different story about African descendants in Brazil. Cuba has also danced between a postabolition race consciousness among Cuban poets and intellectuals and a post-independence call for *cubanidad*—a unifying of Cubans across racial lines. As political, social, and economic change looms in the horizon in Cuba, it will become increasingly important to revisit the precursors to the modern Cuban imagination.

As Frances Harper, Cristina Ayala, and Auta de Souza wrestled with their observations of the world, the emergent poems suggested that freedom would never be a product of denotation but of imagination. That is to say, that the postslavery Americas would not be able to sustain an ideology of freedom delineated solely by legal or political documents. Instead, the Americas would have to engage in a dialectical battle between a history of slavery and a present pursuit after new freedoms.

One of the battlefields was the poetic text. The poetic texts examined here foreshadowed the dilemmas we face even today as we try to develop a new global language. We seek a language that acknowledges the presence of a history that lives on in geopolitically defined nations and at the same time recognizes the need to proactively defend human rights and define freedom today. As literary texts, poems are influenced by currents that complicate categories of race and defy geopolitical lines of nation. Poetry embraces the multivalent systems of language that make up our concepts of individual and collective history and community. The poetic text is a dynamic, internally complex "object." Its multiple and simultaneous meanings do not negate the importance of historical context and extratextual factors in analysis; rather, these factors are critical in both reading and writing poetry. Poetry provokes us to look at the points where dividing lines between national literatures and peoples become permeable. This book urges the reader to recognize the poem as a space of contention in which symbolic and metaphorical language reaches beyond the text to engage the world around it while at the same time preserving a contained aesthetic, an internal dialogue with itself, line by line.

ACKNOWLEDGMENTS

To God for making all possible.

To Professors Werner Sollors and Joaquim F. Coelho for their careful critique and incessant, unfailing support of the project at every stage. To Professor Evelyn Brooks Higginbotham for your feedback and guidance at the early stages of the project.

To Kathy George in the Department of Comparative Literature for your diligence in taking care of us students during your time at Harvard. To Carlos Varon in the department of Romance Languages and Literatures for your consultations on my Spanish translations and general copyediting. To Professor Steven Kaplan for your generous critique.

To my incredibly erudite undergraduate advisees, willing to lend their eyes and ears to the project: Aaron Frazier and Manny Antunes.

To *LitVerlag* for permission to republish a version of "Translations of Transnational Black Icons in the Poetics of Frances Harper: Brazil's Zumbi and Cuba's Maceo," from *Loopholes and Retreats: African American Writers and the Nineteenth Century*; to Dr. Luis Miletti for permission to republish an edited version of "Race and redemption in 19th century 'American' poetry across the Americas: Francis Harper's 'Deliverance' and Cristina Ayala's 'Redención,'" from *Negritud: Revista de Estudios Afro-Latinoamericanos*.

To my mother, Jeanette A. Callahan, for giving me the greatest head start I could ever ask for by being my first teacher.

To my father, Allen D. Callahan, for your advice, feedback, and exampleship.

To my beloved grandmothers: Olivia S. Estes, librarian at heart, and Judith Prescott, poet in spirit.

To my cheerleading team in the day-to-day trenches, for being consistent, for getting me across the finish line a whole person: Melanie S. Ramsey and Albert Owens-Kaplan.

A NOTE ON THE TRANSLATIONS

All translations in this book were done by the author unless otherwise noted.

Between the Lines

Introduction

Esta idea de colonización parece ya perfectamente afianzada, instalada. Pero la historia tiene sus sorpresas, y no se contaba con un elemento imprevisto: el de los esclavos africanos. Traído del continente africano, el negro que llega a América aherrojado, encadenado, amontonado en las calas de buques insalubres, que es vendido como mercancía, que es sometido a la condición más baja a la que puede ser sometido un ser humano, resulta que va a ser precisamente el germen de la idea de independencia.
[This idea of colonization seems to be perfectly secure, established. But history has its surprises, and didn't count on an unexpected element: that of African slaves. Brought from the African continent, the Negro who arrives in America chained, shackled, piled up in the hold of unsanitary ships, who is sold like merchandise, who is subjected to the lowest condition that to which a human being can be subjected, ultimately comes to be the very root of the idea of independence.]

—Alejo Carpentier (quoted in Pérez Cano 2004, 92–93)

The creative imagination has been colonized. . . . We are taught to believe, for example, that there is an American literature, that there is an American cinema, that there is an American reality. There is no American literature; there are American literatures.

—Toni Cade Bambara (1996, 140)

What Is Between the Lines (?):
A Comparative Literature by Nature

Poet Wallace Stevens called a poem the "cry of its occasion." For poets Frances Harper, Cristina Ayala, and Auta de Souza, that cry was that of peoples and nations looking for a way to escape from the inscriptions written on them by language and by law. The occasion was slavery—the condition or fact of being entirely subject to, or under the domination of, some power or influence—manifested in the inscribing of race and gender onto individual and national bodies (definition from *Oxford English Dictionary*). In her own way, each poet stepped into a tradition of writing born out of the legacy of transatlantic slavery in the New World. Their poems demonstrate how language itself—indentured poetically, imbibed politically—became the battleground on which to fight a failing syntax of individual and national identity.

During the abolition eras, the poetry of the New World had to articulate a national ethos and simultaneously amplify voices of dissent and discontent. Derek Walcott champions the New World poet even today as someone who actively defies the notion of history as a static entity. For Walcott, the New World writer "rejects the idea of history as time for its original concept as myth" and, with revolutionary daring, rejects a belief in "historic time." He shows the New World its "simultaneity with the Old," while at the same time carrying an "elemental vision of man," recognizing him as "a being inhabited by presences, not a creature chained to his past" (1996, 354). As Walcott so brilliantly suggests, the poet actively composes history. Her place in New World history is Adamic: she is not merely named but she *names*.

In a poem, language discloses its textures and demands the reader contend with the poem's use of rhyme, rhythm, its stoppages, its diction.[1] On one hand, the units of a poem function as metaphors, generating meaning through a relationship of similarity or familiarity. On the other hand, these units function metonymically by standing in for a larger network of interrelated differences, each amplifying—rather than canceling out—the other. A poem is at once integral and fragmented, at once whole and made up of distinct parts that resonate at multiple frequencies. It is—like the various imagined communities that comprise a nation, a "race," a gender community—characterized by fluidity rather than fixity.

In turn, my claim in this book is that the poetic texts examined here constitute an active process of composing history; they are not simply historicized. They give name to the nation and compose a historical narrative for its denizens. They are literary artifacts, bearing the vestiges of the past while provoking new interpretations. As visionaries and composers of New World history, Frances Harper, Cristina Ayala, and Auta de Souza are a part of a larger process of conceptualizing freedom in the New World that intertwines their poetics.

I use Harper's own transhemispheric poetic gestures to delimit the scope of this book. Harper's poems on Zumbi—leader of a Brazilian free slave society—and Cuban military leader Antonio Maceo draw our attention to the only two countries in which the practice of slavery outlasted that of the United States—Cuba and Brazil.[2] From Harper, I move to Cuban poet Cristina Ayala and Brazilian poet Auta de Souza, whose poetry features thematic and typological elements similar to Harper's. Ayala and Auta were both prolific poets and major literary figures in their time. Both linked their poetics to a larger national discourse. Through her use of allegory and iconography, Harper also implicitly links African Americans in the United States to a larger national project. Unlike Ayala and Auta de Souza, however, Harper goes even further to explicitly articulate a global vision. By exemplifying the kind of readings that can evolve from following one poet's transhemispheric allusions, I hope to both articulate the fundamentally transnational aspect of African American literature in the

United States and inspire more reevaluations of transhemispheric literary currents across national boundaries in *afrodescendente* literatures. (I more fully explain my use of the term *afrodescendente* later in this introduction.)

This book follows a long tradition of studies and anthological work on poetry from the black world across national boundaries: James Weldon Johnson's *Book of American Negro Poetry* (1922), Nancy Cunard's *Negro* (1934), and Lilyan Kesteloot's *Anthologie Négro-Africaine* (1992), among others. The poets examined in *Between the Lines* construct an alternative history in their poetry. Their work declares history a subjective and creative process. Though none was a slave, they avidly interrogate the relationship between slavery and freedom. Furthermore, they specifically address gender as it relates to nation-building. My readings of these poets aim to go beyond analysis of a racially or gender-defined canon of writers or writing. I ask, "What is the semiotic and literary relationship between slavery and freedom in the New World? How does their poetry succeed or fail at articulating this relationship? How do they instruct us about how a poetic use of language can both reinterpret history and create a new vision?"

As a comparative endeavor that focuses on poetry and involves translation, this project engenders certain inevitable challenges. I do not claim that these poetic texts indicate any form of transnational racial solidarity on the part of the poets. My comparative strategy does not ignore difference, but accounts for it by attending to the nuances of each individual text through close literary analysis and extensive contextual readings. But to what extent, in this case, can I justify bringing together a group of texts by poets linked only by virtue of a particular reading of history? What justifies entering a specific set of texts into a closed system to analyze them for similarity and difference?

The answer lies in the question. Any comparative impulse brings with it an implicit context that justifies the comparison. We make choices about how we conceive of our history. These choices help produce meaning. The meaning of a given poetic text and its relationship to other poetic texts is always inextricably linked to the interpretive influence of the accepted historical narratives that surround it. A poem, then, is always at once integral and interconnected at all times. We can say that it mirrors the flux of ideas and tropes throughout the Americas and the multiple imagined communities that inhabit African diasporic space.

The poets I discuss in this book use poetry to both interrogate and construct narratives about the history of slavery and its effects in the New World. In doing so, they project a kind of transnational "nation" of African descendents that is tentative and fluctuating in shape and is in constant negotiation with the postabolition nation-state. We see through these poetic texts that poetry and nation evolve in tandem. Derek Walcott's notion of history itself as a "literary process" reminds us that history and literature do not evolve separately but collaboratively. This "history" is an amalgam of narratives, a collaboration of stories in persistent flux, constantly being told and retold.

Cuban novelist and cultural critic Alejo Carpentier maintained that African slavery was a catalyst for definitions of freedom and independence in the Americas. In his essay, "Lo que el Caribe ha dado al mundo" (What the Caribbean Has Given to the World), he illustrates how the history of African slaves interrupts an illusory myth of colonial "discovery."[3] For Carpentier, African slavery formed the binary opposition necessary to define freedom in the New World.

These understandings of freedom also informed the narrative construction of "nation" as a concept. For Homi Bhabha, the nation is a reflection of ambivalent language and composed of partial meanings. His notion of ambivalence lends to understanding the poem, as the nation, becomes a site where the very process of history and the concept of nation is *negotiated*. As Bhabha suggests in the introduction to *Nation and Narration*, history itself can be "half-made because it is in the process of being made" (1990, 3). He reminds us of the ideological instability of the nation and its reliance on narrative to maintain its integrity. In this book, I am interested in how poetry—in its various forms (narrative, lyric, and didactic primarily)—has contributed to this process of narrating nation and how its borrowings and allusions actually challenge the idea of a nation as a whole ideological concept with definitive boundary lines. Furthermore, I ask what other forms of nation might have been invented in the Americas where many peoples were in diaspora and where the term "nation" was itself ambivalent in form.

Translation and Transnation

As a trilingual project and a theory of reading that links literary transnationalism and translation, this book conjures a unique set of complications.

Let me explain what I mean by transnationalism. Transnationalism is the phenomenon of reaching across or extending beyond predefined national boundaries. Transnationalism offers an alternative to a nation-based understanding of literature and history and an alternative way of theorizing literary texts. Additionally, it introduces translation as a fundamental element of any form of literary analysis. In *Translation and Identity in the Americas: New Directions in Translation Theory*, Edwin Gentzler identifies translation as a "permanent condition in the Americas" (2008, 5). Acknowledging that translation studies in the United States are a relatively recent evolution, Gentzler maintains that translation has been at the very heart of U.S. nation formation. For Gentzler, translation is the very mode by which cultures are constructed; it is not a "neutral site in the Americas, rather it is a highly contested one where different groups, often competing literary or political interests, vie for space and approval" (2008, 3).

In her analysis of Phillis Wheatley—whom she defines as the "invent[or] of transatlantic literature," Colleen Glennes Boggs highlights the multiple connotations of translation (2007, 2). Using Noah Webster's 1828 definition of the term *translation*, Boggs explains how translation depicts both the "literal sense of conveyance" or "movement across space" in the natural realm as well as the transition into a transcendent state in the spiritual sense (2007, 25). Just as a single word might be taken from one lexical context and translated into another for the purpose of attaining meaning, so can a symbolic figure be translated into an "other" lexicon defined by a different geographical, temporal, or cultural space. The act of translation bridges a perceived gap by showing that ultimately there is no gap, that meaning in an "other" context—be it linguistic or nonlinguistic—can be achieved through a bidirectional and persistent negotiation of one with an "other."

A poem in translation is itself a body subject to the inscriptions of "other" languages. It is a metaphor for the kind of encounters and exchanges between peoples that has characterized our national and international histories in the Americas. *Between the Lines* is both a project of comparative literature and a process of translation. The etymology of *to compare* (to pair together or bring together; Latin prefix *com-* + *par*) does not insist on an intrinsic similarity between compared objects, but rather emphasizes the act of bringing them together. In this case, bringing together certain poetic texts through a particular interpretation of cultural and national history in the Americas produces meaning. It signals the interconnectedness of concepts of freedom, slavery, and identity in the Americas. Translation in this context is both a necessary tool for placing texts in conversation as well as a process that belies any myth of fixity of meaning in the texts. As they converse with one another through various levels of translation, the texts acquire new degrees of meaning.

My readings of the poems in this book are themselves a form of translation. As an interpreter of the texts, I wield a degree of power over them. My decision to translate a specific set of poems and place them in a particular historical context is, in and of itself, an act of interpretive violence. These interpretations take on meaning beyond the text as I link them to various narrative histories in the Americas. The act of close reading using a hermeneutic that combines textual with contextual analysis is a vigorous act of translation.

Translations of any kind shed light on a corner of the world that some may never have been able to see otherwise. What texts actually get translated governs the perception nonspeakers of Spanish or Portuguese have of the range of literary voices that truly occupy these language spaces. This book expands the range of voices engaged in the literary critique of race, gender, and nationhood during the second half of the nineteenth century. I hope this initial gesture will lead to more comparative projects that give voice to those silenced by language hegemonies.

Projects that demand translation challenge the illusion of origin in a text, reminding us that the very process of reading is in and of itself a form of translation. As Willis Barnstone so aptly argues, reading is "translation and translation is reading," just as "writing is translation and translation is writing" (1993, 7). This fact, however, does not make a given reading any less *true*. The meanings of texts evolve through a perpetual process of textual and contextual interpretation. In this sense, reading is its own kind of poetics. Ultimately, the poetic texts examined in this book are not entirely fixed in meaning but acquire meaning through interaction, through a *reading between*.

Another form of translation involves a translation onto physical and textual bodies. In his discussion of Toni Morrison's poetic novel *Beloved*, Gentzler expands on this process of translation onto the body: "The story, the memory is translated into a semiotic sign system that extends beyond language, a scarring upon the body . . . the 'rememory' provides a kind of identification, a sense of one's roots and one's past, and offers a kind of healing, recreating history despite the massive oppression, and creating possibilities for a new inscription for the future" (2008, 181). One of the most salient of these inscriptions onto the body is the inscription we refer to as race. The category of afrodescendente literature inevitably invokes this term.

A number of scholars have delineated the particular definitions and manifestations of race in Brazil, Cuba, and the United States. Brazilian anthropologist Gilberto Freyre, for example, argued that racial mixing or miscegenation in colonial Brazil defined the relationship between African slaves and their Portuguese masters. This practice of miscegenation, Freyre maintained, produced a more fluid system of racial categorization in Brazil, described by the term "racial democracy." Racial democracy, according to Freyre, contrasted with the binary system in the United States. In *Slave and Citizen* (1946), Frank Tannenbaum claimed that manumission legislation allowed a racial democracy to evolve in Brazil. Carl Degler (1971) considered the high amount of racial mixing in Brazil, suggesting that it produced a "mulatto escape hatch"—an in-between space that prevented the evolution of a strict black–white binary. Marvin Harris drew attention to the "plethora of racial terms and the abstract and referential ambiguity surrounding their application" in Brazil (1964, 22).

Each of these theories of race in Brazil has been challenged over the past two decades in particular. Nevertheless, many of these nineteenth-century racial narratives maintain strength in the popular imagination. Edward E. Telles refers to the duality between what he calls the "twin pillars of Brazil's racial ideology"—racial democracy and whitening (2004, 45). Though on one hand the notion of a racial democracy invokes an ideology of racial plurality and equity, the ideal of whitening creates a color hierarchy that valorizes whiteness. One drop of white blood could, in fact, permit an individual to classify as the more idealized white (2004, 85). Nevertheless, the systems of valorization promulgated by Western racial ideologies produced a situation in contemporary Brazil where "as with race, one's color in Brazil commonly carries connotations about one's value according to the general Western racial ideology" (2004, 79).

Luiz Alberto Oliveira Gonçalves notes an ideological fusion between slavery and race. The "fusão ideológica entre 'escravidão', 'cor negra,' e 'imoralidade' de um lado," he writes, and the

> fusão entre "cor branca," "ideal moral-religioso" e "status de liberade," de outro lado, fez parte de uma discurso de dominação que foi "inventado" pelo clases dominantes (um discurso que justificava a exploração). (2003, 62)
>
> [The fusion between slavery, black, and immorality on one hand, and white, moral-religious ideal, and free status on the other, formed part of a dominant discourse that was "invented" by the dominant classes (a discourse that justified exploration).]

Over three hundred years of slavery in Brazil laid the foundation for both a culture of racial ambiguity and a precedent of color division, producing social relations, as Gonçalves goes on to say, that are based on "an ideology of mixture and ambiguity" (2003, 57).

A similar ideology of racial and cultural mixing, or *mestizaje*, characterizes Cuban intellectual and social history. Ethnomusicologist and scholar of Afro-Cuban culture Fernando Ortiz devised the term "transculturation" to describe various cultural phenomena in Cuba. According to Ortiz, transculturation signified the "complejísimas transmutaciones de culturas" (extremely complex transmutations of cultures) that comprised the Cuban nation (1987, 93). In the essay "Race and Nation," Cuban poet Nancy Morejón puts forth the concept of "transculturation" as a primary element of Cuban nationalism. Cuban history then, was the history of "intricadísimas tranculturaciones" (extremely intricate transculturations), beginning with the indigenous peoples, followed by white European immigrants and then African slaves (1993, 93).

Building on Ortiz's formulation of the term, Morejón identifies transculturation as the "constant interaction, transmutation between two or more cultural components whose unconscious end is the creation of a third cultural whole . . . The reciprocal influence here is determining. No element is superimposed on the other; on the contrary, each one becomes a third entity. None remains immutable" (1993, 229). Morejón uses this phenomenon to explain the cultural constitution of the modern Cuban nation. Effectively a theory of cultural miscegenation, transculturation characterizes the "in-between" as a third element, an amalgam of two cultural entities that create a third after the original two have been altered. It effectively counters the hegemony of an anthropologically formed national subject (Rojas 2008, 46). In this sense, Morejón's conception of transculturation places afrodescendente writing in Cuba at the epicenter of a process of a distinctively Cuban cultural identity, a constitutive part of *cubanidad* (Cuban-ness). According to Pedro Pérez Sarduy and Jean Stubbs, race in Cuba, though difficult to define, cannot be ignored (2000, xii). They maintain that "Cuba's African-descended identities and cultures are jostled between asserting a sense of difference and recognizing transculturation" (2000, xi).

Recognizing the difficulty presented by the concept of race in Cuba, Cuban novelist Eliseo Altunaga problematizes the term "Afro-Cuban." "I think the term 'Afro-Cuban' is exclusionary, the idea that there was a white Cuban and a black African," says Altunaga. He goes on to say, "the Cuban is what matters, the hybrid meeting of European and African cultures" (2000, 91). Reminiscent of the Brazilian notion of a "racial democracy" in which distinctive races become subsumed in a unified cultural whole, the concept of *transculturación* differs greatly from the legacy of racial absolutism and antimiscegenation in the United States.

In her analysis of Cuban gender and racial politics in the nineteenth and twentieth centuries, Vera Kutzinski cautions against "critical projections of the desire for a 'black aesthetic' onto Cuban, as well as onto other Hispanic-American, literatures, so that the history of Afro-Hispanic American literature can be narrated as a journey toward a thematics of blackness that would compensate for prior elisions of racial issues" (2004, 12). As many scholars have duly noted, the specific cultural manifestations, racial definitions, languages, and implications of this ancestry differ from nation to nation and region to region. Consequently, I do not claim that Harper, Ayala, and Auta de Souza perceived their individual and collective identities through the same racial lens. The extent to which they identified racially or expressed a race consciousness in their work varies not only from poet to poet but also from poem to poem. I maintain, however, that they all perceived their respective national and individual lives in the shadow of racial slavery and that there are traces of this fact "between the lines" of their poetry.

Though categories of identity have become increasingly individualized and relativistic, the lens of "black writing" still allows us to consider the role of collective identities, common histories, and contingent meanings. As a literary phenomenon, "race" is significant in so far as it informs the sociopolitical and historical context in which they were composed.

Ultimately, race, in this book is like Heidegger's "Being"—a term that is "inadequate yet necessary" (Sarup 1993, 33).

Harper's, Ayala's, and Auta de Souza's work demonstrates how the bind between race, ancestry, and slavery was, in turn, bound to conceptions of freedom. As Anthony W. Marx notes, the "modern house of race in each country was built on similar foundations of prejudice, but constructed under varying circumstances" (1998, 10). These "foundations" beg the question of how racial slavery imprints the transnational space of the Americas. From the margins of the literary world, this sampling of poetry by afrodescendente women poets provides an entrance into this line of inquiry.

The comparative framework is a vital means of enhancing and further unpacking texts that may have only been read in a national context. Comparative literature as a discipline engenders projects that challenge and necessarily open up literary canons, disciplines, perceptions of the text, perceptions of identity, and perceptions of history and its relationship to interpretation. The idea of racial ancestry is a by-product of the transnational movement of inscribed bodies, thus making the comparative method vital. Through the lens of a comparative framework, we can see that the writing of history *onto* those bodies is not only a literary process broadly but specifically a *poetic* process of imagining nation and the people that compose those nations. Barnstone continues as follows:

> and the carriers of the word stumble at every step on the road to revelation. . . . They gamble with their talent, and in the end are condemned to surprise and the art and infidelity of re-creation . . . even those things inert, dead, are not fixed but are distorting, translating. The eye itself contributes to that process of re-creation. (1993, 4)

In this sense, the *I* itself contributes to the re-creation of these texts. I consider how the speaker in each of the texts asserts herself as an "eye" and an "I" with the task of re-creating her own identity, the identity of a given group with which she identifies (national or racial) and her conception of history.

Although it necessarily takes into account these disparate racial and cultural ideologies, *Between the Lines* is not a comparative study of people or culture. Instead, it is a comparative analysis of literary texts, recognizing that literary texts are not only products of their sociohistorical contexts but are also involved in what writer George Orwell calls the "historical impulse"—the desire to "see things as they are," and the "political impulse"—the desire to "push the world in a certain direction, to alter other peoples' idea of the kind of society that they should strive after" (1984, 5). Similarly, Theodor W. Adorno presents the art artifact in a constant dialectical give-and-take with "the world." "There is nothing in art," he writes, "not even in the most sublime, that does not derive from the world; nothing that remains untransformed. All aesthetic categories must be defined both in terms of their relation to the world and in terms of art's repudiation of that world" (1997, 138). The poetic text elicits a reading both of its expressed perception of history and the present and of how it pushes the reader toward new ways of seeing.

The translations in this book are not attempts at poeticism, however. They reflect my efforts to produce a companion text in translation that captures a resonance of the poem in its original language and provides, for those who do not read Spanish or Portuguese, access to both the "letter" and "spirit" of the poem. At the same time, the relatively prosaic renderings of many of the poems in translation remind us that access to the full poetic essence of the text relies on access to the language of origin. The translations represent a process of approximation and an effort at communication across linguistic lines. My translations, then, materialize some of the fundamental theories on which I have built this project.

Analysis of these texts requires a particular diasporic theoretical framework whose contours are delineated by a history of the transatlantic and transhemispheric slave trade. This study focuses on a specific portion of this diasporic space—the "New World" or "the Americas"—and gives particular attention to the poets' use of biblical typology and of themes related to slavery and abolition during the second half of the nineteenth century. Ultimately, I put forth a series of close readings that show how the poems speak to each other when contextualized in this way.

Although I am not suggesting that we read poetry as sociologists or political scientists, I am suggesting that canon formation as a means of delineating literary traditions is connected to larger historical processes. As a result, it matters not only *what* is written but also *who* is writing.[4] I focus on what Joyce King refers to as a common experience of "liminality" that links afrodescendente histories—the historical experience of transatlantic slavery.

> Grounded in the sociocultural and historical experience of the liminality of African-descent people, the Black Studies theoretical perspective, as critique, is not merely *another way* of seeing, that is, an alternative way of "constructing" reality, but entails deciphering our contemporary social reality. This perspective of alterity is not due to an inherent biological/racial/cultural difference but is the result of a "historically specific process;" the dialectic of socially constructed *otherness* that prescribes the liminal status of African-descent people (and indigenous American Indian) as beyond the boundary of the normative (Eurocentric) concept of *self/other*. Most importantly, this alterity perspective is centered in the historic encounter of the Red, Black, and White people at the founding of the "Americas" and the colonial domination of Africa. (2006, 27)

The "perspective of alterity" stemming from this liminality allows for an alternative reading of the history of the Americas and "offers a new way of perceiving reality that transcends the personal knowledge of 'personal history' of individuals or a specific group" (2006, 29). At the intersection of a dialectic between slavery and freedom, Saidiya Hartman locates a "basic and troubled association with freedom" (1997, 27) in the literature of African descendants in the New World. The presence of slavery in the New World has informed the practice and the problem of freedom in the Americas. According to Walter Johnson, a "metanarrative of racial liberalism" (2002, 155) in American history informs the stories we tell about African and African American slavery. Johnson questions the simple linearity of the "slavery-to-freedom narrative of American history" (2002, 160–61). His critique suggests that history is characterized by the simultaneity of freedom and slavery, thus making our definitions and experiences of "freedom" *contingent* on—rather than opposed to—slavery. Hartman and Johnson urge us to think more deeply about how forms of slavery inform our conceptions of freedom. I put forward the idea that traces of this interlinking of slavery and freedom inform the corpus of writing we identify as African American, as defined broadly with the term afrodescendente literature. When we read poetry by Harper, Ayala, and Auta de Souza, we can see how the poetic text houses this tension between slavery and freedom while at the same time demonstrating how generative it is as a creative impulse. These poetic texts reveal the workings of language as a creative power, endowed with the ability to write and rewrite history and to inscribe national and individual bodies.

Afrodescendente Writing as a Lens

In *Between the Lines*, I examine the history of poetic representations of slavery and freedom by women of African descent in the Americas. By "the Americas," I mean the geopolitical region called the Western Hemisphere that includes North, South, and Central America and the Caribbean. During the nineteenth century in particular, the question of freedom permeated the Americas and became a literary question and informed the lexical, syntactical, typological, and thematic elements of afrodescendente writing. I use the term *afrodescendente* here to refer broadly to an imagined literary community of writers of African descent.[5] Such imagined communities were constructed not only politically but also through literature, which I define here simply as the craft of telling stories and constructing narratives using the imagination. These imagined communities relied on poetic elements to create collective stories about their history.[6]

Though the hyphenated Portuguese term *afro-descendente* refers to peoples of African descent *in* Brazil, the collapsed *afrodescendente* here refers more broadly to peoples of African descent in the Americas at large. It temporarily replaces specific nation-based terms like Afro-Brazilian, Afro-Cuban, or African American, not as a means of conflating them but as a way of placing them under a larger umbrella of New World literature.[7] The objective of this grouping is to produce a theoretical context out of which we can ask certain kinds of questions of the texts. The term *afrodescendente* also replaces the term "black," for these purposes, in an attempt to account for a wider range of systems of racial categorization in the New World, while at the same time linking them to a common history of transatlantic slavery.

The term *afrodescendente* contains both the "imagined" space of "Africa"—which allows for the concept of diaspora—and the notion of descent or ancestry. It accounts for the terms on which Africans entered colonial societies in the New World but opens up to the distinct cultures and constructions of racial identity that have evolved over the course of the nineteenth and twentieth centuries. An afrodescendente literature designates a particular historical context in which to situate literary texts: a historical context framed by the transatlantic and transhemispheric trafficking of African slaves. As a category, afrodescendente literature elicits the symbolic presence of an imagined, transnational community designated by the tracings of transatlantic and transhemispheric slavery to and throughout the Americas.[8]

Many afrodescendente poets had to account for the not-so-final end of a legacy of slavery in the Americas. Some challenged a Hegelian vision of history as a universal progression toward freedom.[9] Instead, they imagined a malleable history that was highly contingent on narrative, on the interpretive violence of writers, on the incessant rewriting of contending editors. In *Between the Lines*, I compare selected works of three afrodescendente poets who wrote prolifically during the "abolition eras" in the last three countries to abolish slavery in the Western Hemisphere: the United States, Cuba, and Brazil. These poets are North American poet Frances Ellen Watkins Harper (1825–1911), Cuban poet Cristina Ayala (1856–1936), and Brazilian poet Auta de Souza (1876–1901). On one hand, by "between the lines" I refer to the act of reading poems side by side to generate meaning between the two. On the other hand, I refer to the idiomatic meaning of the phrase, the reading of what is *not* said (or in this case, what is not *written*—that is, the specific historical and sociopolitical contexts that encircle the poetic text).

Literary Foundations

To establish a literary context in which to theorize African American poetry, however broadly defined, we must first consider a particular trio of literary powerhouses in the colonial Americas: Phillis Wheatley (1753–1784), Juan Francisco Manzano (1797–1853), and Gabriel de la Concepción Valdés (or "Plácido") (1809–1844). These three afrodescendente poets have become icons of literary tradition in the Americas: to Wheatley is attributed the birth of African-American literature, to Manzano the first and only known hispanophone slave narrative, and to Plácido the mystique of the political poet-martyr of Cuban abolitionism.[10]

Phillis Wheatley

Replete with biblical motifs and Christic typology, Wheatley's poems draw on Greco-Roman mythology and reflect her biblical education and classical training. Her poems begin the literary work of negotiating between a myth of Africa, an evolving myth of America, and the peculiar in-between status of the enslaved African. Both composer of and slave in a "new" England, Wheatley embodies the transnational element in America both by experience—her poetry is literally born out of her physical movement from Africa to America—and by name—she is named after the ship that brought her to America (M'Baye 2009, 24). As she herself traveled transcontinentally to publish and read her poetry, Wheatley's movement demonstrates the movement of literary texts and tropes across the Atlantic and through the Americas.[11]

We see in Wheatley's poems the drama of pioneerism and the expansive idea of an America looming with possibility. In the poem "On Imagination," for instance, she suggests that the poetic process of imagination produces an ability to project "new worlds" into existence.

> *Imagination!* who can sing thy force?
> Or who describe the swiftness of thy course?
> Soaring through air to find the bright abode,

> Th' empyreal palace of the thund'ring God,
> We on thy pinions can surpass the wind,
> And leave the rolling universe behind:
> From star to star the mental optics rove,
> Measure the skies, and range the realms above.
> There in one view we grasp the mighty whole,
> Or with new worlds amaze th' unbounded soul. (in Mason 1989, 78, ll. 13–22)

In "On Imagination," the ability to imagine new freedoms relies on poetics. Imagination, the internal workings of the mind here performed through poetics, produces a cohering of "the mighty whole." The poetic imaginary brings together the parts and asserts a transcendent order that can "measure the skies" and create new worlds. A newly composed, free self, an "unbounded soul," then occupies this new space.

The poem "On Recollection," manifests Wheatley's interest in the relationship between history and poetry. Beginning with an apostrophe to Mneme, the Greek muse of memory, the poem enacts the interplay of memory, the composing of a poetic text, and the pursuit of freedom.

> *Mneme* in our nocturnal visions pours
> The ample treasure of her secret stores;
> Swift from above the wings her silent flight
> Through *Phoebe's* realms, fair regent of the night;
> And, in her pomp of images display'd,
> To the high-raptur'd poet gives her aid,
> Through the unbounded regions of the mind,
> Diffusing light celestial and refin'd.
> The heav'nly *phantom* paints the actions done
> By ev'ry tribe beneath the rolling sun. (in Mason 1989, 76, ll. 8–18)

The speaker hails Mneme as both an aid to the poet and a creative force in human action. She warns against the ills of ignoring the powerful force of memory. Memory "pours" into "nocturnal visions;" it imparts to the poet a surreal realm where she can embrace memory in its fullness. Similar to "On Imagination," "On Recollection" indicates a "free" zone—the "unbounded regions of the mind"—produced from the interactions between the poet and memory. The muse of the text functions in an "other" realm, one that reaches beyond the apparent limitations of language ("Diffusing light celestial and refin'd") but that operates in the human mind. The creative power of the text is both within and between the lines. "Enthron'd within the human breast," memory both pours into the human mind and *is* within (i.e., a product of) it. Ultimately, the interaction between poet and memory becomes a history of the world outside of the text ("paints the actions done / By ev'ry tribe beneath the rolling sun"). As the poet engages memory poetically, she produces history.

In the poem "America," a *new* England is formed at the intersection of this history and language.

> New England first a wilderness was found
> Till for a continent 'twas destin'd round
> From field to field the savage monsters run
> E'r yet Brittania had her work begun
> Thy Power, O Liberty, makes strong the weak
> And (wond'rous instinct) Ethiopians speak
> Sometimes by Simile, a victory's won (in Mason 1989, 125, ll. 1–7)

A new England ushers forward out from a wilderness. It emerges in the midst of an encounter between nations of people. This victorious new England emerges through poetic process ("Sometimes by Simile, a victory's won"). Wheatley's poems prompt us to ask, "How does the poetic text theorize itself?" That is, how does the text explain the process of creating a poetic text, and how does it present the relationship between its internal workings and the themes it addresses? For Wheatley a poem is both textual and performative; it both contains an internal schematic and it projects a new vision.

Juan Francisco Manzano

Primarily known for his autobiography, the only known account of slavery written by a slave in the hispanophone Americas, Juan Francisco Manzano was also a poet. He acquired his freedom in 1837, after which he continued to write. In 1844, he was imprisoned and tortured for his alleged participation in the infamous Conspiración de la Escalera (Ladder Conspiracy)—a rumored collaboration between Cuban *negros* and *mulatos* to violently rebel against slaveholders. Like Wheatley, Manzano was trained in classical literature. His frequent references to Greek mythology and classical poetry and his neoclassical style demonstrate this influence. Manzano's poems amplify the voice of "the slave" in Cuba. The speaker in his poems often takes on the collective burden of Cuban slaves, thereby aligning Manzano with a burgeoning abolitionist movement in Cuba that would be inextricably bound to the struggle for independence.

In many of Manzano's poems, we encounter the sentimental expression of extreme despair so characteristic of Romantic poetry. He uses this convention to demonstrate the tension between the aesthetic beauty of poetic language and the ugly truth of slavery. The first stanza of Manzano's "La Visión del Poeta. Compuesto en un Ingenio de fabricar azúcar" (Vision of the Poet Composed in a Sugar Factory) reads:

> Cuando en la cima allá de un alto pino
> Para morir el ruiseñor se advierte.
> Se postra a saludar con triste himno
> Aquel postrer instante de su muerte;
> Y doliente del mísero destino
> Celebrar él mismo tan funesta suerte,
> Y aparenta que canta, pero llora
> El terrible dolor que le devora. (in Azougarh 2000, 158, ll, 1–8)

[At the very top of a tall pine, the nightingale appears ready to die. It surrenders itself to greet that final moment of its death with a sorrowful hymn; and, exceedingly sorrowful because of its wretched destiny, it appears to be singing, to be celebrating its own ill-fated fortune, but it is lamenting the terrible pain that consumes it.]

The nightingale is in fact the poet himself. The intense suffering of the poet opens the door for the desire for escape. He writes in the face of death as if to confront death and as if life itself depended on the very act of writing. In as much as the poet, like the nightingale, is able to "lament," he exhibits signs of life, though he is positioned in readiness for death. The final stanza of the poem reads:

"O crueldad" repuse, y enseguida
Voló la ilusa sombra fugitiva,
En mi pecho dejando cruda herida

Con la esperanza casi ya perdida,
¿Cómo es posible que tranquilo viva?
Pues al pintar mi cruel melancolía,
Qué sueño, me parece todavía. (401–8)
["Oh cruelty," I replied, and suddenly the innocent, fugitive shadow takes to flight, leaving a raw wound in my chest. How is it possible to live in peace when all hope is almost gone? What a dream it seems to me still when painting my terrible melancholy.]

The poetic act produces the transcendent dream. The speaker emphasizes not only the sentiment but also the act of depicting that sentiment through a creative act ("Pues al pintar mi cruel melancolía, / Qué sueño, me parece todavía"). The transcendence of the dream intersects the creative act. In "La Esclava Ausente" (The Absent Slave) (1823), again the creative act of the poem itself reaches for transcendence. The final lines read:

Y con ambas rodillas en la tierra,
Allá dirijo la esperanza mía;
Allá volara si también pudiera
A buscar en regiones más felices
Vida de miseria menos llena.
Mas "que viva" me ordena el cielo, y vivo.
Hasta apura[r] el cáliz que presentan
Amor y esclavitud cuando se unen,
Y a sufrir sus tormentos nos condenan. (in Luis 2007, 174, ll. 109–17)
[And with both knees to the earth, I aim my hope for beyond, if I could I too would fly beyond to search in more joyful realms for a live less filled with misery. But "live" the heavens command me, and I live. Until drinking the chalice that love and slavery offer when they join together and condemn us to suffer their torments.]

The word *ausente* in Spanish does double work, carrying the meaning "absent"—as we would translate in English as the opposite of present—and also carrying the connotation "daydreaming"—as we associate the state of being physically present but mentally or spiritual absent from a physical world. In the poetic moment, the speaker's pursuit after transcendence meets the word from that transcendent realm. This moment then precipitates the speaker's internalizing of the poetic act and the acridity of the slave experience it has to convey.

In the last stanza of the fifteen-stanza poem "Una hora de tristeza" (A Time of Sadness), Manzano continues to correlate the transcendent dream and a figurative escape from slavery. In this poem this correlation culminates in a cathartic expression of song—an allusion to poetry itself.

> Mas ¡Ay! ¡cuán leve oh Dios y pasajero
> Ese día veloz, que en un momento
> De dicha, ha levantado el pensamiento!
> ¡Rapto fugaz, iluso y visionero
> De un intenso dolor, adusto, fiero!
> ¡oh sombra de placer! ¡oh vanos brillos!
> ¡En vano reflejáis, si entre los grillos
> Está mi mal el corazón ahogando!
> Mis amorosas penas,
> Mis esclavas cadenas
> Condéname a dolor, a eterno llanto . . .
> Suspiro, clamo, pero no me aterro . . .
> ¡Vuele mi acento de la selva al cerro!
> ¡Cantemos, musa, miserable canto! (in Luis 2007, 166)
> [But *Ay*, my God, how light and [quickly] passing this fleeting day, that in a moment of happiness, the thought has arisen! Fleeting rapture, innocent and visionary, of a deep suffering, cruel, severe! Oh shadow of pleasure. Oh empty brightnesses. You reflect in vain if, between my shackles, my ill drowns my heart. My beloved sorrows, my slave chains condemn me to suffering, to eternal lament . . . I exhale, I cry out, but I am not afraid. My voice soars from the forest to the hill! Let us sing, Muse, our wretched song.]

The poetic text is the thumbprint of an imaginative process in which language empowers new interpretations of geographical landscapes. Manzano puts forth the poem as a space in which historical narratives can be rewritten and as a stage for the performance of naming and renaming.

Gabriel de la Concepción Valdés

Accused of being the principal organizer of the Conspiración de la Escalera, Gabriel "Plácido" de la Concepción Valdés was executed by Spanish colonial officials in 1844, allegedly while reciting the poem "Plegaria a Dios" (Prayer to God) (Tarragó 2006, 26). Plácido's poetry addressed a range of themes, including romantic love, the relationship between divinity and humanity, the imminence of death, and the severity of human suffering. His rich repertoire of poetic styles included ballads, sonnets, acrostics and *décimas*—a form of poem rooted in the Spanish oral and folk tradition often written to be sung. Plácido's use of form coupled together with a certain political urgency to speak out against oppression. His poetry was especially controversial because of its often blatant proclamations against slavery and colonialism.

Plácido combined his political ideology with an appropriation of Christian theology particularly in his allusions to the figure of Christ. The sonnet "En la Muerte de Jesucristo" (In the Death of Jesus Christ), narrates Christ's final moments on the cross.

> cuando el monte Gólgota sagrado
> dice el Dios-Hombre con dolor profundo
> <<Cúmplase, padre, en mí vuestro mandado>>
> y a la rabia de un pueblo furibundo,
> inocente, sangiento y enclavado,
> muere en la cruz el salvador del mundo. (79–80, ll. 9–14)
> [At the sacred mountain of Golgotha, the God-Man says with profound suffering, "Father, complete thy will in me" and at the raging hands of a raging people, the savior of the world dies on the cross, innocent, bloodstained, and pierced-through.]

In "Plegaria a Dios," Plácido enacts a kind of intertextual play when he places the words of Christ in the mouth of the speaker, thus identifying the speaker—and in this case the poet himself—as a Christic figure. The final line reads: "Suene tu voz y acabe mi existencia . . . / ¡Cúmplase en mí tu voluntad, Dios mio!" (Your voice sounds and my existence ends. Complete in me your will my God). In this sense, Plácido links Cuban nationalism and biblical history through two speech acts performed within the poems, presenting the poet as a Christ-like martyr for the cause of Cuban independence. With the poem "La Resurrección" (The Resurrection), he alludes to the redemption of Israel by God.

> <<¡Gloria al Dios de Israel en las alturas!>>
> Cual después de tres siglos de miseria,
> De opresión, de temor y de malicia
> Tornó a lucir en la dichosa Iberia
> El sol de Libertad y de Justicia.
> ["Glory to God of Israel in the highest!" who after three centuries of misery, of oppression, of fear and of malice, caused the sun of Liberty and Justice to shine again in blessed Iberia.]

Plácido's God is one who liberates the oppressed; he is the God who freed the Israelites from slavery under the oppressive hand of Pharaoh. "Resurrección," then, takes the messianic theme of redemption—a reference both to the Exodus of the Israelites and the New Testament redemption of "slaves" from sin by Christ—and applies it to slavery and colonialism in Cuba. The poet then takes on the task of declaring national and racial freedom, designating the poem as a space in which an oppositional voice can articulate new freedoms. The poem "Décima" demonstrates this kind of declaration.

> ¿O somos libres o no?
> Pues no burla el orbe entero
> si sois salvajes, no quiero
> morar con vosotros yo.
> Ya el tiempo feudal pasó
> de opresión y oscuridad,
> oid en la inmensidad
> do el regio planeta habita,
> que una voz de gloria grita:
> *¡Habaneros! ¡Libertad!* (125)
> [Are we free or not? Since the entire world does not dissemble, if you are savages, I don't want to live with you. The feudal era of oppression and darkness already passed, hear, in the immense abyss, the royal heavenly body causes a voice to cry out from glory: *Habaneros! Liberty!*]

Mediated by a voice, freedom emerges from a transcendent realm. Similarly the poet mediates the declaration of freedom through the poetic text. The poem itself represents a textual vocalization of a nascent Cuba Libre.

If in "Décima" the poem facilitates the poet's verbal declaration of freedom, in "El Juramento" (The Vow) the poet presents himself as a Christic figure who, in his willingness to be a martyr, will secure freedom from slavery. In the sonnet, "El juramento," the poet vows to stain himself with the blood of "tyrants" if it will ensure that the "yoke" of slavery will be broken.

> Ser enemigo eterno del tirano,
> Manchar, si me es posible, mis vestidos
> Con su execrable sangre, por mi mano
> Derramarla con golpes repetidos;
> Y morir a las manos de un verdugo,
> Si es necesario, por romper el yugo. (in Tarragó 2006, 52–53, ll. 9–14)
> [To be an eternal enemy of the tyrant, to stain, if it is at all possible for me, my garments with his wretched blood, to shed it by my own hand with incessant blows; And to die at the hands of a cruel master, if it is necessary that the yoke be broken.]

As it composes the poetic text, the hand of the poet also engages in a discursive battle against slavery. Within the poem, the speaker translates himself into a Christ figure willing to die to break the "yoke" of slavery in Cuba. In the poem to General Mejicano, called "Despedida" (Farewell) (1839), Plácido expands his poetic vision beyond the island of Cuba and beyond the urgent call for a national body separate from Spain.

> En esas playas que llegar te vieron
> sin libertad, sin patria y sin fortuna,
> y ledas te acogieron,
> cuando el suelo natal abandonaste,
> cansado de vivir cual siervo esclavo,

> y en su suelo seguro
> patria, fortuna y libertad hallaste.
> Es verdad que el camino de la gloria
> tu espada y tu valor te lo han abierto
> marcándote una página en la historia;
> mas también por desdicha es harto cierto
> que hay en tu Patria, hermosa y desgraciada,
> millares de hombres fuertes e instruidos,
> en la inacción y esclavitud sumidos,
> que con valor espada,
> héroes pudieran ser, y no son nada. (125–26, ll. 11–26)
>
> [On those very shores that joyfully took you in without freedom, without homeland, without fortune, when you abandoned the land of your birth, weary of living as an enslaved servant, and in whose secure soil you found country, fortune and freedom. It is true that your sword and your strength have opened to you the glory road, marking for you a page in history; but, unfortunately, it is also very true that in your country, beautiful and yet spoiled, millions of strong and educated men who are overcome by idleness and slavery, who could be heroes with the strength of a sword, but who are nothing at all.]

Plácido puts forth an explicit critique of slavery and its impact on the Cuban nation. The idea of marking a page in history with a sword indicates the violence of colonialism but also alludes to the violence involved in seizing control over what story comes to be understood as historical truth.

Indisputably, these poetic monuments loom large in the literary history of the United States, Latin America, and the Caribbean as harbingers of poetry by peoples of African descent. They are not meant to be representative of a certain aesthetic or topical repertoire. Instead, these poets set the literary stage for a discussion of Ayala, Harper, and Auta's work.[12] To varying degrees, Harper, Ayala, and Auta de Souza echo and build further on the themes, tropes, and literary devices of these early poets. In Wheatley, we see the early rumors of an American nationalism; in Manzano and Plácido, we see the wedding of the literary and the political; in all three, we see a romantic and neoclassical appropriation of biblical tropes and Christic typology. The poets highlighted in this book build on these same themes and tropes, adopting the "problem" of freedom from a national and transnational viewpoint.

The historical "burden" of these poets is the transition between slavery and freedom during the incipient rise of the nation-state. The literary "burden" is a combination of romanticism and neoclassicism and each poet's appropriation of one of the most venerated and most widely read texts: the Bible. Additionally, they add the dimension of gender, inquiring into the definition of freedom not only for African descendants and for the nation but also for women.

I aim not for a feminist reading of the poets, but for a gendered reading of their poetic texts. I resist the notion that any study of literature written by women *must* be inherently feminist in content or methodology. To do so limits the possibilities of such interrogations. Accordingly, my focus is not on any inherent *woman-ness* of the texts, but on the specific ways in which they engage gender and, in doing so, venture claims about women's relationship to the national project. Finally, I emphasize the idea of freedom as a product of a literary process, the creative act as a political act, and a particular appropriation of biblical tropes and figures as a literary signature of afrodescendente poetry.

The Poets. Harper, Ayala, and Auta de Souza

Frances Harper

The most read African American nineteenth-century poet prior to Paul Laurence Dunbar (Foster 1990, 4), Frances Harper spent most of her life at the center of the literary and political life of North America. She was a prolific poet, novelist, essayist, and powerful orator. The thematic content of Harper's poetry and her avid involvement in nineteenth-century racial politics, attest to her commitment to the cause of abolition and racial uplift.

Harper was born into a free family in Baltimore, Maryland, in 1825. She was an active suffragist and avid proponent of abolition in the United States. She was highly vocal about her critique of suffragists like Susan B. Anthony and Elizabeth Cady Stanton who, in their efforts to promote white women, often spoke out against black men (Painter 2002, 51). Though she most often favored the ballad, Harper employed a variety of poetic forms.[13] Harper's poetry conjoined political tenacity and creative ingenuity. Her poems gave voice to the experiences of enslaved women, and her biblically based inversions of an antiblack legacy in American history challenged established scripts of American nationalism. Her body of work demonstrates a sustained critique of slavery and a range of biblical allusions.

Harper traveled throughout the North and the South before and after emancipation, observing the lives of blacks in the United States and giving speeches. Her essays and speeches focused on the plight of the Negro and that of women. In a speech titled "A Room to Myself Is a Luxury" that she delivered in Alabama, she voiced her observations about women in the South after emancipation: "The condition of the women is not very enviable in some cases. They have had, some of them, a terribly hard time in Slavery, and their subjugation has not ceased in freedom" (133–34).

Harper's poetics (re)invent the nation differently from abolitionist literature. Her poetry exposes the hypocrisy of American society as she observed it. "The Slave Mother" (1857) highlights the contradictions in the term "slave mother" and the way the system of slavery interrupts a mother's claim to her own child.

> She is a mother, pale with fear,
> Her boy clings to her side,
> And in her kirtle vainly tries
> His trembling form to hide.
> He is not hers, although she bore
> For him a mother's pains;
> He is not hers, although her blood
> Is coursing through his veins! (in Foster 1990, 59, ll. 13–20)

This use of sentimentalism is characteristic of her work and much in line with abolitionist literature in the United States.[14]

Observing a precarious freedom for blacks in the United States, Harper also envisioned the ramifications of slavery for the future descendants of slaves. She wrote the following in the essay "The Colored People in America":

> Born to an inheritance of misery, nurtured in degradation, and cradled in oppression, with the scorn of the white man upon their souls, his fetters upon their limbs, his scourge upon their flesh, what can be expected from their offspring, but a mournful reaction of that cured system which spreads its baneful influence over body and soul; which dwarfs the intellect, stunts its development, debases the spirit, and degrades the soul? (99)

She describes African (North) Americans as "nominally free," having "exchanged the iron yoke of oppression for the galling fetters of a vitiated public opinion" (99).

Harper's writings demonstrate her distinctive position in relation to a national abolition movement in the United States as she complicates the sentimental guise of the brand of freedom proscribed by white abolitionists. Her poem, "To Mrs. Harriet Beecher Stowe" (1854), appeared in *Frederick Douglass' Paper* in response to the publication and growing popularity of *Uncle Tom's Cabin*. She praises Stowe, beginning with the lines "I thank thee for thy pleading / for the helpless of our race" and concluding in the penultimate stanza that "For the sisters of our race / Thou'st nobly done thy part / Thou hast won they self a place / In every human heart" (in Foster 1990, 57, ll. 17–20).

Stowe aligns Aunt Chloe with the domesticity of the slave kitchen and the empathic bent of Northern abolitionism. Her "self-consciousness" is born out of her status as the primary cook as she is "acknowledged and universally held up to be" (Stowe 1851, 26). Chloe fuels the self-actualization and resolve to action of others—George and Eliza in particular—but she herself does not act outside of the role prescribed for her. Even if we interpret her specific and limited role as symbolic—she metaphorically *feeds* the action of the central characters—Stowe's Chloe stops short of personal reinvention.

Furthermore, Chloe interprets scripture in a way that exposes the hypocrisy of a slave society that would at once claim allegiance to the principles of Christianity and support the enslavement of fellow Christians. In this sense, Stowe portrays Chloe as a kind of weeping prophet, a prophetic voice that freely utters poetically but is, at the same time, restrained in the text.

Harper is far from just a corroborator of the abolitionist agenda. She takes Stowe's characterization of Chloe as a point of departure in her poetic reinvention of the Aunt Chloe figure. Unlike Stowe, she aligns Chloe with literacy and textuality. Harper uses the poetic text as a space in which to rearticulate or *translate* Stowe's portrayal of Aunt Chloe, demonstrating a kind of intertextual, poetical politics. Perhaps the most immediately apparent "translation" of Stowe's Aunt Chloe by Harper is evident in Chloe's speech act. Unlike Stowe's version, Harper's Chloe does not speak in dialect. In place of a language specific to a particular region, race, and class, Harper gives Chloe the syntax and cadence of a poetic orator; she gives her a lingua franca in place of the distinctively "Negro" dialect of the (North) American South. In this sense, Harper nationalizes Chloe through a form of translation.

In "Learning to Read," Aunt Chloe acquires a knowledge that creates a "room" for her, that empowers her with a degree of self-consciousness and paves the way for a sense of independence.

> And, I longed to read my Bible,
> For precious words it said;
> But when I begun to learn it,
> Folks just shook their heads,
> And said there's no use trying,
> Oh! Chloe you're too late;
> But as I was rising sixty,
> I had no time to wait.
> So I got a pair of glasses,
> And straight to work I went,
> And never stopped till I could read
> The hymns and Testament.
> Then I got a little cabin—
> A place to call my own—
> And I felt as independent
> As the queen upon her throne. (in Foster 1990, 206, ll. 33–44)

At the end of *Uncle Tom's Cabin*, Stowe claims abolitionists should take on the task of educating an "ignorant, inexperienced, half-barbaric race" (1851, 626). Harper charges the slave herself with this task. Harper's Chloe defies a community of naysayers and teaches herself how to read. "Learning to Read" underlines Harper's interest in the relationship between text and identity, her belief in the potential of the poem to revise, to re-envision, and to reimagine what has already been scripted into a national narrative. For Harper, the ability to both interpret text and manipulate words is the ability to reinvent. The poem is a space in which to locate the main tenets of a given narrative and challenge them. At the same time, Harper maintains a strict commitment to poetic form, insisting on the aesthetic integrity of this process of translation.

Through her series of Aunt Chloe poems, Harper places a reimagined Aunt Chloe in conversation with Stowe's configuration of the same character; in doing so, Harper enacts a kind of transtextual critique of abolitionism in the United States and its relationship to gender and race politics. Harper's Chloe stands in for a changing nation developing a new kind of literacy; through her engagement with text as she learns how to read the Bible; Harper's Chloe sets herself apart from a larger group. She also represents a racially designated group that is "rising" out of slavery. Like Aunt Chloe, they cannot do so without a text and interpretation of that text. We see here, too, Harper's insistence on the Bible as an important text involved in this process.

The Bible informs much of Harper's poetry. The epic poem "Moses: A Story of the Nile," serves as the title poem for an 1893 volume including "Simon's

Countrymen"—a poem describing the crucifixion of Christ—"The Resurrection of Christ," and "Christ's Entry into Jerusalem." "Moses: A Story of the Nile" follows the theme of the Israelite Exodus, suggesting it as an allegory for the African American experience. The marriage of Harper's poetry and her politics bears witness to her belief: that poetry could in fact transform the landscape of American society. But Harper's vision went beyond the nation. Her transhemispheric sensibility placed national identity in a transnational context. It suggested a symbiotic relationship between U.S. nationalism and "other" nations.

Harper's revision of Aunt Chloe demonstrates her presentation of the poetic text as a dynamic organism capable of challenging predominant narratives through revision. It demonstrates her understanding of literacy and literary practice as a part of the process of reimagining the self. She prompts us to ask: how do we analyze the resonances of a transhemispheric sensibility in Harper's texts, and how might aspects of her work be read as transnational poetic gestures?

Harper extended her critique beyond the national and considered a transnational context for both African American and (North) American identity. Through her use of historical figures outside of the United States—Zumbi and Antonio Maceo—her poetics pose the question: how do we engage U.S. national politics in transhemispheric parlance? In "Bible Defense of Slavery," Harper criticizes the U.S. sanction of slavery and its evangelical rationalization of its "manifest destiny": "Oh! when ye pray for heathen lands, / and plead for their dark shores, / Remember Slavery's cruel hands / Make heathens at your doors!" (in Foster 1990, 60, ll. 33–36). In "Our English Friends" (1872) Harper stretches across the ocean to England, recalling those who "across the distant strand" (. 5) fought for the cause of abolition in America, "When Slavery, full of wrath and strife, / Was clutching at the Nation's life, / How precious were your words of cheer / That fell upon the listening ear" (in Foster 1990, 196, ll. 9–12). In the poem "'Do Not Cheer, Men Are Dying,' Said Capt. Phillip, in the Spanish American War," Harper reflects on the participation of (North) American soldiers in the larger context of the Americas beginning in the first stanza: "Do not cheer, for men are dying / From their distant homes in pain; / and the restless sea is darkened / By a flood of crimson rain" (in Foster 1990, 388, ll. 1–4). Further on in the poem, Harper further reflects on the role of women as "the nation" extends itself beyond its geographical boundary lines.

> Do not cheer while maid and matron
> In this strife must bear a part;
> While the blow that strikes a soldier
> Reaches to some woman's heart.
> Do not cheer until the nation
> Shall more wise and thoughtful grow
> than to staunch a stream of sorrow
> By an avalanche of woe. (25–32)

In general, Harper's subject matter suggests that her work is primarily preoccupied with national concerns. In the poems "Death of Zombi" (1857) and "Maceo" (1896), however, we see rare examples of her transhemispheric sensibility. As I discuss further in chapter 1, the publication of these two poems mark two moments in national history of the United States in which national concern is inextricably linked to international factors.

International laws about slavery, for instance, were a major factor in the famous 1857 *Dred Scott v. Sandford* ruling. The case received much international attention and the UU.S. Supreme Court was subject to intense international pressure in light of a general push to abolish slavery globally (Drown-Marshall 2007, 226). It is ultimately this case that confirms the authority of the Fugitive Slave Law, which, in turn, frames the historipolitical context for Harper's "Death of Zombi." Furthermore, the 1850s marked a period in which Brazilian and Cuban slave markets closed, thereby causing an upsurge in efforts to traffic enslaved Africans illegally. In the same year that Harper published "Death of Zombi," organizations in Cuba employed American ships and flags to maneuver throughout the Atlantic without being intercepted by British cruisers (Strickrodt 2004, 223), thereby reigniting another phase of transhemispheric trafficking.

Nowhere else in her body of poetic works does Harper refer specifically to Brazil or Cuba. The presence of these poems in her body of work, however, suggests that at key moments in the political history of the United States, her poetic vision extended beyond the nation, particularly as such vision might influence (North) African American racial uplift or progress. This fact then demands a revisiting of her entire corpus; it poses new questions to her other less explicitly transnational texts as to what extent might they also reflect a more transnational vision.

Harper's work also points to a larger question: how do afrodescendente writers portray the role of women in the nation as distinct from that of other writers? Even further, how does that portrayal compare to that of white abolitionists in the United States? In addressing this question, however, I emphasize the importance of *not* understanding this project as binary in nature, positing the afrodescendente against a "white" tradition of writing. I suggest rather that the complexities of New World literature, as demonstrated through the poetics of these three women, work against any simplistic construction of national and racial lines, that race and nation, in fact, are often necessary but always insufficient terms that repeatedly fail us as we try to understand literature and history.

Harper's hemispheric sensibility here demonstrates her sensitivity to the concept of "the Americas" and the African diaspora as a construct; it also suggests that she recognized poetry as a space to explore these transnational realities and to engage redemptive narratives and typologies that reached beyond the nation.

Cristina Ayala

One of the first known Cuban women poets of African descent, Maria Cristina Fragas (1856–1936), composed her own "redemption song" titled "Redención" (Redemption) (1889). Fragas wrote "Redención" three years after *La Real Orden* of 1886 formally abolished slavery in Cuba. She was thirty years old. She would continue to write under the pen name Cristina Ayala. As is evident in her collection *Ofrendas Mayabequinas* (1926), Ayala's poetry varied formally and thematically: a balladic ode dedicated to Poetry, a didactic poem on racial uplift, a concise sonnet on faith and belief in a celestial world. Like Harper's, Ayala's poetry addresses the problem of postabolition racial uplift for the "raza negra" in Cuba, while at the same time facing the challenge of national unity on an international playing field. Also like Harper, Ayala ventures to interrogate women's role in that process.

The daughter of a slave woman, Ayala was born free in 1856 in Güines, Cuba. She grew up in the country during Cuba's struggle for independence and emancipation among the *campesinas*, whose race consciousness likely influenced her poetry (DeCosta Willis 2003, xxx). Ayala was a prolific writer during this period and published poetry in over twenty newspapers and journals in Cuba, including *El Pueblo Libre* (Free People) and *El Sufragista* (The Suffragist) (DeCosta Willis 2003, 31). She was a founding editor and regular contributor to the first magazine dedicated to women of color in Cuba, *Minerva: revista quincenal dedicada a la mujer de color* (Minerva: The Bi-weekly Magazine for the Woman of Color)—a magazine that aimed to not only provide a network for black women on the island but also to link these women with expatriates living in places like Tampa and New York (Montejo Arrechea 1998, 35).[15] Moreover, *Minerva* linked black Cuban women with African (North) American women in the United States who both contributed their work to the magazine and helped circulate it in the United States (Montejo Arrechea 1998, 36).

Like Harper, Ayala gave public readings of her poetry. In fact, she was so prolific during this postabolition period and into the early years of the twentieth century that she produced a 240-page volume titled *Ofrendas Mayabequinas* published in her home town of Güines in 1926.

Ayala experimented with a range of forms. Sonnets, romantic ballads, and *décimas* account for most of her poems. Ayala's allusions to literary figures like Cervantes, Spanish poet Salvador Rueda (1857–1933), Puerto Rican poet Lola Rodriguez de Tió (1848–1924), and dedications to Cuban political and intellectual leaders including intellectual and champion for Cuban independence José de la Luz y Caballeros (1800–1862) and Juan Gualberto Gómez (1854–1933), indicate her acute awareness of the political and literary world around her and her determination to engage that world poetically. We find in Ayala's body of work a concern with the local—exhibited in a series of poems reflecting on Güines—and the transnational—exhibited both in her literary and historical allusions as well as her use of biblical tropes.

Ayala was what we might call today a poet laureate of Güines. In "Al valle de Güines" (To the Valley of Güines) an ode to her town of birth, the Cuban landscape is an inspiration for poetry and fodder for Cuban nationalism: "Cuánta rica ilusión, cuanta belleza / este pedazo de cubana tierra" (What rich illusion, what beauty, this small piece of Cuban soil) (Ayala 1926, 11). In a poem written and recited in honor of the fifth anniversary of *Letras Güineras*—a literary magazine published and edited by women and established by poet Rosa Trujillo—Ayala writes:

> Hoy se engarza otra perla en el collar joyante
> que una güinera ilustre lleva altiva y triunfante;
> y la diosa sublime llamada *Poesía*
> a quien ferviente culto le rinde el alma mía,
> viene con su diadema excelsa y luminosa,

a ceñir la alba frente de esa divina Rosa. (Stoner 1991, 208)
[Today is thread another pearl in the jeweled necklace raised high, haughty and triumphant by an illustrious *güinera*; and the sublime goddess *Poetry* whom my soul worships fervently, comes with exalted and luminous diadem to rest the dawn before the ever so divine Rosa.]

The themes in Ayala's work vary greatly, including Cuban nationalism, the importance of education, religion, the struggle between man's will and "Providencia" or fate, the inability of human beings to override fate with their knowledge or achievement, and the precarious balance between "good" and "evil." In the final stanza of "Pensamientos" (Thoughts), she writes about these themes directly.

Y olvidar no debemos los mortales,
que del mundo, los bienes, y los males
tenemos que atacar,
porque los fallos de la Providencia,
¡el hombre más ilustre y de más ciencia,
no los puede alterar . . . (Ayala 1926, 23)
[And we mortals should not forget that we must confront the good and the evil of the world because even the most illustrious man and the man with the most scientific knowledge cannot alter the rulings of Fate.]

Individual agency bows to "the rulings of Fate," also calling into question the efficacy of the individual act of writing as it aims to challenge sociohistorical "rulings." In "La Fatalidad" (Fate) Ayala depicts fate, gendered as female, as a violent predator against human life, exhibiting a kind of female aggression in the text that we see echoed in Harper's depiction of Eliza Harris.

Ella nunca abandona la víctima elegida;
lentamente en sus redes envolviéndola va,
y hasta que al fin la deja extenuada o sin vida,
con insaciable saña, torturándola está. (Ayala 1926, 39)
[She never abandons her chosen victim; she goes about gently wrapping the victim in her arms and, until the victim is layed out or without life, torturing the victim with insatiable rage.]

For this incessant battle between the human soul and fate, Ayala's speaker presents just one escape in the final lines of the poem: "y como único alivio a mi infernal tormento, / ¡sólo a la Muerte invoco . . . *morir es descansar*" (and as the only relief from my infernal torment, I call on Death . . . *to die is to be at rest*). The refrain echoes Auta de Souza's refrain in "Fio Partido" (Broken Thread): "Será morrer?" (Could it be to die?). In both poems, death is consolation and is invoked by the poem's speaker in a climactic moment in the poem. Both present death as an ideal escape from a tormenting life.

Ayala's "Una Rosa después del baile" (A Rose after the Dance) (1890) expresses the speaker's realization that the rose should not be deprived of life simply for the pleasure of the beholder. Underlying the tension between the desire to preserve life and beauty is the reality of a certain fated helplessness and melancholic reality the speaker cannot escape even through the writing of the poem: "¡qué vivan bellas! / yo no las mato, / pues es injusto/privarlas de su vida, / sólo por gusto" (let them live in beauty! I will not kill them, for it is unjust to deprive them of there life only for my pleasure) (Ayala 1926, 25, ll. 38–42).

In the poem "Lamento del Alma" (Lament of the Soul) Ayala places herself in the tradition of Plácido as she identifies with the burden of martyrdom: "¿De una mujer que desvalida y sola / por esta vida va, / ciñendo del martirio la aureola / nadie se apiadará?" (Will no one pity a helpless and lonely woman going through this life wearing the aureole of martyrdom?) (Ayala 1926, 30, ll. 5–8). Ayala adapts the notion of the poet-martyr we see in the figure of Plácido, suggesting that she is in fact a living martyr.

In one instance she alludes to Plácido directly. To memorialize him, she composed and then recited the poem "Mi Flor" (My Flower), a twenty-one-stanza ballad composed in quatrains, at the Sociedad Gran Maceo de Santa Clara in 1911. "Mi Flor" supports the idea that patriotism is a solution for the history of slavery in Cuba.

> Plácido, y si los hijos de aquellos que dictaron
> la inhumana sentencia que tu vida tronchó
> hoy honran tu memoria, ¿qué harán los que lloraron
> tu inmensa desventura cual la he llorado yo?
> Los que en la triste noche de la raza oprimida,
> en nuestro humilde albergue, oímos con horror
> a la madre o la abuela, narrar estremecida
> ¡una *Sangrienta Historia*, temblando de pavor . . .!
> Historia, ¡la más negra, terrible y afrentosa
> que de Cuba en el libro llegose a registrar . . .
> que dejara en nuestra alma huella tan dolorosa,
> que . . . ¡sólo el patriotismo la ha podido borrar! (Ayala 1926, 146, ll. 56–72)
> [Plácido, if the children of those who declared the inhumane ruling that cut down your life at the root, today honor your memory, what will those do who wept for your misfortune as I have wept? Those of the oppressed race who, in the gloomy night inside of our humble shelter, listened in horror to our mother or grandmother, shuddering, tell a *Bloody Story*, trembling with terror. The most black, terrible and ignominious history of Cuba that came to be recorded in the book . . . that would leave its painful mark on our soul that only patriotism has been able to erase!]

Ayala's speaker asks what of those whose ancestors actually heard the stories of Plácido told in their families, those whose families carry the narrative in their mouths. She highlights the role of women—here represented by the mother and the grandmother—in passing on narrative history. Through a collective embracing of Cuban patriotism, she conjoins those whose ancestors oppressed with those who were oppressed themselves.

The oppression of a race of peoples in violent slavery permeates the narrative history of Cuban nationalism. The bloodiness of this history is paramount. The story itself is one of blood. The inscription or *mark* of slavery is erased only through the embracing of a nationalistic Cuban patriotism that heralds Cuban independence from Spain and the end of Cuban slavery simultaneously. The poetic text mirrors the text in which the dark history of Cuba is recorded and yet simultaneously erased to become reinscribed by Cuban patriotism.

In her poetry, Ayala takes on the task of rendering analysis of the relationship between a history of slavery in Cuba, conceptions of postabolition and postindependence freedom, and the role of Cuban national identity in developing Cuban racial identities. Ramon Vasconcelos was a journalist who, in the early twentieth century, started an essay series titled "Palpitaciones de la raza" (Pulse of the Race of Color) in which essayists discussed the problems facing Afro-Cubans at the turn of the century (R. Graham 1990, 56). In a poem dedicated to Vasconcelos ("Al Culto Periodista Ramon Vasconcelos"), Ayala wrote the following:

> Y que llena de orgullo, te proclame una gloria
> de nuestra hermosa Cuba, que agradecer sabrá
> tu labor tan ingente, y sin duda, en la historia
> de sus preclaros hijos, tu nombre inscribirá.
> Y cuando en breve sepas que terminó mi vida,
> que mi alma a lo infinito se ha remontado ya,
> espero, que tu pluma, también, agradecida,
> para mi humilde nombre, un recuerdo tendrá. (Ayala 1926, 117, ll. 25–32)
> [And full of pride, may it declare you a glory of our beautiful Cuba that will learn to appreciate your great labor and, without doubt, will inscribe your name onto the history of your illustrious children. And when you soon discover that my life has ended and my soul has already soared into infinity, I hope that your pen also, thankful for my lowly name, will have a remembrance.]

Here between the lines of the text, Ayala identifies a correlation between historical narrative, ancestry, and the process of naming. She emphasizes the act of applying a name to a physical or imagined body. Writing itself is a part of this process; the use of the word *pluma*—simultaneously meaning pen, feather, and penmanship—reinforces the idea of writing as a means of achieving transcendence but at the same time inscribing a permanent narrative.

In the ode "La Escuela" (School) (1924), Ayala hails education as a redemptive force: "La Escuela ¡Égida santa / que por nuestra gloria vela / y nos protege! ¡la Escuela, / que a la Sociedad levanta!" (Holy protector that watches over our glory and protects us. Education, that raises Society) (Ayala 1926, 207, ll. 11–14). Here the poet's speaker suggests that education will both preserve Cuban "glory" and raise it to a national promised land. She continues, using a biblical allusion to the "promised land," to argue that education would move "nuestra juventud florida" (our blossoming youth) to "la Tierra prometida" (the Promised Land). In the final stanza, Ayala appeals to biblical language. "Bendigamos a la Escuela, / áncora de salvación, / do brota la ilustración / que nos redime y consuela" (We sing praises to Education, our last hope, from it rises up the enlightenment that redeems and consoles us) (Ayala 1926, 208, ll.41–44).

Allusions to Christ and biblical themes are more commonly subtle features of Ayala's work, but we encounter a number of instances where such themes and allusions take center stage. "En la Pasión y Muerte de Nuestro Señor Jesucristo" (In the Passion and Death of Our Lord Jesus Christ) (1924) and "Plegaria ante Cristo crucificado" (Prayer before the Crucified Christ) (1920), for example, feature the figure of Christ as martyr and redeemer. "En la Pasión" (In the Passion) narrates the passion of Christ in a thirteen-stanza ballad of which the final stanzas read:

> Y . . . sentenciado a muerte
> por fin ha sido
> el Divino Cordero,
> que el Creador
> dispuso que a la Tierra
> fuera venido,
> a rescatar el alma
> del pecador . . .
> ¡Oh Jesús Nazareno!
> ¡mártir sublime!
> ¡de estos hijos ingratos
> ten compasión!
> ¡Nuestra alma del pecado
> salva y redime,
> ya que por ella sufres
> Muerte y Pasión! (49–64)
>
> [And . . . the Divine Lamb has been, finally, sentenced to death who the Creator allowed to come to rescue the soul of the sinner . . . Oh Jesus of Nazareth, sublime martyr, have compassion on these ungrateful children! Save and redeem from sin our soul for which you already suffer Death and Passion!]

As Harper does in much of her poetry, Ayala draws connections between slavery and the religious themes in her poems. As I discuss in more depth in chapter 2, the poet uses Christian themes and typology to illustrate the impact of slavery on the Cuban national landscape.

In the poem "Plegaria ante Cristo Crucificado" Ayala presents Christ as martyr and redeemer, emphasizing the personal redemption of the speaker and the poem's structure as an incantatory prayer.

> Cristo mi Redentor, ¡yo me prosterno,
> a tus plantas, transida de dolor . . .
> Tú, que a la diestra estás del Padre Eterno
> ¡ampárame Señor!
> ¡Ten piedad buen Jesús! del alma mía
> que, llena de profunda contrición,
> hoy se abisma, pensando en la agonía
> de tu cruenta Pasión . . .
> Que la sangre preciosa que vertiste

por redimir al mundo pecador;
que la muerte afrentosa que sufriste
sólo por nuestro amor. (Ayala 1926, 227, ll 1–12)
[Christ my Redeemer, I lay myself down at your feet, harrowed with pain . . . You, who are at the right hand of the Eternal Father, help me Lord! Take pity good Jesus on my soul that, filled with deep contrition, today humbles itself, thinking of the agony of your blood-filled Passion . . . that you shed your precious blood to redeem the sinful world; that shameful death that you suffered just for the sake of our love.]

Unlike Harper, Ayala also makes frequent use of Marian typology. In "Himno a María al Pie de la Cruz" (Hymn to Mary at the Foot of the Cross) (1923), Mary appears as an intermediary between Christ's sacrifice and the redemption of the "we" in the poem; Mary's suffering also acquires redemptive power through her sacrifice of her son.

Pues bien, ¡Madre amorosa!
por tu gran aflicción,
por la muerte afrentosa
de su hijo y su Pasión,
te imploro fervorosa
de todo corazón
¡que intercedas piadosa
por nuestra salvación! (Ayala 1926, 232, ll. 33–40)
[Beloved Mother, so good through your great affliction, through the shameful death of your son and his Passion, I beg of you fervently with all of my heart that you intercede, merciful one, for our salvation!]

In "A la Santísima Virgen María" (To the Most Holy Virgin Mary) (1923) (Ayala 1926, 233), the speaker refers to Mary as the "Reina y Señora de la Tierra y Cielo" (Queen and Lady of the Earth and Sky) (l. 10) Ayala's use of Marian typology (and Auta de Souza's as well) reflects the prevalence of Catholicism in South America and parts of the Caribbean as opposed to the Protestantism that dominated the religious ideology of the United States. The fact that Ayala and Harper are influenced by two different strands of Christianity makes their similar appropriations of biblical tropes all the more worthy of critical attention. It is likely that Harper's Protestant background lends to her more explicit connections between the Exodus and North American slavery. Though Ayala's allusions are more subtle, we still see very distinct traces of this similar strategy of biblical interpretation and appropriation.

The first to "break the silence" about race in Cuba in her poetry (DeCosta Willis 2003, 30), Ayala wrote a number of didactic poems that explicitly addressed race in Cuba and the role of women in nation-building. She likely had contact with black abolitionist and president of the Directorio Central de las Sociedades de la Raza de Color, Juan Gualberto Gómez (1854–1933), who served as *Minerva*'s honorary director (DeCosta Willis 2003, 46) and who was a leading intellectual, organizer, and advocate for black Cuban political and social interests in postabolition Cuba. In fact,

Ayala wrote and recited a twenty-one-stanza ballad for Gualberto Gómez titled "Corona al Genio" (To the Genius, a Crown) (1893). Stanzas 9–11 read:

> Aquí, la culta dama, que recrea
> con su palabra dulce y elocuente;
> allí, el varón ilustre, que la Idea
> lanza al espacio con su voz potente.
> Y . . . más allá, ¡distingo emocionada
> al que en mi raza brilla por gigante . . .
> ¡aquel que Cuba contempló admirada!
> ¡permitidme, señores, que le cante . . .
> Que he de cantarle, sí; con deferencia,
> al hombre que fundó todo su anhelo
> en ilustrar la inculta inteligencia
> del triste esclavo en el cubano suelo.[16]

[Here, the refined mistress who amuses with her sweet and eloquent word; there, the illustrious man who, with his powerful voice, thrusts out into open space the Idea. And . . . even further, I am happy to honor him who among my race shines greatly . . . on whom Cuba gazed, astonished! Allow me, gentlemen, to sing his praises . . . I must sing his praises, yes; with deference to the man who has concentrated all his desire on proclaiming the uncultivated intelligence of the pitiful slave on Cuban soil.]

As Ayala positions herself as a poet in relation to Juan Gualberto Gómez in the poem, she suggests also the relationship between poetry and the "idea" or ideology of postabolition Cuba. The poet "sings" the praises of "the idea" as a lyrical vehicle for the idea, thereby the poem sets an aesthetic stage and engages an audience. For Gualberto Gómez the "idea" was to reverse the impact of slavery on the social and moral well-being of black Cubans. He emphasized the importance of moral development and envisioned racial progress as a function of the ability of black Cubans to confront injustice with an ultimate vision of national unity.[17] While highlighting the dynamic and intimate relationship between poetry and political struggle, Ayala also genders the political process of spreading a new ideology.

As Edward J. Mullen suggests, many scholars recognize *Afrocubanismo* during the 1920s and '30s as the beginnings of a black Cuban literature. In fact, what Mullen calls the "genuine Afro-Cuban aesthetic" originated from a series of mid-nineteenth-century debates concerning Cuba's status as a colony of Spain and the concomitant development of a national literary aesthetic (1998, 7). Ayala was both poetically and politically at the center of these debates.

As an early Afro-Cuban writer, Ayala used the poem as a space in which to engage the question of Cuban nationalism and Afro-Cuban identity. In one poem, "Canto a la Raza Española" (Song to the Spanish Race) (1925), she praises the Spanish "race" as a source of Cuban heritage and pride: "¡Oh Raza her[o]ica! Raza de mis progenitores! / ¡Raza donde tan alto el patriotismo brilla!" (ll. 1–2) (Oh heroic race! Race of my ancestors! Race in which patriotism shines high) and as a source of poetic inspiration: "Quiero en tu honor, ¡Oh Raza! de templada lira / arrancar dulces notas que vibren armoniosas, / para cantar aquellas hazañas portentosas / en que mi n[u]men bélico, entusiasta se inspira, / y tu historia consigna en páginas gloriosas" (Ayala 1926, 129, ll. 6–10) (In your honor, Oh Race, I want to draw out from the well-tuned lyre beautiful notes that resound harmoniously, to sing of those marvelous feats in which my warlike numen, enthusiastic, finds inspiration, and to record your history onto glorious pages).[18]

In another poem, "A mi raza" (To My Race) (1888), Ayala locates herself as a part of a racial community in postemancipation Cuba: "Ya es tiempo raza querida / que, acabado el servilismo, / demos pruebas de civismo / y tengamos propia vida" (Now is the time beloved race that, our servitude having ceased, we give proof of our good citizenship and we have a life of our own) (Ayala 1926, 17, ll. 1–4). Ayala's dual use of "raza" suggests a nuanced understanding of the kind of concurrent historical narratives that influenced Cuban identities and that would shape ideas about Cuban nationhood. When she specifically addresses the "raza negra" in the poems "A mi raza" and "Redención," she does so in a way that reflects this duality, emphasizing both racial and national solidarity.

Ayala's involvement with the Cuban magazine *Minerva* also points to her transhemispheric sensibility. The regularity of her contributions highlights the political nature of her life and poetry. She joined a collaboration of women poets of African descent in and outside of Cuba as a regular contributor to *Minerva*. The magazine provided a forum for black Cuban literary and political discourse and served as a platform for transhemispheric cultural exchange (Montejo Arrechea 1998, 35).

We also see Ayala's awareness of and interest in transnational poets and events in her poetics. In "A Las Víctimas de Andalucía" (To the Victims of Andalucía) for instance, she demonstrates this transnational sensibility alongside her rhetorical skill as she urges her readers and listeners to acknowledge the tragedy: "No hay un solo ser piadoso / que no se haya conmovido / cuando ha llegado a su oído / un caso tan lastimoso" (There is not a single pious person that was not moved when it came to hearing of such an unfortunate affair) (Ayala 1926, 14, ll. 31–34). Among her corpus of poems and essays, Ayala refers to a number of her contemporary poets in Cuba, but she also gestures toward poets and writers in Puerto Rico, Spain, and Trinidad.

For Ayala, the poem was a place in which to explore private and public struggle. She used poetry in a variety of forms as a means of engaging with the world around her—literary community, ideas, historical events, the death of friends and fellow poets—to negotiate her own voice in relation to a tradition of writing as well as to a historical context of Cuban politics and writing, even within the context of its struggle for independence. Patriotism, poetry, and her life were inextricably intertwined. Not constrained by one form or topic, her corpus demonstrates her commitment to language as a field of negotiation and of poetry as an expanse (in its manifestations of form, style, and content). Like Harper and Auta de Souza, Ayala was committed to the poem as the "cry of its occasion," where the occasion is quite often the historical moment and, more specifically, the poetic "cry" that calls for new ways of reading the past and of reimagining collective and individual identities.

Auta de Souza

Just as race and nation inform the subtext of Ayala's and Harper's poetry, so they inform that of Auta de Souza. Though less overtly political in her poetics, Auta de Souza is considered one of three women—and the only poet—who comprise the tradition of modern Afro-Brazilian women writers (Durham 1997, 186). This canon was made up of only three women: Maria Firmina do Reis, Carolina Maria de Jesus, and Auta de Souza. A contemporary of such major Brazilian writers as Machado de Assis (1839–1908), Euclides da Cunha (1866–1909), and João da Cruz e Souza (1861–1898), Auta de Souza is a major figure in the canon of nineteenth-century Brazilian poetry. Her work was published in a number of newspapers read primarily by the small educated elite throughout Brazil, including *A Gazetinha* (Recife), *O Paiz* (Rio de Janeiro), *A República* (Natal), *A Tribuna* (Natal), *Oito de Setembro* (Natal), *Oásis*, and *Revista do Rio Grande do Norte*—a magazine that she helped organize (Ferreira Gomes 2001). Her collected works are published in a volume titled *Horto* (2001).

Auta de Souza was at the same time a poet of the educated elite and a poet of "o povo" (the people) in both word and deed. She was born into an elite family very active in the political and intellectual life of northern Brazil. She was raised by a grandmother of African descent (Cascudo 1961, 28) in a region founded on the labor of slaves working in cotton fields. In fact, members of her family owned slaves and worked as financiers of the cotton and sugar trade (Cascudo 1961, 29). In the latter stages of her life, she traveled up and down the eastern coast of Brazil while slaves were being transported en masse to the coffee plantations in the south, another way she came face to face with the realities of Brazilian slavery.

Auta also had considerable popular appeal. Her work was readily adaptable to nonelite audiences. A number of her poems served as lyrics for popular *modinhas*—a form of Brazilian song that came to typify Brazilian national music in the nineteenth century. These musical adaptations of her work were sung both in churches and in the streets. On one hand, Auta's elite education separated her from the larger, mostly illiterate population of northern Brazil, but on the other hand, she was also known to read to groups of illiterate women as well as male and female slaves in *o campo* (Cascudo 1961, 77).

In spite of the fact that Auta composed her poems during one of the most racially charged periods in Brazilian history and the history of the Americas, little is known about how her work might speak to the question of slavery and freedom in and outside of Brazil. Critical work on Auta's poetry has focused on its relationship to Brazilian symbolism and has included sentimental and formalist readings.[19] Like "Fio Partido" and "Minh'alma e o Verso," many of Auta's poems reflect on her personal struggle with physical illness and a tension between the natural and the transcendental worlds.

Placing Auta in a canon of Afro-Brazilian literature comes with complications. In the introduction to *Poesia Negra Brasileira* (Black Brazilian Poetry) (1992), Zilá Bernd questions what constitutes "poesia negra" in Brazil. In his perspective, "não será apenas a utilização de uma temática negra (o negro como objeto), nem a cor da pele do escritor (critério epidérmico) que caracterizariam a existência de uma literatura negra, mas a emergência de uma *eu-anunciador que se assume como negro no discurso literário*" (it is not simply a use of black themes [the Negro as object], nor is it the color of the skin of the writer [epidermal criterion] that characterized the existence of a black literature, but rather the emergence of a *verbalized-I that asserts itself as black* within a literary discourse). According to Bernd, the subsequent notion of "black literature" in Brazil, by this particular standard, lends itself to a concept of black literature and intertextual discourse between such texts contingent on "um modo negro de ver e de sentir o mundo, transmitido por um discurso caracerizado seja no nível da escolha lexical, seja no nível dos símbolos utilizados, pelo desejo de resgatar uma memória negra esquecida" (a black way of seeing and feeling the world, transmitted by a discourse—be it at the level of lexical choice or at the level of symbols that are employed—characterized by a desire to redeem a forgotten black memory) (1992, 13).

Eduardo de Assis Duarte outlines five elements that distinguish Afro-Brazilian literature: theme, authorship, point of view, language, and readership. According to Assis Duarte, "o negro é o tema principal da literatura negra" (the Negro is the primary theme of black literature) (2007, 104) and must be written by Afro-Brazilians. Additionally, he maintains that Afro-Brazilian literature must have a point of view that encompasses "uma visão de mundo indentificada à história, à cultura, logo a todo problemática inerente à vida desse importante segmento da população" (a world vision linked at once to the history, culture, and the issues inherent in the life of this important segment of the population) (2007, 104). Furthermore, the language of Afro-Brazilian literature should reflect a distinctly Afro-Brazilian discourse "marcada pela expressão de ritmos e significados noves e, mesmo, de um vocabulário pertenecente às prácticas lingüísticas oriundas de Àfrica e inseridas no processo transculturador em curso no Brasil" (marked by the expression of rhythms and meanings that are new and, at the same time, from a lexicon belonging to the linguistic practices endemic to Africa and a part of the transcultural process in effect in Brazil) (2007, 104). Finally, Assis Duarte suggests that Afro-Brazilian literature must be conscious of an intended audience of black Brazilians that it simultaneously addresses and constructs. A major part of the Afro-Brazilian literary project, for Assis Duarte, is the "formação de um público específico, marcado pela diferença cultural e pelo anseio de afirmação identitária" (formation of a distinct audience, parted by cultural difference and by the desire to assert identity) (2007, 110).

Auta de Souza's relationship to any canon of Afro-Brazilian literature is tenuous and complicated at best. Her appearance and social status would have categorized her as white for all practical purposes and would likely have informed the way she perceived herself and her writing. Contemporary Afro-Brazilian poet Miriam Alves aligns Auta, however, with a tradition of Afro-Brazilian women's writing (Alves 1994, 9).The possible implications of Auta's African ancestry on our reading of her poetry have been virtually ignored. Luis da Camara Cascudo, who wrote the only biography of Auta de Souza, praises her ability to negotiate in the highest echelons of "cultured" society *in spite of* her color: "A cor jamais determinou à mais longínqua restrição do ambiente caloroso em que viveu" (Color never determined the slightest restriction in the vibrant environment in which she lived) (80).[20] Ana Laudelina Ferreira Gomes suggests that this elision is a form of "embranquecimento" or *whitenening* of the poet.[21] This "whitening" has removed Auta from a larger context of "race" in Brazil as related to the enslavement of "a raça negra."

The complexity of Auta de Souza's relationship to what might be considered Afro-Brazilian literature today forces us to think more deeply about what informs a text written in the shadow of slavery without the "easy" signifiers of "black" and "white" from which to extract meaning. Her poetics urge us to question how poetic texts complicate and become multivalenced when under the microscope of a transnational theory of reading.

In tandem with the literary style of Romanticism, many of Auta's poems express personal sentiment as well as musings on transcendence. Her work demonstrates a preoccupation with death and melancholy examined through images in nature and the unspoken, underlying menace of seemingly tranquil scenes. One example is the poem "Melancolia" (Melancholy), which I include here in its entirety.

> Sinto no peito o coração bater
> Com tanta força que me causa medo . . .
> Será a Morte, meu Deus? Mas é tão cedo!
> Deixai-me inda viver.
> Tudo sorri por este campo em flor
> O Amor e a Luz vão pelo Céu boiando . . .
> Só eu vagueio a suspirar, chorando
> Sem Luz e sem Amor.
> Lutando sempre com uma dor cruel
> Cheia de tédio e desespero, às vezes;
> Minh'alma já tragou até às fezes
> O cálice de fel.
> E o coração no seio a palpitar,
> Como se acaso não tivesse crença,
> Pulsa com a força indefinida, imensa,
> Dos vagalhões do Mar. (Souza 2001, 159)
> [I feel my heart beating in my chest with such a force that it frightens me . . . Could it be death, my Lord? But it is too soon! Let me continue to live. Everything smiles throughout this flowering countryside, Love and Light float throughout the Heavens . . . Alone, I drift into sighing, weeping, without Light, without Love. Striving always with a cruel suffering, at times filled to the brim with tedium and hopelessness; my soul has already swallowed from the most bitter cup. And my heart continues to beat in my breast as if by chance I didn't have faith, it beats with the infinite, eternal strength of the ocean's waves.]

In this poem, we encounter Auta's characteristic use of an introductory question as a point of departure, her appeal to sentiment, and juxtaposition of imminent death and the struggle for life. Auta's poems reach for a level of transcendence, aiming to express a certain melancholic solitude and prayerful posture. Here, the poem itself is an address to God in the form of a prayer. The sea appears as a natural element working metaphorically to signal the eternal force of the speaker's soul as distinct from the imminence of death, a characteristic use of nature in many of Auta's poems.

Melancholy and longing ignite a creative impulse in much of Auta's work. Take for instance these lines from the poem "Saudade" (Longing): "Desde esse dia a minha lira canta / Toda a saudade que lhe inspira o verso!" (From this day forward, my lyre will sing all the longing that poetry inspires in it) (Souza 2001, 205, ll. 23–24). The word *lira* in Portuguese also denotes a lyric poem. Again, as we see in Harper and Ayala, the poem is the space in which the poet performs a kind of alchemy, transforming suffering and death into life and lyricism; the poet draws attention to the performance of a transformative resurrection initiated by a poetic use of language. Like Manzano, Auta suggests the poetic text is a gesture toward transcendence and imagines the dream as a metaphor for the poetic text.

Like Harper's and Ayala's, Auta's body of work is characterized by religious tropes. The figure of Christ and the image of the cross appear in a number of Auta's poems. The poem *"Agnus Dei,"* composed in French, is an ode to Christ (Souza 2001, 259–60). The title poem "No Horto" (In the Garden) is an allusion to Christ's final hours in the Garden of Gethsemane (Souza 2001, 65–68). In the ten-stanza poem in quatrains "Consolo Supremo" (Supreme Consolation), the speaker interprets her own suffering through that of the figure of Christ.

> Se há noites frias, escuras,
> Também há noites formosas;
> Há risos nas amarguras,
> Entre espinhos nascem rosas.
> E rosas também cobriram
> O lenho santo da Cruz
> Quando os espinhos cingiram
> A cabeça de Jesus.
> Rosas do sangue adorado
> —Fonte de graça e de Fé—
> Brotando do rosto amado
> Do Filho de Nazareth.
> • • •
> Ó alma triste, chorosa
> como uma dália no inverno,
> Despe da mágoa trevosa
> O negro cilício eterno!
> Enquanto vires estrelas
> Do Céu no imenso sacrário,
> Na terra flores singelas
> E uma Cruz sobre o Calvário. (Souza 2001, 185–86, ll. 9–28)

[If there are cold, dark nights, there are also pleasant nights; there is laughter in bitterness, between thorns roses are born. And roses also covered the sacred wood of the Cross, when the thorns encircled the brow of Jesus. Roses from the cherished blood—fount of grace and of Faith—flowing from the beloved face of the Son of Nazareth. Oh sorrowful, lamenting soul, like a dahlia in winter, strips the eternal black torment from somber despair. While you see the stars descend from the infinite chamber of the heavens onto the earth's pure flowers and a Cross on Calvary]

The sonnet "Oração da Noite" (Night Prayer) combines Christic imagery with apostrophe to the Virgin Mary.

> Ajoelhada, ó meu Deus, e as duas mãos unidas,
> Olhos fitos na Cruz, imploro a tua graça . . .
> Esconde-me, Jesus! da treva que esvoaça
> Na tristeza e no horror das noites maldormidas,
> Maria! Virgem mãe das almas compungidas;
> Sorriso no prazer, conforto na desgraça . . .
> Recolhe essa oração que nos meus lábios passa
> Em palavras de fé no teu amor ungidas. (Souza 2001, 229, ll. 1–8)
> [On bended knee, oh my Lord, and with hands together, eyes fixed on the Cross, I plead for your grace. Hide me, Jesus, from the darkness that hovers in the despair and the horror of sleepless nights. Mary! Virgin mother of penitent souls, a smile in delight, comfort in misfortune . . . Accept this prayer that passes through my lips in words of faith anointed by your love.]

Two of Auta's popular poems from the collection titled *Versos do Povo* (Poems for the People), demonstrate her tendency to both articulate an audacious female voice and emphasize the particular plight of women.

> [1]
> Não sabes? Num sonho brando,
> O Dia ri quando quer.
> E a Noite vive chorando,
> Somente porque é mulher. (Souza 2001, 230)
> [Don't you know? In a lighthearted dream, the Day laughs whenever it wills. And the Night lives weeping, just because she is woman.]
> [2]
> Mulher é coisa ruim,
> Dizias esta manhã . . .
> Só pode falar assim
> Quem não tem mãe nem irmã. (Souza 2001, 232)
> [A woman is vile thing, you were saying just this morning . . . Only someone who doesn't have mother or sister can speak this way.]

If in Ayala's and Harper's work we encounter the large iconic figures and the collective stories that frame racial and national narratives, in Auta's poetry we enter an interior world of symbolism articulated by a singular voice.

As is the case with any group of poets, the lives and work of these afrodescendente poets are colored by difference in many ways. At the level of the poetic line, however, they grapple with the dynamic relationship between slavery and freedom, ultimately suggesting a dialectic between the two. The implications of this correlation in the texts beg exploration and complicate the meanings of gender, race, and nation during one of the most ideologically turbulent and critically formative periods in the history of the New World. Read side by side in symbolic "conversation," these texts speak to one another through common typological and thematic utterances. Ultimately, this "conversation" constitutes a form of transnational exchange. The transnational framework contributes and is essential to any reading of national literatures. The analysis of afrodescendente literature by women is a means of theorizing this more general observation about literature.

When we place these poetic texts in the larger context of the process of abolition in the Americas, we acknowledge the nature of identity as Elisa Larkin Nascimento defines it: a kind of identity that "can be seen as a kind of existential crossroads between a person and a society, a space in which both are mutually constituted" (2007, 10). Nascimento goes on to say that identity is "not only shaped by an individual's life experience but also by the representation of his or her community and by society's collective experience. . . . Identity is not a static system, but undergoes changes and variations in its relationship with society" (2007, 10). The triangulation of these three poets through the close reading of their work allows for a text-based examination of a transhemispheric afrodescendente poetry in the shadow of slavery and in light of inventions of freedom in the Americas. It allows us to look closely at the poetic (i.e., semantic, thematic, typological) performances of race and gender not simply as political or historical categories but as categories supported by narratives and contingent on slavery in the Americas.

Outline

In chapter 1 I examine Harper's use of transnational black figures in two of her poems as a type of symbolic "translation" of one diaspora experience to another. Through her explicit evocation of two revolutionary black figures outside of the United States, Harper interjects a transhemispheric poetic vision into national discourse. I ask, in what ways does Harper carve out a symbolic space in which her poetic rendering of the deaths of Zumbi—the leader of a community of escaped slaves in colonial Brazil—and Antonio Maceo—a legendary Afro-Cuban leader in the Cuban wars for independence—engages with a larger narrative of freedom and redemption in the Americas? She links the Cuban struggle for political "freedom" from Spanish rule, the organized resistance of Africans in Brazil to Portuguese rule, and the plight of African Americans during the national crisis that evolved into civil war and the racist aftermath of Reconstruction.[22]

Chapter 2 examines Ayala's and Harper's use of the Bible—a text that was used throughout the Americas to support racial slavery unequivocally. I ask, in what ways do Ayala and Harper reconfigure biblical text and reimagine identity for African descendants vis-à-vis the nation? In what ways do they reinterpret the Bible? How do they use similar poetic strategies to allegorize the history of racial slavery in the Americas? Ayala's "Redención" and Harper's "Deliverance" transform the space of the poem into a landscape on which to negotiate—rather than simply reconcile—tensions regarding racial and national identity. Both poems reconfigure the relationship between biblical narrative and the history of African descendants in Cuba and the United States: the enslaved become like the Israelites whose closeness to God empowers them to intercede on behalf of their oppressors. Harper's and Ayala's poetic imaginary posits a reconciled relationship of black peoples with the racist nation-state, a reconciliation that opens the door for active participation in the ideological and symbolic reimagining of the nation. Furthermore, the conversance of their work evokes the notion of a transhemispheric literary imaginary of diasporic black writing.

Chapter 3 examines the intertextual workings of Harper's and Ayala's poetics during heightened moments of political and ideological unrest in Cuba and the United States. This chapter addresses the political implications of their poetics. How did they enlist and extrapolate postabolition political discourse in their poetry? How did they opportune the poetic speech act as a way to engage this discourse? Cristina Ayala's "A mi raza"—written shortly after the legal emancipation of Cuban slaves at the wake of a rekindled movement for Cuban independence—and Harper's "We Are Rising"—published during the heyday of the congressional phase of Reconstruction—present the question of racial uplift as a political and ideological phenomenon and as a summons for poetic intervention. Considered in conjunction with Harper's "We Are Rising," Ayala's didactic poem "A mi raza" more clearly demonstrates a similar preoccupation with the process of redefining the raza negra in a new, "free" Cuba.[23]

The second half of chapter 3 gives attention to Harper's and Ayala's treatment of gender. Harper's "Eliza Harris" and Ayala's "El Arroyuelo y la Flor" (The Stream and the Flower) problematize the role of women and their value in the symbology of nationalism both in the United States and in Cuba. How do these poets answer the construction of the figure of woman ideologically and symbolically by the national project? Can a poetic text express patriotism while at the same time critiquing the exploitation the female figure? If so, what does it accomplish by doing so? "Eliza Harris" places a black mother at the center of national debate about slavery. "El Arroyuelo y la Flor" critiques the interplay of symbolic representations of masculinity and femininity in the pursuit of national identity. Although in both poems the woman figure is somehow subsumed in the process of creating an ideology of nationhood, the differences in Ayala and Harper's treatments reflect the different political contexts with which the poems deliberate. Ultimately, it is not a common use of typology or an explicit use of transnational black icons that links the four poems. Instead, they are linked by a common anxiety about the problem of "renaming" a racial community and (re)defining gender within the context of an evolving national identity. This anxiety surfaces in the structure and language of the poems. They posit the binaries slave-free and male-female not as simple dichotomies but as a site of liminality in which these terms are constantly renegotiated and redefined.

Referring to the silencing effect of slavery and sexism on the voice of afrodescendente women in nineteenth-century Brazil, poet Miriam Alves characterizes the literature of Auta de Souza as an "exceção deste quadro de silêncio" (exception to this picture of silence) (1994, 9). In Auta de Souza's work, the text becomes the site where questions of freedom and identity play out. Chapter 4 examines Auta's poems "Minh'alma e o Verso" (My Soul and Poetry) and "Fio Partido" (Broken Thread), two poems that present freedom and slavery as a dialectic. How does Auta's articulation of *self* in and through language and her invocation of themes of freedom and bondage collaborate with transnational discourse on race and slavery in the Americas?

The Brazilian republic centered on the idea of a nation free from the blight of slavery. Prominent abolitionist Joaquim Nabuco (1849–1910) argued that abolition would effectively renovate Brazilian national consciousness. He described slavery as an "impedimento no caminho do país todo" (obstacle to the progress of the entire country) (1988, 236). He argued that true abolitionists were those who "confiam núm Brasil sem escravos" (who believe in a Brazil without slaves). Chapter 4 examines Auta's poetry through the lens of this kind of discourse.

The poems discussed in *Between the Lines* occupy the space between slavery and freedom, not only in the historical sense as their chronology indicates but also in the literary sense. The contingent idea(l) of freedom informs the constitution of these poems as creative (re)imaginings of identities and (re)writings of history. The specter of race and its particular performances of gender identities among afrodescendente peoples in the New World informs these poetics but does not conform them to a monolithic body of national literature. Afrodescendente poetry in the Americas highlights the power of words to imagine new histories and new forms of identity. In their interplay, the poems tell us certain truths about how the concept of freedom can evolve. They say: "freedom" cannot be understood as a by-product of slavery's abolition. They say: freedom is a poetic process. They say: freedom cannot be merely legislated, it must also be written.

Chapter One

Translations of Transnational Black Icons in the Poetics of Frances Harper

In the introduction to *American Literary History*'s special issue "Hemispheric American Literary History," Caroline F. Levander and Robert S. Levine pose key questions about the purview of American literature:

> What happens to US and American literary and cultural studies if we recognize asymmetry and interdependency of nation-state development throughout the hemisphere? What happens if we let this recognition of the nation as historically evolving and contingent—rather than already formed—revise our conceptions of literary and cultural genealogies? Finally, what happens if the "fixed" borders of a nation are recognized not only as historically produced political constructs that can be ignored, imaginatively reconfigured, and variously contested but also as component parts of a deeper, more multilayered series of national and indigenous histories? (2006, 401)

Though the idea of a nation imposes imaginary boundaries, Levander and Levine challenge the idea of "fixed borders," suggesting that our cultures and literatures are formed through border crossings. Studies of gender and race help deconstruct the boundaries imposed by a nation-based concept of literary studies. They do so by undoing the perceived fixedness of national histories. The forced migration of Africans into the New World is one example. As the descendants of enslaved Africans began to articulate themselves and project a space for themselves in emerging New World nations, they challenged national and hemispheric boundaries. Michael Hanchard (1994) goes as far as to say that the middle passage, as a "symbol of the forced migration of peoples across the Atlantic and their enslaved labor in multiple colonial and imperial societies" represents a "moment of globalization" (151).[1]

For African American writers in particular, the scope of "America" extended beyond the national boundaries of North America proper. In his *Book of American Negro Poetry* (1922), for example, one of the first attempts to document a cohesive African American poetic canon, James Weldon Johnson included references to nineteenth-century writers in Cuba, Brazil, Haiti, and Mexico, such as Cuban poets Gabriel de la Concepción Valdés or "Plácido" and Francisco Manzano, and Brazilian poet Machado de Assis.[2] Whereas anthologies like Johnson's demonstrate the fact that *afrodescendente* peoples have written prolifically throughout the Western Hemisphere, Frances Ellen Watkins Harper's poetics suggest the possibility of a transnational and hemispheric discourse in the early poetry of African Americans writing in the United States. Frances Harper's artistic and intellectual contributions are already well documented (Boyd 1994; Foster 1990; Hill 1981; Still 1872). Her popularity made her one of the first black women to earn a living as a poet. She toured the United States giving lectures and reading her poetry to blacks (free and enslaved) and whites alike and was a strong advocate of both racial and gender equality. What has yet to be sufficiently explored, however, is the degree to which we might consider her work in the context of a larger, transnational discourse on race and nation in the nineteenth century.

There are, in fact, two outstanding instances in which it is clear that Harper is *explicitly* transnational and hemispheric in her poetics. Her treatment of Zumbi, in "Death of Zombi, the Chief of a Negro Kingdom in Latin America" (1857) precedes more recent appropriations of Zumbi by a century.[3] Brazilian black nationalists, writers, artists, and scholars during the twentieth century in particular have appropriated Zumbi—leader of a society of escaped slaves in colonial Brazil—to represent Afro-Brazilian resistance to oppression. Harper suggests that his significance extends beyond the Brazilian national sphere. Zumbi's struggle in "Death of Zombi" mirrors the struggle of African Americans in North America during the nineteenth century who had to daily negotiate the choice between a life of slavery and death. Like Zumbi, general Antonio Maceo has emerged as an iconic figure in Cuban history. His role in the Cuban struggle for independence at the end of the nineteenth century made him one of the most well-known Afro-Cuban leaders in world history. Harper's poem "Maceo" (1900) draws attention to the complex intersection of North American nationhood and Latin American struggles for national sovereignty. She depicts Maceo as a martyr for the cause of Cuban independence and uses his death to question the reality of freedom in the United States. In doing so, Harper bridges hemispheric struggles for freedom in the Americas.

In a second phase of its Manifest Destiny, the United States sought to extend its national sovereignty to new territories beyond the boundaries of the continent. The post-Reconstruction era saw African blacks systematically stripped of the legal rights gained after the Civil War and subjected to unchecked racial violence. Moreover, the U.S. victory in the war with Spain—a war fought primarily in Cuba with a predominantly Afro-Cuban Cuban Liberation Army—which made the nation an imperial power, caused African Americans to question their status vis-à-vis the colonized people newly under American control. Through her representation of Maceo—a man who emphasized the ideological connection between Cuban national freedom and that of black slaves in and outside of Cuba—Harper suggests that the freedom of nations was inextricably linked to the freedom of oppressed peoples. She conjoins the struggle for freedom in the United States not yet realized by African Americans with that of nations that, like Cuba, were struggling for national freedom. In doing so, Harper characterizes African American identity in the nineteenth century as a negotiation between a North American politics of race and a transnational politics of race manifested largely in debates about racial slavery and national sovereignty.

"Death of Zombi" (1857) was published in the wake of the Fugitive Slave Act and "Maceo" (1896) during the nadir of Reconstruction and in the aftermath of the United States victory in the war with Spain. In these poems, Harper links the organized resistance of Africans in Brazil to Portuguese rule and the Cuban struggle for political "freedom" from Spanish rule, to the plight of African Americans during the national crisis that evolved into civil war and the racist aftermath of a failed Reconstruction. She bridges the gap between Cuban, Brazilian, and U.S. legacies of slavery and struggle for an ideal of national freedom. At two critical periods in its national history when the United States was internally conflicted about the terms of its own nationhood, Harper uses poetry to challenge African Americans to conceptualize identity beyond national borders. She posits African American identity as what Paul Gilroy calls "a process of movement and mediation" (1993, 19) characterized by transnational movement not only of people but also of ideas, tropes, and symbols.

Harper's treatment of Maceo and Zumbi constitutes a form of translation. Not only does she effectively translate these figures through the act of memorializing them poetically—that is, facilitating their transition from the physical world to a transcendent world of collective memory—she also moves these figures across an imaginary hemispheric space, ultimately making them relevant to North American slavery and struggles for freedom.

> From the beginning, however, it should be carefully emphasized that the slave trade was accompanied stride for stride by slave revolts and rebellions. In the sixteenth century there were revolts by black slaves in America, and the organized rebellions by slaves called Maroons had already begun in Cuba, Jamaica, Haiti, Mexico, and Brazil. Du Bois points out, as the trade increased, so too did the rebellions. Throughout the seventeenth century actual wars went on against slavery. There were nine major revolts in Jamaica, Barbados, Haiti, and the forming of an independent state, Palmares, in Brazil. This state was founded by Afro-Brazilians fighting against the Portuguese slavers—they were called Zombis! The name has been used as a negative and metaphysical term to characterize these warriors as rising from the dead and being unkillable, because of the ferocity with which these Afro-Brazilians fought against slavery. (Baraka 1984, 228)

"The Death of Zombi": Harper's Mythology of Black Resistance

For leading figure of the Black Arts Movement Amiri Baraka, the enslavement of African peoples went hand in hand with an unrelenting determination on the part of the enslaved to pursue freedom through active resistance. He uses the term "Zombi" to characterize Afro-Brazilian fugitive slaves and their efforts to secure their freedom, thereby suggesting a transnational context in which to locate the themes of freedom and resistance in the history of African American peoples. In the Brazilian context, Zombi, more commonly written Zumbi, was the name of the last chief of the republic of Palmares, a *quilombo* (society of escaped slaves) now legendary in Brazil. Baraka's appropriation suggests that African Americans and African descendants as a larger "imagined" community of afrodescendentes, might understand their own history by seeing Zombi as an immortal legacy of human agency against slavery and its dehumanization of black peoples.

Baraka was far from the first to venture such a claim. Perhaps we might expect that as an aesthetic sister to and historical contemporary of the Black Power Povement, the Black Arts Movement and its political engagement would result in such a pan-African sensibility. Less predictable, however, is Harper's allusion to Zumbi over a century before Baraka's in the poem "Death of Zombi, the Chief of a Negro Kingdom in South America" (in Harper 1857b). Harper constructs a narrative of this leader of a fugitive slave community, presenting him as a heroic figure who chooses physical death rather than accepting the "death" (i.e., demise) of a realized ideal of freedom and citizenship in a community. She thereby translates Zombi from a tragic figure, contained in the historical time period and geographical space of seventeenth-century northern Brazil, to a nineteenth-century icon for resistance to the oppressive forces of racial slavery in North America. Ultimately, Harper translates Zombi from a symbol of African resistance in Brazil to a figure for the transnational phenomenon of black resistance in the Americas as a whole.

Harper's "Death of Zombi" narrates the invasion and eventual destruction of Palmares and culminates in the heroic suicide of Zumbi (1655–1695). One of the most legendary and longest lasting societies of fugitive slaves in the Americas, the republic of Palmares flourished for almost a century in the northern region of Brazil in the Barriga Mountains between Alagoas and Pernambuco. Pernambuco was one of the major centers of Portuguese colonial activity in Brazil. By the end of the sixteenth century, there were sixty-six *engenhos* (sugar mills) in Pernambuco and approximately 10,000 African slaves. Both numbers continued to grow over the next century as the Portuguese imperial economy became more and more dependent on the sugar industry (Gomes 2005, 43). Together with its plantations and slaveholders, Palmares maintained a thriving society of fugitive slaves.

Primarily of Angolan descent, the citizens of Palmares, or *palmaristas*, had been brought from Africa to Brazil. For the duration of its existence, Palmares was under the constant threat of attack, first by the Dutch and then by the Portuguese. Eventually, at the end of the seventeenth century, Palmares was destroyed by the Portuguese. Harper's dramatic monologue "Death of Zombi" begins at the moment of the Portuguese invasion.

> Cruel in vengeance, reckless in wrath,
> The hunters of men bore down on our path;
> Inhuman and fierce, the offer they gave
> Was freedom in death or the life of a slave. (1–4)

As Harper's speaker, a member of this community attacked by a cadre of "inhuman" hunters, retells the story, the reader participates as listener and is urged to recognize the speaker as a human survivor of an *in*humane attack. The musicality and rhythmic structure of the lyrical ballad evokes the rhythm of speech, further emphasizing this speaker–listener interaction. The reflection of the "inhuman and fierce" attackers on the faces of the people of Palmares further highlights the humanity of the palmaristas in their encounter with the inhumane and oppressive forces of the colonial invaders. The primary opposition here, however, is that of death and freedom. By choosing death over enslavement, Zombi gains freedom and becomes a mythological symbol of resistance to slavery. The resolution of this opposition through self-sacrifice complicates the relationship between life and death in that it suggests that freedom in life can be achieved through physical death.

In the same year that "Death of Zombi" was published, the U.S. Supreme Court declared Dred Scott an illegal fugitive, ineligible for citizenship because of his race. Scott was reenslaved after living "free" in Illinois for close to ten years. The *Dred Scott* ruling highlighted the fact that the presence of slavery in North America was no longer bound to regional demarcations of "free" and "slave" states. Just seven years earlier, Harper herself was forced to flee her home state of Maryland after the passing of the Fugitive Slave Law as a part of the Compromise of 1850 marked the legal denial of self-ownership to African Americans and threatened the nominal freedom of the small population of free blacks in the United States. Harper suggests that even "free" blacks—a major contingent of her audience—had to walk the line between freedom and slavery as they negotiated a life of second-class citizenship and the constant threat of slavery posed by the Fugitive Slave Law.

Although Harper's involvement with the Underground Railroad placed her in close contact with a large number of fugitive slaves in North America, they are not the subjects of her only poem depicting such a community. She does not write about the many fugitive slave communities in Virginia or South Carolina. Nor does she write about any of the other approximately 20,000 fugitive slaves and descendants of fugitive slaves living in maroon societies in the United States between the seventeenth and nineteenth centuries (Price 1996, 152). Instead, Harper transports her readers to seventeenth-century Brazil via a narrative poem about the demise of a free "Negro Kingdom" there. As fugitive slaves in North America faced death in the pursuit of freedom (or at the very least virtual death through reenslavement), Harper suggests a larger historical and mythological scope within which to place their experience, one that takes into account the presence of enslaved afrodescendentes throughout the Americas and proposes an "imagined" transhemispheric space.

Zumbi was born in Palmares and fought in the final war against the Portuguese. Though it is documented that he was in fact captured by the Portuguese and publicly beheaded, a version of the story survives through folklore that he chose to commit suicide rather than be captured. By using this version of the story, Harper emphasizes the significance of his self-sacrifice as a resolution to the threat of reenslavement. Turning to poetry to actively construct memory rather than to simply represent historical fact, Harper treats Zumbi as both a historical and a mythological figure.

Harper continues to contrast the humanity of the palmaristas and the inhumanity of their attackers.

> The cheek of the mother grew pallid with dread,
> As the tidings of evil around us were spread,
> And closer and closer she strained to her heart
> The children she feared they would sever apart.
> The brows of our maidens grew gloomy and sad;
> Hot tears burst from eyes once sparkling and glad.
> Our young men stood ready to join in the fray,
> That hung as a pall 'round our people that day.
> Our leaders gazed angry and stern on the strife,
> *For freedom to them was dearer than life.*
> There was mourning at home and death in the street,
> For carnage and famine together did meet.
> The pale lips of hunger were asking for bread,
> While husbands and fathers lay bleeding and dead. (5–18; emphasis added)

Harper highlights the intensity of the desire for freedom among the palmaristas as her narrator claims that "freedom to them was dearer than life." The desire for freedom is coupled with a natural hunger for "bread." The speaker emphasizes the loss of "husbands and fathers," thereby humanizing the palmaristas. In contrast to the palmaristas who are depicted as members of a family, the colonists are portrayed as "hunters of men," lacking domestic titles. As "tempests of wrath," the colonists acquire an elemental quality (natural in their force, but not human) that stands in opposition to the familial humanity of the palmaristas. Harper concludes the first section of the poem by emphasizing the death of the kingdom as it yields to the force of history itself.

> For days we withstood the tempests of wrath,
> That scattered destruction and death in our path,
> Till, broken and peeled, we yielded at last,
> And the glory and strength of our kingdom were past. (19–22)

When death and destruction overwhelm the palmaristas to the point of complete acquiescence, Zombi enters as a heroic figure. Harper presents the figure of "Zombi" as a figure in which the contending forces of life and death, freedom and slavery, humanity and inhumanity resolve themselves. His introduction into the narrative interrupts the pattern of oppositions.

> *But Zombi*, our leader, and warlike old chief,
> Gazed down on our woe with anger and grief,
> The tyrant for him forged fetters in vain,
> His freedom-girt limbs had worn their last chain.
> Defiance and daring still flashed from his eye;
> *A freeman he'd lived and free he would die.*
> So he climbed to the verge of a dangerous steep,
> Resolved from its margin to take a last leap;
> For a fearful death and a bloody grave

Were dearer to him than the life of a slave.
Nor went he alone to the mystic land—
There were other warriors in his band,
Who rushed with him to Death's dark gate,
All wrapped in the shroud of a mournful fate. (23–36; emphasis added)

At this point the poem shifts from the invasion story to focus on the story of Zombi and his heroic rejection of slavery through suicide. His resistance to physical enslavement demonstrated in his rejection of "fetters" and chains on his "freedom-girt limbs," culminates in a rejection of physical life. For him "a fearful death and bloody grave / Were dearer to him than the life of a slave" (31–32).

Zombi emerges in the poem, then, as a symbol of resistance to the colonial rapacity. Harper contrasts the freedom of his limbs with the "chains" and "fetters" of the colonial "tyrant," using parallelism to reinforce his defiance—"A freeman he'd lived and free he would die." Here life and death are *linked* by freedom, rather than in tenuous conflict with one another. The image of Zombi gazing down on the scene hearkens back to the moment of the invasion when the leaders "gaze" at the Portuguese attack. As a god-like presence, Zombi observes the scene and transcends the binary oppositions. He lives free and dies free, becoming a symbol of resistance to colonial imperialism and slavery. He leads his followers into a "mystic land," a place where the freedom they fought to maintain in life can be sustained in death.

Harper's narrator, who has witnessed the event in the past, now relays it in the present, taking us from the "reckless wrath" of the ensuing attackers to the fated death of Zombi and his followers. As a performance of telling, "Death of Zombi" becomes meaningful in its performance of this re-membering of a collective history of escaped slaves. This type of re-membering suggests that the pursuit of freedom on the part of African descendants—rather than a passive acceptance of enslavement—constitutes a tradition of struggle for freedom in the Americas. The poem also serves as a testament to the existence of African descendants outside of the United States whose lives are inscribed by the tension between a desire for freedom and the reality of slavery in the Americas. Additionally, Zombi functions as a link between the past and the present. This linkage is again mirrored in the structure of the poem. After the speaker and the other palmaristas have been "broken and peeled" and succumb to the colonial invaders, "Zombi" enters as a redemptive force.

In "Death of Zombi," Zumbi becomes a figure for "Negro" freedom, while demonstrating the double bind confronting enslaved peoples for whom the terms of "freedom" require physical death. By commemorating Zombi's "freedom in death," the poem confers immortality on its protagonist. By alluding to this double bind in which death in fact becomes synonymous with freedom and life under slavery becomes a type of death, Harper highlights the dialectic between freedom and death imposed by the system of racial slavery. Zombi emerges as a type of resolution, synthesizing freedom and death in a single act of heroic self-sacrifice.

As Zombi transitions into the "mystic land" of death, "fearful death" and the "bloody grave" become "dearer" than a life of slavery. Zombi's act of resistance reconfigures the relationship between freedom, slavery, life and death. Unable to realize freedom in life, the fugitive redefines the very terms of freedom itself. As the slave system creates a cosmos in which life becomes synonymous with death, the fugitive who faces death heroically sustains the spirit of resistance. It is this process that Harper portrays in "Death of Zombi," thereby arriving at the more familiar notion of the *zombie* as a person in a liminal space between life and death.

The *Dred Scott* decision affirmed slavery's hold on the South and confirmed the fact that freedom for blacks in North America—like that of the palmaristas—was under constant threat of attack. Through her depiction of Zumbi as the quintessential fugitive hero who defies slavery in life and achieves freedom in death, Harper highlights the transnational context of slavery and black experience in North America. The poet effectively "translates" the history of fugitive Brazilian slaves into the language of African Americans in the United States, whose autonomy was also threatened by slaveholders. Harper's celebration of one man's choice of death over slavery in seventeenth-century Brazil challenged her readers in the United States—black and white alike—to recognize not only the pervasive nature of slavery in the Americas but also the legacy of heroic black resistance to it.

> En nuestra desgraciada patria ha sonado nuevamente el grito de ¡Libertad! Ha llegado el momento oportuno de que hagamos conocer al mundo entero que el cubano sabe morir por la redención de su patria . . .
>
> [In our wretched country the cry of Freedom has sounded once again! The opportune moment has arrived that we will make the whole world know that the Cuban knows how to die for the redemption of his country . . .] (Maceo 1879 [2002])

The "Bronze Muse" and the "Bronze Titan"

Harper thematizes black resistance to not only racial slavery but also colonial oppression. One instance of black resistance to colonial oppression is that of the largely Afro-Cuban Independentista army against the Spanish Crown during the late nineteenth century. One the best-known leaders of this army was Antonio Maceo y Grajales (1845–1896) who famously demonstrated his willingness to die for the "redemption" of Cuba. His leadership in the Cuban wars of independence won him the sobriquet "the Bronze Titan." Just four years after his death, Harper's poem "Maceo" appeared in her 1900 collection *Poems* published in Philadelphia.

Beginning as an elegy lamenting and commemorating Maceo's death, the poem also incorporates elements of the dramatic monologue and eventually evolves into a prayer. Maceo's death prompts the anonymous speaker to interrogate the role of death and bloodshed in struggles for freedom.

> Maceo dead! a thrill of sorrow
> Through our hearts in sadness ran
> When we felt in one sad hour
> That the world had lost a man. (1–4)

In very first stanza the oxymoronic notion of a "thrill of sorrow" alludes to what will not only emerge as a commentary on Maceo but also on the implications of his life and ideology for the United States, a nation riddled with its own contradictions. The rise of the Jim Crow system in the Southern states reflected the belief of many white Americans—namely, that white supremacy was indeed the solution to "the problem of black freedom" (K. Clark 2005, 193). Racial violence increased dramatically in the South as blacks were systematically excluded from politics (K. Clark 2005, 194–98).

Ironically, war in Cuba provided a pretext for U.S. national unity, a unity reinforced by a belief in white supremacy. According to Kathleen Ann Clark, the Spanish-American War and the rise of North American imperialism "further fueled both national reconciliation and racial antagonism. As Northern and Southern whites joined together to defeat a common—and darker—foe, they celebrated the decline of 'sectional feeling' and bolstered the power of white supremacy at home and abroad" (2005, 194). Politicians and journalists began to represent the Spanish-American War as continuation of the Civil War, promising to "re-unite North and South in a united fight and heal the wounds and divisiveness of internecine war" (Kaplan 2002, 122). In fact, convinced that black Cubans were also unfit to rule themselves, the U.S. government used the racial composition of the Cuban Liberation Army to justify its intervention in Cuba. The blurring of racial lines in the military—on both the Cuban and U.S. side—threatened the integrity of domestic racial divisions (Kaplan 2002, 124–28). This thinking ultimately led the U.S. government to implement a Jim Crow system in Cuba during its four-year occupation. Rumors spread throughout the United States, Cuba, and Spain about the predominantly black presence in the Cuban Liberation Army as it fought vehemently for Cuban independence. Maceo and other leaders of the army denied such claims but at the same time advocated a Cuba free of any outside intervention, even that of the United States. A number of black newspapers sided with black Cubans and argued against the exportation of American racism through their imperial presence in Cuba (Kaplan 2002, 135).

"Death of Zombi" explores the relationship between human life and freedom in the shadow of the transatlantic slave trade; "Maceo" likewise engages the theme of freedom but does so in national rather than individual or even regional terms. Harper uses the death of Maceo—a black leader internationally known for his struggle against racial and national oppression—to prescribe a solution for a racially divided United States, a nation whose avid pursuit of nationhood too often coincided with racial violence and the disenfranchisement of African Americans. She calls for heroic men who, like Maceo, can lead the country toward a utopian vision of nationhood rooted in biblically based morality. The poem's celebration of Maceo's manhood—expressed in his willingness to fight and die for an ideal of freedom and his vision of national independence and racial equality—highlights the failure of the United States to realize its own ideals.

As Amy Kaplan notes, the black male body posed a problem for American national identity. "Black and white male bodies," she asserts, "had different symbolic resonance, a different signifying function in the political landscape. The foundation for the construction of the white male body as figure for American nationhood lies in the subjugation of black male bodies at home and abroad" (2002, 142). It is significant, then, that Harper begins her poem with a reference to Maceo's manhood and uses it as an entry point for her vision of an integrated American nation that embraces the goal of global peace.

Harper expounds on the vision of a *free* Cuba as the literal and figurative link between Maceo's life (i.e., his "latest breath") and his death.

> He had clasped unto his bosom
> The sad fortunes of his land—
> Held the cause for which he perished
> With a firm, unfaltering hand.
> On his lips the name of freedom
> Fainted with his latest breath.
> Cuba Libre was his watchword
> Passing through the gates of death. (5–12)

Harper evokes the image of Maceo holding "the sad fortunes of his land" to his chest and "the cause" of freedom in his hand. In his death, he "names" or identifies freedom as "Cuba Libre," his "watchword."

An iconic symbol for the struggle for Cuban independence, Maceo pursued a delicate and strategic balance between Cuban nationalism and a species of New World black transnationalism. While he fought for a collective and racially integrated Cuba Libre, Maceo also believed that the history of slavery in the Western Hemisphere had inextricably linked the history of Cuba and those of other countries with a similar legacy of racial slavery.

In an effort to garner support for the cause of Cuban independence, Maceo traveled to Jamaica, Haiti, and the United States to talk with black leaders. As secretary of the Cuban Anti-Slavery Committee, black abolitionist and separatist Henry Highland Garnet (1815–1882) addressed a mixed crowd of Cubans and North American blacks at a meeting in New York in 1872. Garnet assured the Cuban "defenders of freedom" (1872, 16) that African Americans who had "passed through the terrible ordeal of the struggle for freedom and equal rights" would recognize the similar plight of their "enslaved fellow-men" in Cuba (15). In 1878, the same year that Maceo visited the United States, *La Verdad* (a newspaper in New York) published a letter to Maceo from Cuban Anti-Slavery Committee chairman S. R. Scrotton. "The friends of liberty in America as in Europe," Scrotton wrote, "have their eyes anxiously fixed on you, hoping that perhaps you will save that noble Cuban army which successfully sustains the flag of liberty" (quoted in P. Foner 1963, 270).

Regarding himself as an "emissary for a slave 'people,'" Maceo believed Cuba and Haiti had a connection based on a common history of racial slavery. He wrote the following in a letter to the Haitian General José Lamothe:

> La historia de Cuba es igual a la de Haití; es la historia de todas las colonias . . . allí, la mayor parte de la población compuesta de hombres de nuestra raza, se ve privada de todos los derechos políticos y civiles y sujeta a las más estúpidas preocupaciones y allí, en fin, 350 mil hombres yacen aún en la más dura servidumbre y nacen y mueren bajo el férreo yugo de la esclavitud. . . . Me bastaría decirle que hay en Cuba cerca de medio millón de hombres que son de la propiedad exclusiva de unos cuantos

que tienen sobre ellos derechos de vida y muerte, que pueden comprarlos y venderlos, que les hacen trabajar día y noche sin ninguna retribución, que los mandan azotar por la más ligera falta y que asimilándolos completamente a las bestias, les niega hasta el derecho de tener una familia.

[The history of Cuba is the same as that of Haiti; it is the history of all colonies . . . there, the majority of the population is comprised of men of our race; they are deprived of all political and civil rights and subject to the most frivolous concerns and there, lastly, 350 thousand men remain still in the most harsh servitude and are born and die beneath the iron yoke of slavery. . . . I can tell you myself that in Cuba there are almost half a million men who are the sole property of a few who have the rights over their life and death, who can buy and sell them, who can make them work day and night without retribution, who can order them to be whipped for the slightest fault, and considering them to be completely equivalent to beasts, deny them even the right to have a family.] (Maceo 2002b, 48)

Maceo believed that it was the obligation of "hombres de color que hemos tenido la fortuna de no nacer en la esclavitud" (men of color who had the fortune of not being born into slavery) to liberate the enslaved who were "cansados del látigo y de las cadenas" (tired from the whip and the chains) and "demasiado débiles para romperlas por sí solos" (too weak to break them by themselves) (Maceo 2002b, 49). His contention that the African slave trade and its legacy in the Americas were intrinsically linked to the pursuit of cross-racial freedom significantly informed his conception of the Cuban national project. Maceo, the Cuban nationalist, then, did not separate the legacy of black oppression in Cuba from the cause of liberty in Cuba. In his speech "A Los Cubanos de Color" (To Cubans of Color; 2002a), Maceo identified the Cuban government, in its loyalty to the Spanish Crown, as "enemigos de la humanidad negra" (enemies of black humanity), while in the same breath he called black Cubans to arms united with "los blancos, hijos del país que os defienden vuestros derechos" (the whites, sons of the country, who defend your own rights) (50).

By identifying himself as the emissary of an enslaved "people" fighting for independence, Maceo linked the pursuit of freedom for and by afrodescendente slaves and the national freedom of Cuba from the "yoke" of European colonialism. He drew parallels between the enslavement of "el hombre negro" (the black man) in Cuba and that of the Cuban nation, "yoked" under the colonial grip of Spain. For Maceo, the rise of the "bandera de Cuba" (Cuban flag)—that is, the new, independent, egalitarian Cuba that was an expressed ideal of the independence struggle—would effectuate the freedom of the slaves and of the Cuban nation (Maceo, 1879 [2002], 46).

Maceo's pan-African sensibility, integrated with the struggle for Cuban independence, made him the object of much criticism. News of the Cuban wars for independence with a largely Afro-Cuban army began to fuel white fear in Cuba, Spain, and the United States of another slave revolt like the Haitian Revolution in 1791 (Helg 1995, 49–51, 80, 89). Maceo was accused of favoring his black troops and trying to build a "Negro republic." He denied these accusations vehemently and repeatedly expressed his commitment to an integrated struggle for Cuban independence. Identifying himself as a member of "the colored race," he believed in an integrated and egalitarian nation that would "recognize no hierarchy" of races and stated that he "entered the revolution for no other reason than to shed his blood to see the slaves and his country free" (P. Foner 1977, 62–63).

Harper's poetic rendering of Maceo's death emerges out of this larger historical and political context. By the time she published the poem, Maceo was already an established figure closely aligned with racial and national struggles for freedom. Harper not only celebrates his life but also links him to the continued struggle of African Americans for social and political freedom in the United States as well as to the American nation's failure to realize its ideals. By aligning Maceo with Christ, Harper challenges an American nation founded on Christian ideology to observe the contradiction between Christian values and racial or colonial oppression.

After identifying Maceo with Cuban national freedom in the first three stanzas, Harper's speaker calls on other Christians to consider Maceo's death in light of Christic typology.

> With the light of God around us,
> Why this agony and strife?
> With the cross of Christ before us,
> Why this fearful waste of life?
> Must the pathway to freedom
> Ever mark a crimson line,
> And the eyes of wayward mortals
> Always close to light divine. (13–20)

Like Christ, Maceo is martyred because of the ignorance of "wayward mortals" with "eyes . . . close[d]" to the divine who make the "pathway to freedom" one of bloodshed and death.

Harper's typological linking of Christ and Maceo places her within a tradition of American writers who, from the seventeenth century on, as Werner Sollors notes, "develop Christic parallels" in their work, relating a secular American history to biblical types (1986, 51). Both Maceo and Christ walk the "pathway of freedom." They shed "crimson" blood on behalf of the freedom or redemption of mankind. Both gain immortality through death. As Maceo becomes immortal through the eulogizing process of the narrative, Harper opposes him to "mortals."

As Christ's death brings about a plan for a spiritual redemption, Maceo's death redeems Cuban nationhood by making him the quintessential citizen of a new Cuba—one that, in his own words, "sabe morir por la redención de su patria" (knows how to die for the redemption of his country) (Maceo 1879 [2002], 46). Maceo's heroic self-sacrifice for the "redemption of his country" aligns him with the crucified Christ, who shed his blood to redeem others. Furthermore, Maceo's disappearance in the poem is as meaningful as his initial appearance. Although the poem bears his name, Maceo is not explicitly mentioned after the third stanza. However, I suggest that this "disappearance" is actually a textually implied metamorphosis. After "passing through the gates of death" Maceo disappears, effectively *becoming* Christ as we are prompted to perceive him in the "light of God."

Harper does not reject Christianity; she reinterprets it. Her appropriation of Christic typology places her within a tradition of biblical reinterpretation in African

American poetry. Allen Dwight Callahan cites the Negro spirituals as prime examples of such a phenomenon. He maintains that the Negro spirituals in fact created a context in which the Old and New Testaments were *correlated* rather than dichotomized.[4]

> But in the Negro spirituals, the New does not supersede the Old. The two Testaments, Old and New are correlated to each other. Moses is not a "type" of Jesus. Both bear witness-eternally, equally valid witness-to what God has done and is doing in the world. They are placed side by side with others in the Bible, that "great cloud of witnesses," as the writer of the Epistle to the Hebrews puts it, who *corroborate* each other's testimony. (Callahan 2006, 189)

Joshua does not "foreshadow Jesus" but is identical to Jesus, his New Testament antitype (Callahan 2006, 193). On the one hand, Maceo's suffering and death in "Maceo" ties him to the New Testament Christ, a correlation that is performed in the very structure of the poem. On the other hand, his heroic and militaristic death identifies him with the often vengeful God of the Old Testament as well as the vision of Christ predicted in the Book of Revelation.

This connection between Maceo and Christ not only places "Maceo" in a tradition of African American literary meditations on Christ, it also suggests that the poem has implications that go beyond religious symbolism. The speaker suggests that Maceo's death repeats Christ's sacrifice and questions whether the eyes of the global community are truly open to the "divine light." In doing so, Harper evokes the contradictions that plagued nineteenth-century North American national consciousness.

For instance, Harper's critique of American nationalism aligns her with her contemporary Frederick Douglass, who also drew a line between the "Christianity of Christ" and the Christianity of the American nation. In his autobiography, Douglass called the "religion of this land" a "corrupt, slave-holding, women-whipping, cradle-plundering, partial and hypocritical" Christianity (1960, 155). Yet American nationalist rhetoric thrived on the idea that the United States was a Christian nation. In his observation of a burgeoning American nation, French political scientist Alexis de Tocqueville asserted that "America [was] nevertheless still the place in the world where the Christian religion [had] retained the greatest true power over souls" (2000, 132). America fulfilled its desire for a distinctly American character, a national character, by positing itself as a nation chosen by God, a "Promised Land" (Friedman 1975, 164; Grosby 2002, 221–24).

Harper's meditation on Maceo's death in her poem suggests that this "promised land" of freedom had yet to be fully realized in the Americas. Maceo's death and the ongoing wars for independence in Cuba signaled this fact. The correlation between the fight for freedom and death—death being the "pathway to freedom" that "mark[s] a crimson line"—recalls "Death of Zombi," in which freedom becomes associated with bloodshed. Christianity being a central component of nineteenth-century American nationalism, Harper tropes on this dialectic between freedom and death through an allusion to Christ in the context of Maceo's death, considering his death in a larger discourse about freedom and Christianity.

This correlation also resonates with the American Civil War, for which the relationship between freedom and national unification was central. Harper's speaker questions a world that kills its "heroes," and she calls for human and *humane* intervention.

> Must the hearts of fearless valor
> Fail 'mid crime and cruel wrong,
> When the world has read of heroes
> Brave and honest, true and strong?
> Men to stay the flood of sorrow
> Sweeping round each war-crusted heart;
> Men to say to strife and carnage—
> From our world henceforth depart. (21–28)

After questioning a failing humanity, Harper's speaker addresses God directly in a plea for the "reign" of Christ as "redeemer."

> God of peace and God of nations,
> Haste! oh, haste the glorious day
> When the reign of our Redeemer
> O'er the world shall have its sway.
> When the swords now blood encrusted,
> Spears that reap the battle field,
> Shall be changed to higher service,
> Helping earth rich harvests yield. (29–36)

This redemption is not transcendental or escapist. Instead, the "higher service" is the act of causing the Earth to be fruitful. The God here is one of nations *on Earth*. Harper's "Redeemer" does not "reigns" over an earthly kingdom. Harper grounds the "heavenly" in the earthly world of the poor, the widowed, the orphaned child.

> Where the widow weeps in anguish,
> And the orphan bows his head,
> Grant that peace and joy and gladness
> May like holy angels tread.
> Pity, oh, our God the sorrow
> Of the world from thee astray,
> Lead us from the paths of madness
> Unto Christ the living way. (37–44)

Beyond its moralistic or didactic function, the assertion of movement *toward* Christ from the "paths of madness" suggests a subtle but specific interpretation and appropriation of Christ. Harper identifies Maceo with a Christ who himself became a victim, "the 'lamb that was slain' . . . whose perennial wound signifies his suffering" (Callahan 2006, 238). This suffering Christ, however, brings peace and change to the downcast and the marginalized.

> Year by year the world grows weary
> 'Neath its weight of sin and strife,
> Though the hands once pierced and bleeding
> Offer more abundant life. (45–48)

From this point on, the poem becomes an intercession. It extends beyond the specific Cuban national context and acquires a transnational, even global scope. After lamenting the condition of a world that "grows weary '[n]eath its weight of sin and strife," the speaker asks that the "old and sweet refrain" be sung until there is peace.

> May the choral song of angels
> Heard upon Judea's plain
> Sound throughout the earth the tidings
> Of that old and sweet refrain.
> Till our world, so sad and weary,
> Finds the balmy rest of peace—
> Peace to silence all her discords—
> Peace till war and crime shall cease.
> Peace to fall like gentle showers,
> Or on parched flowers dew,
> Till our hearts proclaim with gladness:
> Lo, He maketh all things new. (49–60)

Addressing a higher power that might grant this request for peace, the speaker intercedes on behalf of a world plagued with "war and crime." This peace is not simply a transcendental peace of death in which death functions as a metaphor for a mystic translation into heaven. In fact, heaven does not appear here at all. Maceo's new "Cuba Libre" remerges at the end of the poem in the form of a new Earth. Like Zumbi, the iconic figure of Maceo effects a peculiar relationship between life, death, and freedom, such that freedom is achieved only in and by death. Maceo's death in the first line of the poem culminates in "all things new" in the last. In both cases, freedom requires death, the shedding of blood.

In connection with the overall structure of "Maceo," Harper's sensibility for oral performance becomes particularly important. The poem functions as a quasi-sermonic performance, beginning with an event, commenting on that event using biblical allusions, and finally ending in a prayer. The implied audience in "Maceo" is divided between "the people" (i.e., in the United States) and God himself, as it culminates in a collective prayer. In this sense the poem progresses from the regionally specific and isolated death of Antonio Maceo toward a collective prayer on behalf of "nations" and "worlds." Maceo is transformed from individual to icon, signifying a symbolic redemption. Harper adopts the figure of Christ—with its biblical notions of freedom through self-sacrifice—and aligns it with the cause of earthly (political, economic, racial, social) redemption through the death of Maceo. Maceo becomes a black Christ—the synthesis of sacrifice and struggle. In her translation of Maceo, Harper configures him as a *sign* for the African American struggle for freedom during the post-Reconstruction era in United States.[5] Harper urges blacks facing government-sanctioned violence and persecution to see their fight against oppression in a larger, transnational context of the struggle African descendants. Harper suggests that this struggle calls into question the very tenets of North American national identity. For her, the progress and spiritual health of an evolving United States at the turn of the century depends on recognizing the death of men like Maceo as both tragic *and* redemptive.

Conclusion

Harper's emphasis on the common humanity of blacks and whites falls in line with many other abolitionists at the time who made a deliberate effort to counteract the belief that blacks were less than human. In a speech delivered to the New York Anti-Slavery Society in 1857, Harper asked

> Could we trace the record of every human heart, the aspirations of every immortal soul, perhaps we would find no man so imbruted and degraded that we could not trace the word liberty either written in living characters upon the soul or hidden away in some nook or corner of the heart. The law of liberty is the law of God, and is antecedent to all human legislation. It existed in the mind of Deity when He hung the first world upon its orbit and gave it liberty to gather light from the central sun. (Harper 1857a)

Not only does Harper allude to a common, transcendent humanity, she also argues that liberty is fundamental to any conception of the human. The "law of liberty" precedes any legislation or epistemological theory that might place limitations on humanity and the human desire for and entitlement to freedom. In "On How We Mistook the Map for the Territory," Sylvia Wynter explains how a secularized, "biocentric" definition of "Man" evolved in the second half of the nineteenth century, a European conception of "man" that became synonymous with the definition of "human" and precipitated in the othering (i.e., the dehumanization) of Native Americans and especially Africans (2006, 119). It also produced a color line that then translated into the idea of race. This process was intimately related to conceptions of "races" of people and to a racial hierarchy in which white was ultimately superior and black (and to some degree nonwhite peoples in general) bore the weight of *désêtre*, or "wrongness of being" (Wynter 2006, 118). Both "Death of Zombi" and "Maceo" challenge such definitions of humanity influenced by Darwinian and positivist thought.

Harper *explicitly* transnationalizes the question of freedom and humanity for African Americans in the nineteenth century. In a country torn between a national rhetoric of freedom and a social and economic dependency on slavery, she offered a vision of a free black republic, evoking the history of what later became a celebrated symbol of struggle against colonial imperialism—the republic of Palmares. Four decades later, in the aftermath of a failed Reconstruction leading to racial violence and the exclusion of blacks from full citizenship, Harper wrote about a black Cuban leader who fought to quell racial conflict in his country for the sake of national unity and independence. By using black figures outside of the United States, she suggests that the scope of African American experience extends beyond regional and national boundaries.

The idea that a Negro kingdom could exist in Brazil and be relevant to the history of African Americans suggests the peculiar relationship of afrodescendente peoples to their national identities—identities that evolve from a condition of exile—and shows that neither African American racial identity nor North American national identity respected national borders. This New World black consciousness is born out of a fundamental condition of diaspora. It is neither simply a desire for a return to Africa nor an essentialist concept of blackness or of African ancestry. Rather, it is a product of an interweaving of historical process contingent on the multidirectional movement not only of people but of narratives, symbols, typologies, and other such literary elements.

Likewise, Harper appropriates Maceo's death in an effort to resolve a perceived inconsistency between human behavior and a transcendent morality that might restore black (and white) humanity and create "free" nations. As Cuba Libre (i.e., a new, free Cuba) here becomes synonymous with freedom, Maceo's death acquires a larger meaning with implications beyond the Cuban context. By inserting this text into this larger discourse, Harper also places American nationalism in a transnational context.

Well before the Harlem Renaissance and Negritude movements popularized internationalism in poetry, Harper began using poetry to challenge African Americans to conceptualize identity beyond national borders. Her appropriations of Zumbi and Maceo are signs not only of her pan-African sensibility but also of her early transnational African American poetics, a poetics demanding a certain kind of critical analysis—one that recognizes the permeability of national boundaries. Because her work demonstrates a keen transhemispheric sensibility, future scholarship on Harper should take into account the transnational currents instigated by the transatlantic slave trade and their influence on her poetry. In fact, as part of a collection of transnational poetic allusions in African American literature, Harper's "Death of Zombi" and "Maceo" suggest that transnational readings of African American poetry need to go beyond the scope of such explicitly pan-African movements as Negritude and the "third-world consciousness" of Black Arts Movement poetics and consider all African American writing within a persistent transnational context that has influenced black literary aesthetics from the earliest moments of black literary production in the New World. To do so, African American literary studies requires a transhemispheric—and therefore multilingual, multicultural, and pan-American—conceptual framework.

Chapter Two

Signs of Blood: Redemption Songs and "American" Poetry beyond Borders

Wherefore say unto the children of Israel, I am the Lord, and I will bring you out from under the burdens of the Egyptians, and I will rid you out of their bondage and I will redeem you with a stretched out arm, and with great judgments.

—King James Bible, Exodus 6:6

It returns us to Eliot's pronouncement, that a culture cannot exist without a religion, and to other pronouncements irradiating that idea, that an epic poetry cannot exist without a religion. It is the beginning of the poetry of the New World. And the language used is, like the religion, that of the conqueror of the God. But the slave had wrested God from his captor.

—Derek Walcott, "The Muse of History" (1996)

Old pirates, yes, they rob I,
Sold I to the merchant ships,
Minutes after they took I
From the bottomless pit.
But my hand was made strong
By the hand of The Almighty.
We forward in this generation
Triumphantly.
Won't you help to sing
These songs of freedom?
'Cause all I ever have
Redemption songs
Redemption songs.

—Bob Marley, "Redemption Song"

Biblical Re-Vision: Defining Freedom through the Narrative of Slavery

Biblical allusions to the "hand of God" are and have been at work in the literary and political lives of African Americans for centuries. In the case of African Americans in the United States, the Negro spiritual represents a definitive form of poetic reinterpretation of the Bible. According to Benjamin E. Mays, the tradition of African American spirituals—which he categorizes as a form of "mass" literature (1938, 19)—interprets slavery "in terms of Egyptian bondage," and thus implies that "as freedom came to the Hebrews it would come to the Negro" (1938, 28). The spirituals serve as a clear precedent for biblical reinterpretations evident in the African American literary tradition. For example, the poet Frances Harper's sixteen-stanza ballad "Deliverance" (1893), presents the biblical exodus of the Israelites from Egypt as an allegory for the experience of African Americans in the United States. Although Harper's specific use of the exodus evolves out of a uniquely African (North) American tradition of biblical reinterpretation, we can also see traces of a similar type of re-vision at work in the poetry of other *afrodescendente* poets in the Americas. Cristina Ayala's "Redención" (Redemption) traces the history of slaves in Cuba using allusions to the biblical Israelites and to the figure of Christ.

In spite of Harper's canonical status in the tradition of African American literature, little has been written about her relationship to other afrodescendente women poets in the Americas who were faced with similar challenges presented by the postabolition era. Read alongside Ayala's "Redención," Harper's "Deliverance" reaches beyond the national context of the United States. It presents the problem of racial uplift as a global predicament and the challenge of representing the history of racial slavery in the Americas as a poetic endeavor.[1] This chapter examines the role of women of African descent in the poetic reimagining of the postabolition "Americas" through a close, comparative analysis of Harper and Ayala.

When renowned Cuban poet Nancy Morejón accepted the 2001 Premio Nacional de Literatura (2001 National Literature Prize), she invoked Ayala's name: "He buscado sin tregua" (I have sought tirelessly), Morejon asserted, "darle voz a un coro de voces silenciadas que, a través de la historia, mucho más allá de sus orígenes, su raza o su género, renacen en mi idioma" (to give voice to a chorus of silenced voices that, throughout history, well beyond their origins, their race or their gender, are reborn in my language) (2002a, 8). Ayala is virtually unknown outside of Cuba, but her work constitutes a major contribution to and critique of a period in Cuban history fraught with questions of racial and national identity. Even within Cuba Ayala's work has yet to receive adequate critical attention as a part of Cuban literary history (DeCosta Willis, 2003, xxxi). Negotiating race, its history, and social implications was a critical part of the transition into the post-Reconstruction era in the United States as it was in the postabolition era in Cuba. This period was also characterized by the movement of people and of ideas between Cuba and the United States.[2]

Harper and Ayala were both formally educated. Neither was a slave. One was born in the United States, the other, in Cuba.[3] The similarities in Ayala's and Harper's typological appropriations in "Redención" and "Deliverance" suggest a linkage that transcends national boundaries. Harper's poem posits black Americans as contemporary

Israelites delivered from the "Egypt" of American slavery. "Redención" incorporates a more subtle appropriation of the biblical figure of Christ, comparing Christ-as-martyr to black Cubans recently "redeemed" from slavery. The collective "raza negra" in Cuba emerges as a contemporary Christ figure, a "redeemer" of the Cuban nation by its self-sacrifice and intercession. "Deliverance" and "Redención" both appropriate biblical typology as a means of (1) creating a narrative to understand the history of peoples of African descent in the United States and Cuba, presenting afrodescendente peoples as an "imagined community" constructed by a narrative of slavery and emancipation; and (2) expressing the role African descendants played as both participants in and creators of new nations.

The traces of biblical allusion in Ayala and Harper are evident; the explanation for the uncannily similar way in which they appropriate them is not. Their use of biblical narrative places the texts in conversation and thereby suggests that the strategy of biblical reinterpretation in the construction of racial and national identities in Cuba and the United States did not respect the arbitrary boundaries of geographical or even linguistic "nations." The denotation of the terms *deliverance* (the act of delivering or setting free) and *redención* (deliverance from sin or the act of freeing a slave by payment) roots both texts etymologically and symbolically in the slave-free binary. Furthermore, these interlocking terms place the poetic texts in the larger context of New World slavery. Ayala's and Harper's use of biblical typology—Ayala through the figure of Christ and Harper through the Exodus—demonstrate an early form of secular typology in the framing of a collective history of African descendants in the New World. Both poems inscribe a narrative of freedom. They propose a particular way of envisioning the emancipation of peoples of African descent in Cuba and the United States during the second half of the nineteenth century.

Delivering Memory: Exodus and Harper's "Deliverance"

> Slavery chain done broke at last,
> Going to praise God til I die . . .
> And de days were with head bowed down
> And my broken flesh and pain.
> I did know my Jesus heard me,
> 'Cause de spirit spoke to me
> And said, "Rise my child, your chillun,
> And you shall be free.
> I done 'p'int one mighty captain
> For to marshall all my hosts
> And to bring my bleeding ones to me
> And not one shall be lost."
> Slavery chain done broke at last, broke at last,
> Slavery chain done broke at last,
> Going to praise God til I die.
> —Negro Spiritual

> The great problem to be solved by the American people, if I
> understand it, is this—whether or not there is strength
> enough in democracy, virtue enough in our civilization, and
> power enough in our religion to have mercy and deal justly
> with four millions of people but lately translated from the
> old oligarchy of slavery to the new commonwealth of
> freedom: and upon the right solution of this question
> depends in a large measure the future strength, progress and
> durability of our nation.
>
> —Frances Ellen Watkins Harper, "The Great Problem to Be Solved" (1990a)

By the time the "slavery chain" broke in the United States, African Americans had been interpreting freedom for themselves for centuries. One of the major ways they did so was through their creative use of the Old Testament. In "Deliverance," Harper draws a direct parallel between the experience of the Israelites and that of African Americans, using the Exodus as an allegory for the history of African Americans in the United States. The poem begins at the beginning of the end. It begins before the end of Pharaoh's reign over the Israelites, a nation whose enslavement African Americans would identify with their own. In the first two stanzas, Harper's speaker describes the Israelites' escape from slavery in Egypt.

> Rise up! rise up! Oh Israel,
> Let a spotless lamb be slain;
> The angel of death will o'er you bend
> And rend your galling chain.
> Sprinkle its blood upon the posts
> And lintels of your door;
> When the angel sees the crimson spots
> Unharmed he will pass you o'er. (Harper, "Deliverance," in Foster 1990, 335, ll. 1–8)

The repetition ("Rise up! rise up!") invokes the theme of racial uplift. As the Israelites rose up out of ancient Egyptian slavery (as told through the biblical Exodus narrative), so would African Americans rise up out of modern slavery. Internal rhyme ("death will o'er you *bend* / And *rend* your galling chain") and end-rhyme ("Let a spotless lamb be *slain*; / And rend your galling *chain*") reinforce the theme of biblical sacrifice as a precedent for redemption.[4] The image of an "angel of death" breaking the chains of the Israelites directly precedes instructions for applying the mark that would ensure freedom from death ("Sprinkle its blood upon the posts / and lintels of your door / When the angel sees the crimson spots / Unharmed he will pass you o'er"). The twelfth chapter of Exodus tells the story of God's "passing over" the Israelites, exempting them from plagues and death.

> For I will pass through the land of Egypt this night, and will smite all the firstborn in the land of Egypt, both man and beast; and against all the gods of Egypt I will execute

judgment: I am the Lord. And the blood shall be to you for a token upon the houses where ye are: and when I see the blood, I will pass over you, and the plague shall not be upon you to destroy you, when I smite the land of Egypt. (Exodus 12:12–13)

After a series of plagues failed to free the Israelites, God instructed them through Moses to sacrifice an unblemished lamb and place its blood on their doorposts as a mark. This *mark* would designate the Israelites as the chosen children of God. Not only would this blood mark the chosen Israelites, it would also cause an angel to "rend [their] galling chain." It would guarantee their freedom from slavery in Egypt and identify them as a part of an "imagined" community.[5] There is a space between the physical body and the blood mark placed on the doorposts; this space mirrors the space "between the lines" in which the identity marker binds to an imagined community of people. Ultimately, the blood mark comes to represent the physical—though textual and dependent on narrative—racial mark of African slaves in the New World.

Harper follows the Exodus narrative, describing the Israelites' preparation for escape from Mizriam (i.e., Egypt) led by Moses.

> Gather your flocks and herd to-night,
> Your children by your side;
> A leader from Arabia comes
> to be your friend and guide.
> With girded loins and sandaled feet
> Await the hour of dread,
> When Mizraim shall wildly mourn
> Her first-born and her dead. (9–16)

The importance of remembrance continues as a motif throughout the poem. The feast that would "mark [the] day" of the Israelites' freedom would also ensure the memory of their deliverance and thus keep it alive for future, "unborn generations."

> The sons of Abraham no more
> Shall crouch 'neath Pharaoh's hand,
> Trembling with agony and dread,
> He'll thrust you from the land.
> And ye shall hold in unborn years
> A feast to mark this day,
> When joyfully the fathers rose
> And cast their chains away. (17–24)

The enslaved here, as the "sons of Abraham," are placed in the lineage of Christ. They are freed from their chains by God, who delivers them from Pharaoh, the prototypical slavemaster.

The poem continues to follow the Exodus narrative, echoing the instructions of God to the Israelites while simultaneously calling attention to the act of "re-membering." The connection between racial uplift and a redemptive freedom that we see first in stanzas

1 and 2 reemerges here in the context of remembering the past ("When joyfully the father's rose / And cast their chains away"). The admonition to remember, or to "hold in unborn years / [a] feast to mark this," echoes the scriptural directive found in the Old Testament book of Exodus: "And this day shall be unto you for a memorial; and ye shall keep it a feast to the Lord throughout your generations; ye shall keep it a feast by an ordinance for ever" (Exodus 12:14). Passing on the story from generation to generation provides a means of preserving a particular memory of African American history.

> When crimson tints of morning flush
> The golden gates of day,
> Or gorgeous hue of even melt
> In sombre shades away,
> Then ye shall to your children teach
> The meaning of this feast,
> How from the proud oppressor's hand
> Their fathers were released. (25–32)

The "crimson spots" resurface here as "crimson tints of morning." They no longer signify the blood mark as they did in stanza 2. The future relies not on the redemptive act alone but on the memory of it. Meaning is preserved, then, through the act of transmitting the narrative through consecutive generations.

> And ye shall hold through distant years
> This feast with glad accord,
> And children's children yet shall learn
> To love and trust the Lord. (33–36)
> Ages have passed since Israel trod
> In triumph through the sea,
> And yet they hold in memory's urn
> Their first great jubilee.
> When Moses led the ransomed hosts,
> And Miriam's song arose,
> While ruin closed around the path
> Of their pursuing foes. (37–44)

The narrative voice shifts after beginning in the present and hearing the story of the past. The narrative moves abruptly to the future-present. It shifts away from the Israelites and directs our attention toward "we who stood lately redeemed": African Americans.

> Shall Israel thro' long varied years
> These memories cherish yet,
> And we who lately stood redeemed
> Our broken chains forget? (45–48)

Here, one narrative ends and another begins. The admonition to remember is now directed toward the project of African American collective consciousness. Without this re-membering, the victorious climax of the Exodus narrative might easily dissolve into the tragic mis-remembering of Harper's audience, another "redeemed" people. In *The Talking Book: African Americans and the Bible*, Allen Callahan maintains that an African American "subversive reading" of Exodus creates a separation between the "faith of the master and the faith of the slave" (2006, 87). As slaves in the "promised land" of their masters, enslaved African Americans reinterpreted the Exodus for themselves. They envisioned themselves as modern Israelites and perceived America as the Egypt from which they would be delivered. Harper's poetic reinterpretation of the exodus suggests that although the exodus was an emblem of the past for the early white American settlers, for African Americans it was an anticipated promise of the future.

> Should we forget the wondrous change
> That to our people came,
> When justice rose and sternly plead
> Our cause with sword and flame?
> And led us through the storms of war
> To freedom's fairer shore,
> When slavery sank beneath a flood
> Whose waves were human gore?
> Oh, youth and maidens of the land,
> Rise up with one accord,
> And in the names of Christ go forth
> To battle for the Lord.
> Go forth, but not in crimson fields,
> With fratricidal strife,
> But in the name of Christ go forth
> For freedom, love and life. (49–64)

The "wondrous change" here refers to the passage from slavery to freedom, a change reinforced through the opposition of "freedom's fairer shore" and the demise of slavery ("When slavery sank beneath a flood / Whose waves were human gore"). Ultimately, the allusion to the blood referenced in prior stanzas ("in crimson fields") is replaced with Christ ("in the name of Christ"), thus translating the narrative from Old Testament to New Testament, from ancient to modern, from a completed redemption to an anticipated one. Harper's speaker makes a specific appeal to the "youth and maidens of the land," the least anticipated and most historically uninvolved in national politics. It is the women and children—not the white, predominantly male "Redeemers" of the South and not the cadre of male abolitionists of the North—who receive "the call" to function as Christ-as-redeemer and to realize the constitutional ideals of "freedom, love and life." Harper ties the language of the Constitution together with the history of slavery and recent emancipation of black slaves in the United States. Admonished to "go forth"—a repetition that echoes that of the opening lines of the poem—they "go forth" having acquired a new *name*.

> Harper concludes with opposition, not resolution.
> Go forth to follow in his steps,

Who came not to destroy,
Till wastes shall blossom as the rose,
And deserts sing for joy. (65–68)

The oppositions are resolvable only through an act of linguistic violence, the changing of denotative and connotative *meanings* of the signs. The "wastes" must blossom. The "deserts" must sing.[6] In this sense, Harper draws attention to the role of language in framing the past, present, and future of the nation. Reaffirming the opening lines of the poem ("Rise up! rise up!"), she calls on black women as members of a racial community to whom the "wondrous change" of freedom has come. She urges them to "rise up with one accord," to reassert the Christian ideals of America—the pursuit of "life and liberty" as asserted by the Constitution and reaffirmed in the Emancipation Proclamation. Harper exhorts these women to remember the Civil War ("when justice rose and strong plead / our cause with sword and flame") as it brought emancipation to black slaves and the promise of equality to free and recently emancipated African Americans alike. "Rise up! rise up! Oh Israel" in the first line echoes later in the sixth stanza when the speaker refers to the "youth and maidens of the land." By the repetition of this refrain, Harper suggests that these women and children are in fact the Israel of the first stanza. She admonishes black women and children to sustain the history of slavery in their memory and to use it to mobilize in the name of the biblically based ideals of American nationalism.

As Albert Raboteau indicates in his analysis of slave religion, emancipation left African Americans a "less than complete" freedom (1978, 320). The "historical identity" that slaves acquired through their appropriation of the "archetypal event" of the biblical Exodus, however, represents their efforts to incorporate it into their "mythic past" in such a way that would create meaning out of the experience of slavery (1978, 311). In evoking the exodus as a metaphor for black experience in the United States, Harper follows a tradition of American national discourse but does so in a way that challenges its tenets. She expands on the use of the exodus in Western thought (Walzer 1985, 7) and American national ideology (Bercovitch 1978, 141; Sollors 1986, 44). The American Revolution had already established a strong tie between a biblically based morality and nation-building. In fact, due to the Great Awakening, America by the eighteenth century had become what Richard Hofstadter calls "a concentrated repository of the Protestant Ethic" and "a center of ascetic Protestantism" (1971, 293). During the revolution, moral asceticism and republicanism were melded together (Takaki 1991, 4). As Smith and Dawson suggest in their analysis of "American" national identity in the last decade of the nineteenth century, American nativism grew ever stronger as a "fading Europhilia" met an "increasingly emergent 'Americanness'" (2000, 3). One of the major expressions of this Americanness was religious metaphor. Biblical narrative, more specifically the Exodus, helped construct North American national identity. According to Steve Grosby, Americans believed they were chosen to create an "American Israel," a "promised land" for those displaced because of religious persecution (2002, 221).[7] But "Deliverance" does not only treat the exodus narrative itself. "Deliverance" also demonstrates a preoccupation with the *memory* of the event and the means by which it became a narrative through the passing down from one generation to the next.

The violent backlash of a failed Reconstruction in the South proved that deliverance for African Americans remained to be seen. Recognizing the parallels between a past legacy of slavery and the present violent repression of blacks in North America, Harper encourages her readers to reaffirm the ideals of a collective national unity. At the height of lynch law in the South and the violence of the post-Reconstruction era, Harper uses biblical allegory to frame the story she wants to tell about African Americans in the United States. She first calls them to remember the "redemption" (i.e., legal emancipation) of slaves and then challenges the nation to realize its own ideals. Harper's "we" is simultaneously African Americans specifically—literally freed from slavery—and the American nation as a whole—freed from the pervasive system of slavery.

African American slaves read the Exodus in a particular way distinct from that of their masters. There is a tradition of allegorical use of the Exodus narrative and Christic typology to articulate African American experience in the New World. Reading the Exodus in this way identifies Harper with this tradition. "Deliverance" focuses on the exit from Egypt, not the entrance into Canaan. By the end of the poem, the American "Canaan" of "freedom, love, and life" is yet to be realized. We do not end with deliverance but with the *anticipation* of deliverance. The "promised land" is not the physical terrain of unexplored territories in and out of the United States; instead, it is a second "jubilee" to follow the "first great jubilee" (stanza 10) of freedom from slavery. It is a symbolic space that has no physical territory, an "imagined" territory located outside of the physical and ideological boundaries of American nationalism. It is a space whose contours are determined within the poetic text itself.

Redeeming Cuba: The Slave and the Free in Ayala's "Redención"

Just as the "promised land" in Harper's "Deliverance" extends beyond the physical boundaries of North America, the story of African slaves in the Americas crosses over the arbitrary boundaries inscribed by colonial expeditions. The descendants of Africans in Cuba during the final decades of the nineteenth century also faced the task of writing themselves into a Cuban national script. Cristina Ayala's "Redención" (1889) is one such inscription.[8]

"Redención" begins with a description of a passing storm, a metaphor Ayala uses to articulate the "passing" of an era of slavery in Cuba.[9]

> Cual tras negra tormenta, un claro día
> lucir suele con bellos esplendores
> y cual brilla en un rostro la alegría
> tras un cúmulo inmenso de dolores,
> así mi pobre raza, que llevaba
> una vida de mísera agonía

y bajo el férreo yugo que la ahogaba
en dura esclavitud triste gemía . . . (in Ayala 1926, 20, ll. 1–8)
[As after a black storm, a clear day
comes to shine with radiant beauties
and what happiness shines on a face after
such an immense cloud of pains,
so my poor race,
that endured a life of miserable anguish
and under the iron yoke that choked it
under harsh slavery, groaned in sorrow.]

The juxtaposition of the "negra tormenta" (black storm) and the "claro día" (clear day) establishes a pre- and postslavery dichotomy. Once subject to the "iron yoke" of slavery and its "cúmulo inmenso de dolores" (immense cloud of pains), the "pobre raza" now experiences the present "claro día" (clear day) of abolition. The cries of the "raza" (race) under the "férreo yugo" (iron yoke) of slavery echo the "cries" of the Israelites under the "yoke" of Egyptian slavery (emphasis added). Leviticus reads: "I am the LORD your God, which brought you forth out of the land of Egypt, that ye should not be their bondmen; and I have broken the bands of your *yoke*, and made you go upright" (26:13). After Moses leads the Israelites out of slavery, they sing songs of their deliverance.

Although "Redención" presents a collective black race framed by a history of racial slavery, the poem does not elaborate on a single moment of "deliverance" but focuses on a vision of freedom.

hoy se encuentra feliz, pues con sus galas
la hermosa Libertad augusta y santa
la cubre, y adornada de esas galas
bate las palmas y sus glorias canta. (9–12)
[today finds itself joyful, as beautiful Liberty, august and holy, covers it with its
royal gowns and, clothed in these gowns, it claps its hands and sings its own glories.]

The speaker praises the raza for bearing the burden of slavery, admonishes it to sing its own "glorias" (glories) now that it was adorned with the "galas" (gowns) of "Libertad" (Liberty). That is, it should evoke the memory of the history of slavery and emancipation.

In the next stanza, the poem shifts toward the nature and character of the "raza negra" and its recent encounter with "la Libertad." Here we encounter an allusion to the figure of Christ.[10]

Raza humilde, sencilla y laboriosa,
modelo fiel de abnegación constante,
que vertiste tu sangre generosa
al impulso del látigo infamante. (13–16)
[Humble race, simple and hard-working, so faithful a model of constant abnegation that
you shed your generous blood at the crack of the infamous whip.] (translation mine)

The "raza humilde" is a humble, selfless martyr, a sacrificial lamb that sheds its blood generously under the oppression of slavery. The *sangre* (blood) here is not the cursed blood of Ham, but the redeeming blood of a divine sacrifice.[11]

> By the second to last stanza, the enslaved is transfigured.
> ¡Canta tu gloria sí; pues no es posible
> que al cesar tu baldón y tu tortura,
> una plegaria mística y sensible
> no se exhale de tu alma con ternura . . .
> Haz que hasta el Solio del Eterno suba
> tu acento, y di con voz que tierna vibre:
> ¡Perdón, Señor, te imploro para Cuba!
> ¡Ya su cr[i]men borró! ¡ya el negro es libre . . . (17–24)
> [Sing of your glory, yes; for it is impossible when your dishonor and torture ceases, that a mystical and empathic prayer not exhale tenderly from your soul . . . Make the sound of your voice rise up to the throne of the Eternal One, and say with a voice that trembles with tenderness: Pardon me, Lord, I implore you for Cuba! It finally erased its crime! At last the Negro is free . . .]

Now freed after an encounter with la Libertad, the recently emancipated "raza negra" becomes the benevolent imparter of pardon, freeing Cuba from its past sins. The word "redención" comes from the Latin *redimere*, meaning to "buy back." In Ayala's "Redención," the purchased becomes the purchaser; the redeemed slave becomes the redeemer. The liberty of the slave is inextricably linked to the redemption of the Cuban nation. Like Christ, the raza sheds its blood in a willful act of sacrifice. It removes the "stain" of slavery and ultimately indicts the Cuban nation. This "baldón" (dishonor) also can be translated "stain" or "blot," which both allude to the moral stain of slavery on the face of Cuban national history. As Christ brings freedom from sin to humankind, the black race brings freedom to Cuba through its own emancipation.

"Cuba" is summoned through the speaker's prayer in the next to last stanza of the poem. This prayer links the plight of the emancipated "raza negra" to the collective project of Cuban nationhood. The speaker instructs the "raza negra" to pray for an imagined free Cuba.

> Pide al Hado feliz, que tu Derecho
> respetado en el mundo siempre veas,
> y exclama desde el fondo de tu pecho:
> ¡Oh Santa Libertad! ¡Bendita seas! (25–28)
> [Ask of joyful Fate that you see always your Rights respected in the world, and proclaim from the depths of your soul: Oh Sacred Liberty! Blessed be!]

The realization of Cuba is contingent on the freedom of the slave. It is the experience and history of black Cubans here that provide the historical and linguistic material with which to build a concept of libertad. The poem extends beyond the national scope to a global one.

The reference to the derechos (rights) for Cubans of color in the final stanza ("Pide al Hado feliz, que tu Derecho / respetado en el mundo siempre veas") speaks to the political climate created by the wars for independence and the thrust of abolition. Cuban military leaders like General Antonio Maceo (1848–1896) joined in the early stages of the wars against Spain. A series of battles culminated in slavery's abolition in 1886. Convinced that the end of Spanish rule would increase their status and opportunities in a new Cuban nation, Cubans "de color" participated in great numbers.[12] As Rebecca J. Scott notes, African descended Cubans struggled for civil rights in a colonial society that made political and civil rights difficult to attain for anyone due to the sovereignty of the Spanish Crown (1985, 277). Following the legal abolition of slavery in Cuba, Cubans "de color" faced opposition to integration in public places, schools, and businesses (1985, 272–73). Although the Cuban government did not explicitly sanction racial segregation or discrimination, it often failed to enforce laws and policies that would ensure the legal and social freedom of Cubans "de color" (1985, 273).

Juan Gualberto Gómez confirmed the ongoing struggle for full emancipation following the abolition of slavery in Cuba in 1889 when he wrote:

> Today we are trying to emancipate ourselves not from slavery which has vanished never to return, but from the bad vices which it has engendered throughout society. Today we are trying to [deal with] the burdens of all the injustices that history has thrown at us; finally, we are trying to make known to the world that we are able to make it on the path of human progress, if we have the same opportunities of the rest. (quoted in Howard 1998, 191)

Gualberto Gómez stressed the importance of fixing what slavery had broken. He was particularly interested in addressing the intangible effects of slavery as they extended beyond the reach of legislative reform. Ayala implies a similar imperative in "Redención," suggesting that black Cubans should remember slavery but also support a unified front against Spain in the name of national unity. The poem presents a symbolic "raza negra" empowered to verbalize in a prayer the possibility of a free Cuban nation.

Ayala challenges a sentimental polarization of slavery and a "free" Cuba. She challenges the kind of sentimentalism present in poetry like that of her contemporary Mercedes Matamoros (1851–1906). In "Esclavitud" (Slavery), Matamoros glorifies the Cuban landscape, opposing it to the underside of slavery.

> Las vírgenes de Cuba son palomas
> por su casta modestia y su dulzura;
> y la madre y el hijo son modelos
> de santa abnegación y de tenura.
> Desciendo de una raza infortunada,
> la tierra de los indios es mi tierra;
> la quiero libre y venturosa y grande
> con los tesoros que en su seno encierra . . .
> Porque todo es delito bajo el yugo,

y ante los fuertes buitres carniceros,
la verdad, la razón y la justicia
se ocultan como tímidos corderos.
¡Oh! ¡Qué dolor tan grande el que el esclavo
siente en su corazón hora tras hora!
que cada día reconviene y clama!
que en todo tiempo se lamenta y llora. (Matamoros 2006, 80–81, ll. 29–44)
[The virgins of Cuba are doves because of their modest class and gentleness; and mother and child are models of holy abnegation and tenderness. Descending from an unfortunate race, the land of the Indians is my land; I love it free, fortunate, and great with treasures imprisoned in its breast. Because everything is a crime under the yoke, and before those mighty, carnivorous vultures, truth, reason and justice hide themselves like timid lambs. Oh! What great pain the slave feels in his heart hour after hour that reprimands and cries out, that complains and weeps always.]

Slavery stood at the crossroads of Cuban national and racial discourse, but abolition did not have a religious component in Cuba. In fact, the Catholic Church in Cuba largely supported slavery. Protestant missionaries from outside of Cuba—the United States, Jamaica, London, and Santo Domingo in particular—began to disseminate antislavery ideas. Many of them made specific reference to the Israelites and the experience of African Americans in the United States to support their claims (Castillo Téllez 2003, 6–7). The conflict between supporters of the Spanish Crown and the *independentistas* manifested as an ideological battle between Catholicism and Protestantism.[13] A by-product of the bidirectional wave of immigration between Cuba and the United States in particular, the Protestant church in Cuba came to be identified with the Cuban independence movement (Castillo Téllez, 43–45).

Members of the *criollo* elite believed firmly that Cuba should be "free" from the colonial grip of Spain. However, many of these same elite Cubans had supported a plan for independence that would preserve the institution of slavery. Instrumental in fashioning the Cuban Constitution, Joaquín Infante proposed an independent Cuban republic fashioned after the French Constitution of 1791. His proposal advocated for the continuance of slavery in Cuba and supported a legal and social system that designated the status of free *mulatos* and *negros* by the proportion of "black blood" in their veins (Carreras 1985, 21).

Even after slavery was abolished, the racial hierarchy it imposed continued to influence Cuban politics. The government supported white Spanish immigration to Cuba, or "whitening," as a means of ensuring white supremacy in Cuban society and politics (Howard 1998, 173). The association between black Cubans and barbarism was heavily rooted in a biblical justification for the enslavement of Africans in Cuba. Cubans of African descent were faulted for the lack of moral progress of the Cuban nation.[14] "Redención" challenges this correlation by linking the "raza negra" with freedom. It posits black Cubans as the symbolic martyrs for the cause of Cuban nationhood and designates them as the "redeemers" of the nation. They are not irrevocably cursed by their racial inheritance, but help define the meaning of national freedom through this inheritance.

Ayala's speaker makes reference to a "Cuba" associated with the crime of slavery, only redeemable as an imagined "nation" by the prayer of the recently emancipated "race." As the "modelo fiel de abnegación constante" (faithful model of constant abnegation), the emancipated slave serves as interlocutor between God and Cuba. Like a priest after the Catholic orthodox order, the "raza negra" is intercessor, mirroring the Christ figure as intercessor on behalf of a fallen human race. Like Christ, the "raza negra" willfully concedes the lashes of those it eventually "redeems" through an equally willful act of propitiation and pardon. The "férreo yugo" (iron yoke) that physically and metaphorically binds the black slave also binds the enslaver to the crime of slavery. The "plegaria mística" (mystical prayer) of the "raza negra" is a petition for Cuba on behalf of "Cuba," an emergent nation no longer in covenant politically or ideologically with Spain.

Ultimately, the "redemption" of "el negro" signifies the redemption of the oppressor within Cuba (i.e., *criolle* slaveholders) and paves the way for a nation free from external oppression. In direct contrast with the racist "sons of Ham" theory and the Cuban elite's appropriation of racial eugenics, Ayala suggests that the recently emancipated slave strengthens the moral integrity of a future Cuban nation. As the Catholic Church became synonymous with the Crown and sought to maintain its hold on its Cuban territory, "Redención" removed Cuba's fate from the hands of Spain and placed it in the hands of emancipated slaves. Ayala suggests that black Cubans not only knew the meaning of freedom but also played a major role in determining what that freedom would look like in postabolition Cuba. Her work not only speaks to the question of Cuban nationhood but also stands at the intersection of Cuba's national and racial politics. Like Harper's "Deliverance," Ayala's "Redención" demonstrates the transnational circulation of biblical narratives as they informed beliefs about race and nationhood.

Conclusion

Ayala's "Redención" and Harper's "Deliverance" speak to each other through echoes. Both poems share a topical concern for how the narrative of slavery and emancipation becomes written and sustained in national memory. In "Redención," slavery represents part of a colonial past facing its demise in the wake of an imminent Cuban independence. In "Deliverance," a history of slavery both influences and challenges the constitutional rhetoric underlying North American nationalism. Either explicitly or implicitly, both Ayala and Harper use the Bible—a text that was used throughout the Americas to support racial slavery either in word or in deed—to reconfigure the relationship between biblical narrative and the story framing the history of African descendants in the Americas. Ayala's subtle manipulation of biblical allusions to Christ as martyr and redeemer and Harper's allegorical use of the Exodus narrative to articulate African American experience both function as a counternarrative to the semantic and scientifically sanctioned denigration of African descendants in the New World.[15]

"Redención" draws together the biblical representation of Christ and the collective representation of a black race in Cuba. It does so by linking the figure of Christ as martyr and intercessor with the "figure" of a black race in Cuba. "Redención" links the memory of slavery and the prerogative of freedom in Cuba. The "raza humilde" in the poem is identified with a Christ-like humility as mediator between Cuba and God. The liberated race, though in covenant with a legacy and memory of slavery, is both Mosaic—asking Jehovah for forgiveness for the sins of an aberrant people—and Messianic—enduring persecution from the very people its shed blood would redeem. By Americanizing African Americans, Harper also addresses the problem of race and nationalism simultaneously. In "Deliverance," the enslaved are likened to the Israelites who, as God's elect, are empowered to intercede on behalf of their oppressors. Ayala and Harper posit a reconciled relationship of African descendants with the racist nation-state. This reconciliation opens the door for active participation in the ideological and symbolic reimagining of the nation. They suggest that the specter of slavery extended beyond the particular experience of slavery as defined by national regions.

Just as the similarities in the poems demonstrate similar strategies of biblical revision, the differences between the narrative strategies and literary devices in these poems speak to the political differences of blacks in Cuba and the United States. In the United States, the idea of America as a "promised land" was lodged in the national ideology. Harper allows the Exodus to inform the formal and thematic elements of "Deliverance." In Cuba, the wars for independence brought the question of national sovereignty to the forefront. In "Redención" Ayala identifies the problem of Cuban nationhood with the postemancipation plight of African descendants. In both cases, the symbolic space of the poem transforms into a landscape on which to articulate, though certainly not wholly reconcile, tensions regarding slavery and nationalism.

Chapter Three

Write the Vision: Gender and Nation beyond Emancipation

Sin aire, la tierra muere. Sin libertad, como sin aire propio y esencial, nada vive.
[Without air, the earth dies. Without freedom, just as without proper and essential air, nothing lives.]

—José Martí, 1883

Few men ever worshipped Freedom with half such unquestioning faith as did the American Negro for two centuries. To him, so far as he thought and dreamed, slavery was indeed the sum of all villanies, the cause of all sorrow, the root of all prejudice; Emancipation was the key to a promised land of sweeter beauty than ever stretched before the eyes of wearied Israelites. In song and exhortation swelled one refrain—Liberty; in his tears and curses the God he implored had Freedom in his right hand. At last it came,—suddenly, fearfully, like a dream.

—W. E. B. Du Bois (1907, 5–6)

Freedom is not inherent to the human condition, historian Orlando Patterson proposes. Instead, it has been "generated from the experience of slavery" in the history of Western Civilization (1991, xiii). For Patterson, this freedom is a double-edged sword. Those who possess freedom can indeed "create and transform their worlds." But they are also free to "brutalize, to plunder and lay waste . . . to rape and humiliate, to invade, to conquer, uproot and degrade" (1991, 403–4). This understanding of freedom highlights an idea central to this chapter's reading of Ayala's and Harper's work: inherent in the practice of freedom is the dialectic it forms with slavish oppression.

This chapter further examines the ways Cristina Ayala and Frances Harper's work demonstrates the interdependence of slavery and freedom. Through a close reading of four poems—"A mi raza" (To My Race) (1888) and "El arroyuelo y la flor" (The Stream and the Flower) (1893) by Ayala and "We Are Rising"(1876) and "Eliza Harris" (1854) by Harper—I discuss how the problematic relationship between freedom and slavery appears at the level of the poetic line. In distinct ways, each poem uses symbolism and allegory to explore concepts of racial, national, and gender freedoms. Although the poems differ formally and thematically in a number of ways, each features a precarious freedom that relies on the symbology of slavery to define itself.

"No olvidemos que el deber del hombre es obtener el derecho de tal" [Let us not forget that the duty of man is to obtain the right of man] (Morúa Delgado 1957).

Ayala: "A mi raza"

"Ya es tiempo raza querida / que, acabado el servilismo, / demos pruebas de civismo / y tengamos propia vida" (Now is the time beloved race that, our servitude having ceased, we give proof of our citizenship and we have a life of our own) (Ayala 1926, 17). So read the first lines of Ayala's thirteen-stanza ballad "A mi raza." Composed just two years after the legal abolition of slavery in Cuba, "A mi raza" is a literary response to the problem of postemancipation "racial uplift" in Cuba.

The transnational aspect of racial uplift theories in the United States is already well established. Black intellectual and political leaders like Henry Highland Garnet (1815–1882), Alexander Crummell (1819–1898), Martin Delany (1812–1885), and Henry McNeal Turner (1834–1915) all proposed solutions to the "Negro problem" that were transnational in scope. Garnet advocated for black emigration to Mexico, West Africa, and the West Indies; Crummell encouraged blacks in the United States to help form a black republic in Liberia; Delany proposed the transhemispheric emigration of blacks in the United States to Central and South America, placing particular emphasis on Cuba, which he perceived as the bastion of black revolutionary activity. Turner linked African Methodist Episcopal (AME) churches in the United States to those in Africa and sent black missionaries to Cuba and Mexico. Even W. E. B. Du Bois, though not in favor of any form of black emigration, looked to other parts of the world to develop theories about the condition and future of African Americans in the United States.

Scholars like Evelyn Brooks Higginbotham and Carole Boyce Davies have documented the political, intellectual, and social influence of black women on such movements for racial uplift. Less explored, however, has been the role of women in the discourse of racial uplift and how women of African descent *outside* of the United States addressed the problem of postabolition racial and national (re)formation.

A direct response to a pamphlet titled "Cuba y su gente" (Cuba and Its People) that disparaged black Cubans and women (Ayala 1926, 17; DeCosta Willis 2003, 30), "A mi raza" presents a practical theory of racial "self-help" to contemporary black Cubans. Ayala introduces the second stanza with the repetition of the opening phrase "Ya es tiempo" (Now is the time).

> Ya es tiempo raza querida
> que, acabado el servilismo,
> demos pruebas de civismo
> y tengamos propia vida.
> Ya es tiempo de comprender
> —pues está probado el hecho—
> que es imposible el Derecho,
> si no se cumple el Deber.
> Y, lo que el Deber nos traza
> en tan solemne momento,
> es, redoblar el intento
> de mejorar nuestra raza.
> No es la raza negra, no;[1]
> aunque en tal sentido se hable,
> la que ha de ser responsible
> de "aquel tiempo pasó."
> Pero no puede eludir
> la responsabilidad
> que es suya en la actualidad,
> para con el porvenir. (1–20)

[Now is the time beloved race that, our servitude having ceased, we give proof of our civility and we have a life of our own. It is time to understand—since it is a proven fact—that Rights are unattainable if Duty is not fulfilled. And, what Duty indicates in such a grave hour as this, is that we intensify our intent to improve our race. No, it is not the black race, even though they speak as if it were, that is responsible for "that era that has passed." But it cannot avoid its responsibility in the present day for that which is to come.]

The repetition of the first line "Ya es tiempo" (Now is the time) introduces time as a trope. The present ("Ya es tiempo"), past ("aquel tiempo que pasó"), and future ("el porvenir") converge in the context of an imagined racial community—the silent audience in the poem. Each quatrain, rhyming *abba*, builds on the preceding stanza semantically. The end-rhyme, both through alliteration (Deber, Derecho) and assonance—that is to say, internal rhyme—(dEbEr, dErEcho), creates a semantic link between the words *derecho* and *deber*: "es imposible el Derecho / si no se cumple el Deber." By linking these words, Ayala reinforces the relationship between derecho and deber. Ultimately, "A mi raza" projects the political message that black Cubans should not expect legal rights without performing the duty of improving the race.

In spite of legal dictates for the gradual abolition of slavery, "A mi raza" presents a clear pre- and postslavery vision of Cuban history. It assumes a radical break from a past in slavery and proposes its own postabolition vision.

> Evitemos ese mal,
> teniendo perseverancia
> para extirpar la ignorancia
> de nuestra esfera social.

Mas, si hemos de conseguir
tan nobles aspiraciones,
he aquí las indicaciones
que hemos todos de seguir:
Los hombres han de estudiar;
hay que abandonar el vicio
y salvar el precipicio
en que se van a estrellar.
Comprendiendo la razón,
tratarán de congregarse
para unidos, procurarse
la mayor ilustración.
Y, nosotras las mujeres
cumpliendo nuestra misión,
tenemos la obligación
de entender nuestros deberes.
Que si todos por igual
—sin que haya rémora en eso—
buscamos en el progreso
nuestra perfección moral. (21–44)

[Let us avoid this mistake, having perseverance in order to eradicate ignorance from our social sphere. But, if we are to achieve such noble aspirations, here are the instructions that we must all follow: The men must study; they must abandon vice and escape the abyss into which they are falling. Understanding the reason, they will try to join together in order to, united, strive for the highest enlightenment. And we the women, carrying out our mission, we are obligated to understand our duties. That if we all equally – unhindered—seek in progress our moral perfection.]

The speaker acknowledges a racially defined community and at the same time advocates a patriotic duty to the nation. Furthermore, the speaker allocates distinct roles to black men and women in Cuba. To remove what slavery has left behind ("para extirpar la ignorancia de nuestra esfera social"), the speaker claims, black Cubans should realize a gendered vision of progress in which black men pursue education and black women come to understand their "duties." This designation of black womanhood distinguishes Ayala from her contemporary América Font, who, like Ayala, contributed regularly to *Minerva*. The final lines of Font's opinion editorial which appeared on the front page of *Minerva*'s fourth volume in 1888, "la mujer debe aspirar, repito, [a] salir de la esclavitud de la ignorancia; y para poder ser libre, en este concepto, debe ser instruida; pues donde no hay instrucción, no hay libertad" (the woman should aspire to flee the slavery of ignorance and to be free, in this sense, she must be educated; for where there is no education, there is no freedom) (Font 1888, 3). Ayala specifies the role of black Cuban men but leaves the role of women more ambiguous, suggesting that women have an implicit understanding of the internal workings of the "esfera social" (social sphere) and their role in it. The "perfección moral" (moral perfection) of the race is contingent on women's understanding of their relationship to the project of racial uplift. The ultimate goal of this uplift is to produce the "mayor ilustración" (greatest enlightenment).

"History" itself is the abstract surface on which to inscribe the *name* of the newly emancipated race.

> tal vez tendremos la Gloria
> para que el mundo se asombre,
> de consignar nuestro nombre
> con honra y prez en la Historia.
> Y si tal éxito alcanza
> el noble esfuerzo que haremos
> el estigma borraremos
> que la Sociedad nos lanza. (22–52)
> [perhaps we will achieve the Glory—such that the world is astonished—of writing our name down in History with honor and fame. And if this noble effort meets such success, we will erase the stigma Society places upon us.]

The verb *consignar* comes from the Latin *consignare*, meaning to mark with (*com-*) a sign (*signare*); *estigma* derives from the Latin and Greek *stigma*, referring to a mark on the skin produced by a hot iron. The *Diccionario de la Lengua Española* (2001) defines *estigma* as: "una marca o señal en el cuerpo; desdoro, afrenta, mala fama; marca impuesta con bierro candante, bien como pena infamante, bien como signo de esclavitud" (a mark or sign on the body; blot, indignity, bad reputation; mark imposed with a hot iron as a punishment for infamy or a mark of slavery). Embedded in the denotation of the word is the notion of a *mark* imposed on the body. Slavery was written onto the collective bodies of enslaved and "free" black Cubans as a *mala fama*. The two images in these final stanzas—a name being written and being erased—conjoin here as integral parts in a process of (re)naming these bodies.

In his discussion of the Dion Boucicault play *The Octoroon* (1859), Werner Sollors describes how the myth of the descendants of Ham became linked with the curse of Cain. A visible mark on Cain's forehead would be an eternal sign of his crime. Sollors notes, "the curse of Ham served both as a myth of origin and as a racist description: blacks had become black because of some misdeed and malediction in the past; their blackness was a result and proof as well as permanent punishment" (1997, 95). The story, as it was applied to the bodies of *afrodescendentes*, informed their various forms of identity in the New World. "A mi raza" addresses this very phenomenon. It presents the transition from slave to free as both a problem of a collective politics of identity, requiring social change on the part of black Cubans, *and* a problem of semiological signification, requiring the removal one system of signification (el estigma borráremos que la sociedad nos lanza) and replacing it with another (consignar nuestro nombre / con la honra y prez en la Historia).

North American afrodescendente poet James Madison Bell's "The Triumph of Liberty" (1870) alludes to a similar process.

> *The century bound and fettered slave*
> Shall grasp the hilt of freedom's sword

And rush amid the struggling brave
And write his liberties restored;
He shall have faith where others doubt
And onward press to lead the van,
Till slavery's stain he washes out
In treason's gore, and stands a man. (Bell 1994, 126, ll. 29–36; emphasis added)

In this poem, as in "A mi raza," the removal of the "stain" of slavery requires the *writing* of freedom. Freedom is *not* an inevitable by-product of slavery's abolition but rather must be *written*; it must be imagined through the poetic process of renaming.

Ayala's unabashed address to the "raza negra" runs across the current of José Martí's theory, which he declared three years later in his most famous essay "Nuestra América" (Our America): "No hay odio de razas, porque no hay razas" (2001, 27). Ayala's speaker's stance falls more in line with intellectual leader Juan Gualberto Gómez (1854–1933).[2] Gualberto Gómez was a strong advocate of racial solidarity and racial uplift through social integration in Cuba. While in exile in Madrid just a year before he returned to Cuba, Gualberto Gómez wrote extensively about the challenge political leaders faced to effect reform in postemancipation Cuba. He perceived the history of Cuba in *black* and *white*—"el blanco," who monopolized cultural and wealth, and "el negro," who was brought to live as a slave (1954b, 231). According to Gualberto Gómez, blacks were prohibited from wealth and power while whites were free to exercise economic freedom. He believed that the problem of "la elevación del elemento negro" (the elevation of the black element) was in fact a problem of the country as a whole.[3] Gualberto Gómez emphasized the importance of addressing the past in reform efforts in an essay titled "La Cuestión de Cuba en 1884" (The Question of Cuba in 1884).

> Se notará en nuestro trabajo este doble aspecto: una severa condenación del régimen existente; censura enérgica a los hombres y a los procedimientos del pasado; pero, a la vez, un manifiesto espíritu de respeto, de transacción y de deferencia y consideración para todas las soluciones del porvenir, por todos los mantenedores de las ideas progresivas y por todos los que tienden a la reforma. (1954a, 214)
> [in our work it will be noted this dual quality: an avid criticism of the existing regime; strong censuring of the men and methods of the past; but, at the same time, in all who hold progressive ideas and all who tend towards reform, a manifest spirit of respect, of compromise and of deference and consideration for the solutions of the future.]

For Gualberto Gómez, an ideal critique of Cuban society would look critically at the past and its vestiges in the present, while at the same time creating a space in which to imagine the future. Drawing particular attention to the question of slavery and the social integration of Cuban blacks, Ayala appropriates this same duality in the structure of "A mi raza" where the past and the present engage dialectically.

Cuban intellectual and supporter of independence, Martín Morúa Delgado (1856–1912), also believed in the self-elevation of black Cubans. Unlike Gualberto Gómez, Morúa Delgado believed that "mulatto" constituted a distinct race in between blacks and whites in Cuba. Looking forward to the approaching end of slavery in Cuba, Morúa Delgado was convinced that if Cuban *mulatos* and *negros* wanted to be truly free, they would have to learn *how*—"Queremos ser libres? pues aprendamos a serlo" (Do we want be free? We must learn to be) (quoted in Estuch 1957, 284).[4] Morúa Delgado's approach to the idea of social integration certainly differed from that of Gualberto Goméz; he even voted against legalizing the Independientes de Color as a political party. Ayala's poetic conception of Cuban history and present confronts the ideological and political climate of Cuba in its abolition era.

As immigration of Europeans to Cuba increased as part of a plan to "whiten" the island, Afro-Cuban *cabildos* or "societies of color" and other pan-Afro-Cuban organizations worked to fully integrate black Cubans into mainstream society. They raised consciousness about social problems facing Cubans "de color" and tried to counteract the undesirable social effects of slavery. They did so primarily by reshaping beliefs and conceptions about work, family, religion, and education among black Cubans (Howard 1998, 183). This effort translated to a platform of racial unity based on a rhetoric of rights and a push for legal change in favor of equal rights for blacks in Cuba (Howard 1998, 187).

Ayala's "A mi raza" employs the language and diction of didactic Cuban *folletos* and essays published by leading intellectuals such as Morúa Delgado (1856–1910), Antonio Maceo (1845–1896), and Gualberto Goméz (1854–1933). It also uses a language of duty and rights reminiscent of the language of racial uplift in the United States. Ayala's use of the didactic form in "A mi raza" counters the sentimentalism of the Romantic era's poetic treatment of slavery and abolition. She builds on the tradition of Latin American Romantic poetry in its concern with the sociopolitical problem of slavery and the theme of abolition (Kirkpatrick 2002, 402, 412). "A mi raza" does not, however, feature the voice of a sympathetic observer as many abolitionist poems did. Ayala diverges from this tradition by projecting a voice from "within" the raza negra that interprets its own history. "A mi raza" presents abolition as a symbolic event that emerges from and actively influences precipitant concepts of "freedom."

Presenting the raza negra as an imagined community, "A mi raza" both represents and analyzes the literary aspect of the national project. The poem is a site of semantic play, a dance between pragmatism and theory, between naming and erasure. In this sense, Ayala approaches the question of race and gender in Cuba not simply as a political challenge but as a literary one. The process of destigmatization of black Cubans as a literary as well as social process informs the very structure of the poem. It presents the possibility of a complete freedom, achieved in the realization of a new name.

Harper: "We Are Rising"

> After all whether they encourage or discourage me, I belong to this race, and when it is down I belong to a down race; when it is up I belong to a risen race.
>
> — Harper (1990b, 128)

> Knowledge is power, the great mental lever which has lifted man in the scale of social and racial life.
>
> — Harper (1990a, 275)

> We believe that the first and greatest step toward the
> settlement of the present friction between the races—
> namely the Negro Problem—lies in the correction of the
> immorality, crime, and laziness among the Negroes
> themselves, which still remains a heritage from slavery. We
> believe that only earnest and long continued efforts on our
> part can cure these social ills.
>
> — Du Bois (2003, 138)

In her poems and speeches, Frances Harper, like Cristina Ayala, also addressed the problem of postabolition racial uplift. For one instance, she wrote and recited the poem "We Are Rising" (1876) for the unveiling of the Allen Monument, a memorial statue dedicated to Bishop Richard Allen, founder of the African American Episcopal Church. Though structurally and typologically distinct from Ayala's "A mi raza," "We Are Rising" presents a similar problem of postemancipation racial uplift. In this eight-stanza ballad, Harper traces a similar process of renaming. Like "A mi raza," "We Are Rising" emphasizes the need for collective progress (i.e., racial uplift) in the postemancipation United States and uses a popular poetic form to do so. Harper mimics the structure of traditional gospel hymns by emphasizing the repetition of a refrain and using a version of ballad meter commonly used for such hymns. As a result, the very structure of the poem builds on an African American tradition of congregational participation (Maultsby 2001, 84).

"We Are Rising" is structured around the biblical paradigm of God and his "people."

> We are rising as a people,
> We are rising, to the light;
> For our God has changed the shadows
> Of our dark and dreary night.
> In the prison house of bondage,
> When we bent beneath the rod,
> And our hearts were faint and weary,
> We first learned to trust in God.
>
> We are marching along, we are marching along,
> The hand that broke our fetters was powerful and strong.
> We are marching along, we are marching along,
> We are rising as a people, and we're marching along. (in Foster 1990, 237–38, ll. 1–12)

Reminiscent of a lyrical ballad in its structure, "We Are Rising" echoes a narrative of collective African American experience but focuses on the speaker's emotive exhortation of black Americans to "rise" as a people. Their experience of the "prison house of bondage" establishes their relationship with the God of the Old Testament Bible. Like the biblical Israelites, black Americans move out from the darkness of slavery and into the "light" of freedom.

The juxtaposition of darkness and light, slavery and freedom continues throughout the poem, reinforced by the simple pattern rhyming *xaxaxbxb* (with the exception of the refrain). The rhyme scheme also links *rod* and *God*, underscoring the idea that suffering in slavery linked black peoples to God.

For the sighing of the needy,
God, himself did bare his hand,
And the footsteps of his judgments,
Echoed through the guilty land:
When the rust of many ages,
On our galling fetters lay,
He turned our grief to gladness,
And our darkness into day.

We are marching along, we are marching along,
The hand that broke our fetters was powerful and strong.
We are marching along, we are marching along,
We are rising as a people, and we're marching along.

Unto God, be all the glory,
That our eyes behold the sight
Of a people, peeled and scattered
Rising into freedom's light
Though the morning seemed to linger,
O'er the hill tops far away
And the night was long and gloomy,
Yet he was our shield and stay.

We are marching along, we are marching along,
The hand that broke our fetters was powerful and strong.
We are marching along, we are marching along,
We are rising as a people, and we're marching along.

Help us, Oh! great Deliverer,
To be faithful to thy Word,
Till the nation's former bondmen,
Be the freemen of the Lord.
Teach, Oh, Lord, our hands to battle
'Gainst the hosts of vice, and sin,
And with Jesus, for our Captain,
The victory we shall win.

We are marching along, we are marching along,
The hand that broke our fetters was powerful and strong.
We are marching along, we are marching along,
We are rising as a people, and we're marching along. (13–48)

Both the rhythmic structure and the repetition of marching are reminiscent of the "The Battle Hymn of the Republic"—a hymn whose lyrics, penned by Julia Ward Howe, were inspired by the Union Army troops and appeared in the *Atlantic Monthly* in 1862. The refrain in "We Are Rising" echoes that of the "Battle Hymn": "Glory, glory Hallelujah, his truth is marching on." Through this allusion, Harper revisits the rhetoric of the Civil War in the face of a failed Reconstruction and what was the eve of one of the most intense periods of racial violence and antiblack discrimination in the history of the United States. Using this cross-textual gesture, Harper constructs a bridge between one period in history and another while at the same time projecting a vision for the future. Recognizing the poem as an imaginative space where this kind of work can be wrought, Harper articulates an evolving narrative that would inform the way black Americans would interpret their history for decades.

The repetition of the refrain mimics the verse-chorus structure used in black churches as a syncretism of traditional Protestant hymnody and West African cultural elements (Maultsby 2001, 82). The semantic and syntactic repetition in the refrain not only establishes its rhythmic shape but also, in its use of trochaic or "falling" meter, simulates the repetitive motion and rhythm of marching. These rhythmic and syntactical devices call attention to the poem as a *speech act* that even in its structure invokes the presence and participation of an audience.

The call-and-response dynamic mirrors the interplay in the poem between darkness and light, which ultimately culminates in the transformation from bound to free. Each stanza suggests a movement from a figurative darkness to light. Stanza 1: "We are rising to the light / For our God has changed the shadows / Of our dark and dreary night." Stanza 2: "He turned our grief to gladness / And our darkness into day." Stanza 3: "Rising into freedom's light." In the final stanza the darkness to light metaphor is replaced by a reference to the transformation from "bondmen" to "freemen." The realization of "freedom," however, is both anticipated (that is, not yet present in the poem) and contingent on narrative. The literal fight against "the hosts of vice and sin" conjures another type of entanglement with the specters of slavery: the tug-of-war between a history of slavery and a freedom yet to be realized.

A slight shift in the stressed patterns signals a heightened moment in the final stanza ("Help us, Oh") and an interjection ("Oh"). In this climactic moment, the end-rhyme pattern implies a link between "Deliverer," "Word," "bondmen," and "Lord." The word *deliverer* denotes one who sets free, one who assists in giving birth, one who speaks, sings, or utters. The speaker seeks full deliverance, to be translated from slave ("bondmen") to free by the word. The *word* is a type of Christ as highlighted in John 1:1: "In the beginning was the Word, and the Word was with God, and the Word was God." The kind of freedom in "We Are Rising" is not one of absolute detachment from a master. Instead, it is a substitution of one "lord" for another ("Till the nation's former bondmen / be the freemen of the Lord"). Harper interrogates the connection between the word and the deliverance of the enslaved. The "people" *rise* and are translated into a *new* "people." In this sense, the poem highlights a process of signification that occurs in the space between slavery and freedom—a space mediated by language.

We can perhaps best see how language mediates this space through the lens of another poem Harper wrote five years earlier. "We Are Rising" might even be considered a response to this six-stanza poem, "Fifteenth Amendment," which appeared in the first issue of Frederick Douglass's newspaper the *New National Era* in 1870. Stanzas 4–6 of "Fifteenth Amendment" read as follows:

> Shake off the dust, O rising race!
> Crowned and brother and a man;

> Justice to-day asserts her claim,
> And from thy brow fades out the ban.
> With freedom's chrism upon thy head,
> Her precious ensign in thy hand,
> Go place thy once despiséd name
> Amid the noblest of the land.
> O ransomed race! give God the praise,
> Who led thee through a crimson sea,
> And 'mid the storm of fire and blood,
> Turned out the war-cloud's light to thee. (in Foster 1990, 189–90, ll. 13–24)

The "rising race" rises to change its *name*: "Go place thy once despiséd name / Amid the noblest of the land." Slave becomes "brother and man," reminiscent of the "bondmen" becoming "free" in "We Are Rising."[5]

On one hand, "We Are Rising" is an appeal for "racial uplift" through the adoption of Christian values. It also traces the process of "renaming" of a racially defined "people." The poem begins and ends with the refrain: "We are rising as a people, and we're marching along," never arriving but always in the process of determining what freedom will look like. The poetic space is one where this tension can be seen in the form of semantic play—figurative images of light and dark, the allusion to the removal of one layer of a fragmented identity (a people peeled and scattered). Again, the space between freedom and slavery constitutes a liminal space where renaming can occur.

Harper: "Eliza Harris"

Harper's "Eliza Harris," which appeared in *Poems on Miscellaneous Subjects* (1854), draws on a central character in Harriet Beecher Stowe's best-selling novel *Uncle Tom's Cabin* (1851). Stowe's sentimental novel forged an ideological attack on the institution of slavery. A major character in the novel, Eliza Harris is the "quadroon" slave of plantation owner Thomas Davis. After receiving news that her son is to be sold away from her, Eliza crosses the Ohio River into free territory. A thirteen-stanza poem in quatrains rhyming *aabb*, "Eliza Harris" elaborates on the moment of Eliza's escape. It appeared in *The Liberator* shortly after the publication of *Uncle Tom's Cabin* and placed the slave mother at the center of the national debate over slavery. Consistent with Stowe's sentimental treatment of this slave mother, Harper presents the image of Eliza fleeing from slave-catchers with child in hand. Both literally and metaphorically positioned on the line between freedom and slavery, Eliza's crossing becomes a meditation on the precariousness of "freedom" in the national context and the implications of slavery for the construction of national identity.

> Like a fawn from the arrow, startled and wild,
> A woman swept by us, bearing a child;
> In her eye was the night of a settled despair,
> And her brow was o'ershaded with anguish and care.
> She was nearing the river—in reaching the brink,

> She heeded no danger, she paused not to think!
> For she is a mother—her child is a slave—
> And she'll give him his freedom, or find him a grave!
> It was a vision to haunt us, that innocent face—
> So pale in its aspect, so fair in its grace;
> As the tramp of the horse and the bay of the hound,
> With the fetters that gall, were trailing the ground. (in Foster 1990, 50–61, ll. 1–12)

Forced to choose between the threat of death and freedom for her child ("For she is a mother—her child is a slave— / And she'll give him his freedom, or find him a grave"), Eliza's instinctual (like a fawn) and yet maternal figure becomes larger than life in this moment of escape; she is "wild" and yet "a woman . . . bearing a child" approaching the river, the dividing line between "slave" and "free." At the center of the narrative rests the "vision to haunt us"—a slave mother and her child in the liminal space between freedom and slavery. This image is a catalyst for the speaker's meditation on slavery, nationhood, and the process of reconciling the two.

> Oh! how shall I speak of my proud country's shame?
> Of the stains on her glory, how give them their name?
> How say that her banner in mockery waves—
> Her "star spangled banner"[6]—o'er millions of slaves?
> How say that the lawless may torture and chase
> A woman whose crime is the hue of her face?
> How the depths of the forest may echo around
> With the shrieks of despair, and the bay of the hound? (13–20)

The poem modulates in stanza 4, effected first through an interjection that interrupts the rhythm followed by a series of rhetorical questions. Eliza is temporarily substituted for another silent protagonist—the American nation. No longer speaking as a part of a collective ("It was a vision to haunt *us*") but rather as "I" ("Oh! how shall *I* speak of my proud country's shame?"), the speaker's positionality is ambivalent. We must ask: is the speaker an observer in the moment? One of the slave-catchers? A narrator telling the story in a future present? Eliza's flight prompts the speaker's internal struggle to reconcile a tension between her image (i.e., the slave) and that of the "star spangled banner" (i.e., the nation).

The problem of naming emerges again. The image of the slave mother evokes the "stain" of slavery signified by the "hue of her face." To name the "stains" is to also name the "millions of slaves" that challenge the validity of the American flag as a symbol of freedom. The "country's shame" is its hypocrisy as signified by the presence of slaves under the awning of its national *sign*—the American flag.

The specter of race appears in the "hue" of Eliza's face, her only crime, as she confronts her "lawless" pursuers. Sound clashing in the forest—Eliza's and the hounds—echoes the dissonance of her slavery and the ideals of the nation. *Stains* on the flag represent the imprint of black skin on the woman. The forest is a metaphor for the dark, uninhabited space of the American consciousness where the realities of racial slavery take root; these realities are ignored by American rhetoric of freedom as the "shadow" of slavery is cast on the backdrop of America's ideological landscape.

> With her step on the ice, and her arm on her child,
> The danger was fearful, the pathway was wild;
> But, aided by Heaven, she gained a free shore,
> Where the friends of humanity open'd their door. (21–24)

With her "step on the ice," Eliza steps into the *slippery* liminal space between slavery and freedom. Her crossing is at once metaphorical and prophetic. The slave mother—propelled by maternal instinct—transcends the seemingly natural boundary line that defines her. As an allegory for national progress, this crossing refers prophetically to the future of an American nation that might "cross over" into new legislative and ideological realms—a "free" United States.

> So fragile and lovely, so fearful and pale,
> Like a lily that bends to the breath of the gale,
> Save the heave of her breast, and the sway of her hair,
> You'd have thought her a statue of fear and despair.
> In agony close to her bosom she press'd
> The life of her heart, the child of her breast:—
> Oh! love from its tenderness gathering might,
> Had strengthen'd her soul for the dangers of flight. (25–32)

The pursuit of freedom—fueled by maternal love—transforms Eliza from the "fragile and lovely" statuesque figure, to the fugitive mother, gripping her child in hand.

> But she's free—yes, free from the land where the slave
> From the hand of oppression must rest in the grave;
> Where bondage and torture, where scourges and chains,
> Have plac'd on our banner indelible stains.
> Did a fever e'er burning through bosom and brain,
> Send a lava-like flood through every vein,
> Till it suddenly cooled 'neath a healing spell,
> And you knew, oh! the joy! you knew you were well?
> So felt this young mother, as a sense of the rest
> Stole gently and sweetly o'er *her* weary breast,
> As her boy looked up, and, wondering, smiled
> On the mother whose love had freed her child.
> The bloodhounds have miss'd the scent of her way;
> The hunter is rifled and foil'd of his prey;
> Fierce jargon and cursing, with clanking of chains,
> Make sounds of strange discord on Liberty's plains.
> With the rapture love and fullness of bliss,
> She plac'd o his brow a mother's fond kiss:—

Oh! poverty, danger and death she can brave,
For the child of her love is no longer a slave. (33–52)

A slight variation on the rhythmic pattern of the poem, coupled with a shift to the present tense ("But she's free—yes, free"), produces another heightened moment. Free from the "stain" of slavery, the child crosses over. The speaker describes this transition as a "burning through bosom and brain." This passage between the liminal space between freedom and slavery renames the child.

Freedom is not fully reconciled in the poem, however. Instead, there are subtle traces of discord. The "discord" persists in the space between freedom and the notion of "Liberty" as an American national ideal: the echoes in the forest, the sound of "jargon and cursing," the "clanking of chains." The stains reappear on the flag as "indelible stains" that cannot be removed. The narrative descends back into past tense until the final two lines of the poem ("Oh! poverty, danger and death she can brave / For the child of her love is no longer a slave"). From this point forward the poem emphasizes the freedom of the child and never again refers to Eliza's freedom.

The interaction between the past and present effects a type of polyphony that models the relationship between text and reader. One voice experiences the moment of Eliza's escape; another interprets it. "Eliza Harris" is as much about the process of naming the "stains on [the] glory" of the American flag as it is to giving a narrative to this slave mother figure. The speaker maintains an active presence in the poem, grappling with the contradictions and hypocrisy of an American rhetoric of freedom. The reader is also implicated in the crime as a passive observer or perhaps even complicit in the slave-catchers' pursuit of the slave.

Just as the text vacillates between concrete and abstract images and between visual and aural images, the speaker vacillates between observer and participant—a model for the reader's experience. The nineteenth-century reader grappled with the problem of slavery and of freedom that divided the nation. "Eliza Harris" becomes a meta-discourse on the process of reconciling images and text, of naming and producing signification. The gendering of both the mother and the nation links the two, suggesting that as Eliza escapes to ensure the freedom of her child, somehow the nation must also take steps toward the freedom of its children—African American slaves. The Southern paternalism characterizing an idealized image of Southern slavery is replaced by a national maternalism. The slave woman appears here—as she did in abolitionist rhetoric—as a symbol of motherhood. As Eliza realizes freedom through the freedom of her child, so would America realize freedom through the freedom of African Americans.

Ayala: "El arroyuelo y la flor"

Ayala's "El arroyuelo y la flor" (The Stream and the Flower) further explores the relationship between gender and nation-building. In twenty-six quatrains rhyming *abba*, this narrative poem centers around a dialogue between *el arroyuelo* and *la flor* and ultimately reads as an allegory for the divergent social roles of men and women vis-à-vis the Cuban nation. "El arroyuelo y la flor" explores the process of linking the natural world and the stories we tell about it; it also examines the ways in which language as a *literary* system mediates and (re)imagines the social world. An *apólogo*, the poem is a species of didactic poetry in that it conveys a message of moral or ethic instruction. It is at once a meta-discourse on a system of social relationships and a meditation on the formulation of signification within the poetic space.

The narrative begins with an Edenic scene—an enchanted garden occupied by a river and a flower. Rooted at the edge of the arroyuelo and observing itself in the constant flux of the river's water, the flor begins to question the arroyuelo.

> Al pie de una selva umbría
> en un valle encantador,
> rápido y murmurador
> un arroyuelo corría.
> Una flor que en su ribera
> su lozanía ostentaba
> y en su linfa se miraba,
> le increpó de esta manera:
> "¿Dime arroyuelo, a do vas
> en cont[i]nua corriente
> y por qu[é] lánguidamente
> siempre murmurando estás?
> ¿Alguien te ha ofendido aquí?
> ¿Pues no rodeamos tu lecho?
> ¿Por qué no estás satisfecho?
> ¿Por qué te alejas así?
> ¿Acaso allá en la pradera
> hallarás cosas mejores?
> ¿No estamos aquí las flores
> perfumando tu ribera?
> Detén tu curso un momento
> para que calmes mi anhelo
> y le des algún consuelo
> a mi sentido lamento. (Ayala 1926, 26–27, ll. 1–24)

[At the foot of a shadowy forest in an enchanting valley ran a stream rapid and murmuring. Displaying its luxuriance at the edge of the stream, a flower looked into its clear waters and questioned it, saying: "Tell me stream, where are you going with your constant current and why do you always murmur languidly? Has someone offended you? Do we not surround your bed? Why are you dissatisfied? Why do you run away? Perhaps in the meadows you will find something better? Are we flowers not here bringing fragrance to your banks? Stop for a moment to calm my longing and to give some consolation to my sorrowful cry."]

The presence of a lugubrious and ambivalent darkness in the form of the shadow cast by the tree foreshadows a less romantic underside to the scene. The flor's fixed position on the margin contrasts the movement of the arroyuelo; as an object on display ("su lozanía ostentaba"), the flor enacts agency only through observation ("se miraba") and verbal interrogation ("le increpó de esta manera"). As an object on the side of the arroyuelo, the flor literally speaks from the margin. In the face of absorption into a male "current" representing the limitless bounds of masculinity, woman speaks; the poem is a space where the female voice becomes audible.

> ¿No te acusa la consciencia
> al ver que a una flor vecina
> si a t[i] su corola inclina
> la destrozas sin clemencia?
> Pues de tu corriente en pos,
> en revuelta confusión
> arrastras sin compasión
> a esa flor, obra de Dios.
> Dime ¿qué causa sagrada
> influye Arroyuelo en tí,
> para que corras así
> sin que te detenga nada?" (25–36)

[Does not your conscience accuse you when you see a nearby flower, if it turns its petals towards you and you destroy it mercilessly? And while pursuing your current in a riot of confusion you uproot that flower, God's creation. Tell me what sacred cause motivates you *Arroyuelo*, why do you run allowing nothing to detain you?"]

Questioning the arroyuelo about the reason ("causa sagrada") behind its movement, the flor uses a moral argument of conscience to try to convince the arroyuelo to detain its course. Identifying itself as an "obra de Dios" (work of God), the flor further emphasizes its quality as an ornate object, aesthetically pleasing and yet ephemeral.

> El arroyuelo que oyó
> la queja de aquella flor,
> mirándola con amor
> de este modo contestó:
> "Yo, de mi corriente, en pos
> te arrastro. ¡flor inocente!
> más, no soy inconsecuente
> a los decretos de Dios.
> Que El, en su saber profundo,
> dictó leyes inmutables;
> ¡arcanos impenetrables
> para los ojos del mundo!
> Y El permite, que cumplida
> sea por todos, la misión
> que por su disposición
> cada ser trae a la vida. (37–52)

[The stream, hearing the lament of that flower, looked at it lovingly assured it saying: "I, in following my current, pull you up, innocent flower! But I am following the laws of God. He, in his profound knowledge dictated unchangeable laws, mysterious, impervious to the eyes of the world. And he makes it possible for us all to complete the purpose that, by his (or her) talent every individual brings to life.]

While the arroyuelo begins as subject (Yo), the flor identifies itself as an object even its first speech act (Dime). The arroyuelo's subjecthood is contingent on the destruction of the flor. This destruction is sanctioned by the divine laws of nature ("de mi corriente, en pos / te arrastro ¡flor inocente!"). Instead of looking into the river to see its reflection—such that the arroyuelo would become, as it was for Narcissus, a reflection of the self—the flor sees the arroyuelo (i.e., the man) only. Ultimately the force of the masculine river uproots her.

God reenters the "garden" as the dictator of natural law, a force determining the relationship between the symbolic protagonists of the poem. God consigns the inevitable destruction of the flor by the arroyuelo's current as a part of a predetermined purpose.

> Tú, para que tu hermosura
> brille con más esplendor,
> necesitas ¡pobre flor!
> que yo te dé mi frescura.
> M[a]s . . . también es mi destino
> correr incesantemente,
> y a impulso de mi corriente
> arrastrarte en mi camino.
> Tu fin es, buscar mi apoyo;
> ser hermosa un solo día,
> y con tranquila alegría
> sumergirte en en arroyo. (53–64)

[You, poor flower, need me to give you my cool water so that your beauty might shine brightest. But, it is also my destiny to flow ceaselessly and to pull you up in my path by the impulse of my current. Your end is to seek my help, to be beautiful for only a day and then, with a calm contentment, submerge yourself in the stream.]

The arroyuelo's violent assertion of identity conjoins the "destino" (destiny) of the flor—a brief performance of aesthetic beauty, and then it is subsumed in the current of the arroyuelo. The flor is enslaved, locked into a symbiotic relationship that enslaves it to the arroyuelo's pursuit of freedom. Ironically, this relationship prefaces its destruction.

> Yo, corriendo sin cesar,
> procuro afanosamente
> convertirme en afluente
> y hallar entrada en el Mar.
> ¡En ese abismo profundo!

¡Esa inmensidad sin nombre,
que aun a despecho del hombre
habrá de absorber al Mundo!
No te quejes, pues los dos
aunque por distinta senda,
rendimos cumplida ofrenda
a los designios de Dios." (65–76)
[I flow without ceasing and avidly seek to become a tributary and find an entrance into the Sea. Into that deep abyss! That nameless expanse that even in spite of man will have to absorb the World! Don't complain, for we both, though in different ways, render a complete offering according to the design of God.]

In pursuit of transformation, the stream's current propels it toward a "nameless abyss." The incessant flow of the arroyuelo, a constant flux, leads ultimately to an absence of signification that overrides any attempts to intercept it. Finally submerged in the arroyuelo, the flor will also be consumed in the nameless sea ("ese abismo profundo / esa inmensidad sin nombre").

The two offer themselves up to the purpose of the "designios de Dios," or the higher system of designation within the structure of language. They are fitted into roles like the signifier and the signified that link to determine the sign. The second half of the poem conveys the *meaning* produced in this exchange.

At this point, the narrative voice reemerges.
Calló la flor, convencida
al oir este consejo,
que es un perfecto reflejo
de lo que pasa en la vida.
Pues la mujer, cual la flor
que se mira en el arroyo,
busca del hombre el apoyo,
y le consagra su amor. (77–84)
[Convinced upon hearing this counsel, which is a perfect reflection of what happens in life, the flower grew silent. For the woman, like the flower that looks into the stream, looks for support from the man and devotes her love to him.]

The narrator instructs us to read the first nineteen stanzas as allegory ("un perfecto reflejo / de lo que pasa en la vida").

Pero él, en su alma anida
otro amor más grande y fuerte,
¡que a veces de la muerte
y a veces le da la vida!
Que al igual del arroyuelo,
le hace corrrer sin cesar,
para internarse en el mar
donde le lleva su anhelo.

> y ese amor sublime y santo
> por quien el hombre se olvida
> de la mujer más querida
> y que le seduce tanto,
> ese fuego que arde en su alma
> cual una pira bendita,
> que a llevar le precipita
> del noble mártir la palma,
> ¡a una excelsa trinidad
> se lo consagra su pecho!
> que se llama, ¡su Derecho;
> su Patria y su Libertad! (85–104)
>
> [But in his soul he harbors a greater and more powerful love that sometimes gives him death and sometimes gives him life! That, like the *arroyuelo*, makes him flow ceaselessly and bury himself in the sea to which he brings his desire. And this sublime and holy love for which the man forgets his most beloved woman and that seduces him so, this fire that burns in his soul like a blessed pyre, that hastens the triumph of the noble martyr, a sublime trinity to which he devotes his heart, it is called his Law, his Country, and his Liberty.]

The male figure is seduced into an abyss of namelessness by the ideal of a national vision. Woman is reconfigured in this process, renamed in the man's pursuit of transformation. The female sign is destroyed only to resurface in the rhetoric of nationhood as a newly named beloved. The flor—symbolizing woman—is substituted for *another* "amor" (love) that propels the arroyuelo—symbolizing man—toward transformation. In a liminal space between life and death, "esa amor" (this love) manifests as "una excelsa trinidad / se lo consagra su pecho! / que se llama, ¡su Derecho / su Patria y su Libertad!" (a sublime trinity to which he devotes his heart, it is called his Law, his Country, and his Liberty). The adjectives describing this amor evoke the sacred ("sublime," "santo," "bendita," "excelsa"). Once the anonymous flor, "love" gains a name. Once again, an allusion to this biblical trilogy provides a metaphor for social phenomena. In this case, it is the triangulation of law, country, and liberty characterizing the rhetoric of the wars for independence. The love for a certain sacred, tripartite ideal of a new Cuba Libre—a revision of the Father–Son–Holy Ghost trinity—seduces the man.

The idea of libertad in nineteenth-century Cuba had two connotations—that of freedom from Spain and freedom from slavery. Like "A mi raza," "El arroyuelo y la flor" stands in contradistinction to a sentimental portrayal of Cuban nationalism. Cirilio Villaverde's popular novel *Cecilia Valdés* (1882 [1995]) appropriated the female protagonist Cecilia as a symbol of an internally conflicted Cuban nation. More generally, the *mulatta* in particular served as a symbol for Cuban nationalism as it sought to distinguish itself from Spain. The female body became the site for the contention of unsolved problems of race and class inherent in a nation trying to reconcile with a history of slavery and colonialism.

Defining womanhood became problematic as women saw themselves in the "mirror" of a male-defined national project. As Ada Ferrer indicates, women were "excluded from the symbolic birth of the nation" and were most commonly represented as bodies that were "physically incapable of producing anything other than Cuban patriots" (1999, 127). The figure of the *mambisa*—the mother-patriot who fought in the wars of independence and sacrificed all for the cause of the nation (Stoner 1991, 19)—was praised by independence leaders as a symbol of "national sovereignty" (1991, 29). Ayala's "Arroyuelo y la flor" considers the costs of this revolutionary ideal of nationhood in which women were objectified as aesthetic symbols and sacrificed in the pursuit of nationhood. As the structure of the first half of the poem indicates, we as readers, just as the flor questions the arroyuelo, are expected to question the narrator's tone in the second half of the poem and the poem's apparent resolution. "Man" escapes into a sea of new significations, whereas "woman" remains trapped on the margins, a slave to her own inevitable destruction.

The flor's permanence and ultimate subsumption in the arroyuelo reads as an allegory for the symbolic fashioning of "woman" for the purpose of nationhood. The Judeo-Christian creation narrative places the first male and female in the Garden of Eden, out of which flows a single river. As the Garden of Eden represents a point of origin for gender difference, the place in which God created male and female, "El arroyuelo y la flor" problematizes the male–female relationship as a sociopolitical and literary enterprise.[7] The masculinized love for a rhetorical ideal of nationhood causes an upset in gender relations on the "shadowy" backdrop of an illusory Edenic paradise; the nationalist thrust disrupts an idealized, romanticized vision of male–female love and also calls into question the role men played in silencing women's protest. We can contrast Ayala's "El arroyuelo y la flor" with "Reconciliación" by José Antonio Echeverría (1815–1885)—poet, abolitionist, political activist, and contemporary of Ayala—where an *arroyo* and *la flor sepulcral* appear in the last two stanzas.

> Como el arroyo que corre
> Por bajo fresca sombría,
> Que apenas la luna fría
> Lo vé ni la luz del sol:
> Así nuestra vida oscura
> Corra en secreto, ignorada,
> Bajo la sombra encantada
> De las alas del Amor.
> Y cuando la muerte corte
> Nuestra amante alegre vida,
> Y en nuestra tumba escondida
> Crezca la flor sepulcral;
> Al curioso viajante
> La triste gente, inmutada,
> <<Se amaron>> dirá, bañada
> En tierno llanto la faz. (17–32)

[As the stream that runs beneath the dismal evening air, scarcely seen by the cool moon or the light of the sun: so may our dark life run on in secret, obscure, beneath the enchanted shadow of the wings of Love. And when death cuts off our luminous loving life, And within our hidden grave grows the sepulchral flower; the mourners, changed, will say, to the curious traveler "They were in love," their faces bathed in tender lament.]

In "Reconciliación," the arroyo is compared to the secret life of a love reconciled between two lovers. La flor appears not as metaphor for a woman ultimately subsumed in the masculine pursuit of nationhood but as a sign of the lovers' union even in death. Transformation (La triste gente, inmutada) occurs in the observers as a result of a love that transcends death. Ayala's "El arroyuelo y la flor" answers this reconciliation by problematizing this romanticized union. Love does not assert life in the face of death, but rather causes a form of death as it consumes woman.

The enslavement of woman to the purposes of national symbolism produces a problematic freedom. Ultimately, Ayala highlights the process of creating allegorical relationships between the natural world and social phenomena, thus illustrating the literary aspects of gender and nationalism. "El arroyuelo y la flor" asserts a type of meta-discourse on the process of poetic metaphor. This critique challenges the symbolic appropriation of the female figure that effectively marginalized women in the national project. The problem of namelessness provides the subtext, a chaos out of which the poem orders itself.

Conclusion

Harper's and Ayala's poetry is both informed and formed by the political and literary process of constructing collective identity. A comparative reading of these poems suggests not that the Cuban and North American historical contexts and literature are identical, but that the prerogative of "race," gender, and nationalism in postabolition Cuba and postabolition United States was inflected by a series of interlocking ideas. This interlocking produced a similar set of rhetorical and literary responses to them.

"A mi raza," "Eliza Harris," and "We Are Rising" explicitly problematize freedom and link it to slavery, more specifically, slavery as experienced and historicized by afrodescendentes in the United States and Cuba. "El arroyuelo y la flor" does not make explicit reference to race or slavery, but more implicitly juxtaposes the free motion of the arroyuelo and the fixedness of the flor. The female voice "from the margin" offers a critique of its own destruction. The freedom of one is contingent on the enslavement of another. Consistent with abolitionist rhetoric, Harper places emphasis on the sentimental in "Eliza Harris," depicting Eliza as the (voiceless) image of maternal love and thereby indicting the system of North American slavery. Ayala wrote "El arroyuelo y la flor" at the height of the Cuban separatist movement, just two years before it culminated in the War of Independence (1895–1898)—a time when national solidarity was essential to the separatist cause. Slavery and race do not appear as explicit themes in "El arroyuelo y la flor"; instead, the problem of gender emerges in the context of a tension between Cuban nationalism—posited as a male ideological pursuit—and the sentimental ideal of unconditional female devotion and male desire for a female beloved.

Cuban poet Africa Cespedes wrote the following in response to abolition and Cuban independence:

> ¡Alguna compensación había de alcanzar la familia negra, del heróico sacrificio de
> la sangre generosa de tantos mártires derramada, en holocuasto de la patria en la

epopeya de los diez años! ¡Algun dia había Cuba de ser la virgen pura e inmaculada que, como estigma infamante, llevaba impresa en su candorosa frente! . . . Ya, ¡á Dios gracias! puede la mujer, se cual fuere su condición, dedicarse con entera libertad á los quehaceres que le son propios y entrar con la exigencia lógica del derecho moderno, en el estado civil que la elevará a la categoría de consideraciones y respeto. Hoy, Cuba, tus poetas se inspirarán regocijados en la expressión magnífica de tu pródiga naturaleza, que asila á un pueblo de colonos libres; hoy pueden cantar con entera libertad los encantos mil con que te dotó la Providencia. (1889, 3)

[Some compensation must come to the black family for the heroic sacrifice of noble blood shed by so many martyrs in the country's holocaust during the epic of the Ten-Year War! Some day Cuba must be the pure and immaculate virgin that bore the mark on her innocent brow like a shameful blight! Finally, thank God, a woman can be fully free to dedicate herself to her own affairs, regardless of what her condition was, and with the logical demand for modern rights, can enter the civil state that will raise her to the level of due regard and respect. Today, Cuba, your poets will become inspired, delighted by the magnificent expression of your rich nature, an asylum for a community of free colonists; today they can sing with full freedom the thousands of accolades that Providence gave you.]

What Teresa Prados-Torreira refers to as the "project of a free Cuba" did *not* involve a concerted effort to renegotiate gender roles in Cuban society, thus making the implications and meaning of independence and progress less defined for women than for men (2005, 6).

As a form of deliberation, "A mi raza" and "El arroyuelo y la flor" thematize the presence-absence of women in a discourse of national freedom, while at the same time providing an avenue for the female voice to be heard. In "A mi raza," Ayala's speaker's didactic apostrophe and call-to-arms echo her own voice and urge black women to see themselves through the lens of their "duties" in service of racial uplift. "We Are Rising" both formally and thematically reiterates the ideology of racial uplift and the ongoing process of translation from slave to free, whereas "Eliza Harris" indicates the ways the figure of the black slave mother challenged the system of slavery in the United States. Each poem is undergirded by an anxiety about the semiological and metaphorical constitution of categories of race and gender and the process of creating a national identity. They highlight the literary process involved in negotiating these categories. In this sense, the poems are concerned with the language of "uplift": the "lifting up" of one designation for another as a means of removing a mark—the imprint of one narrative of race—and replacing it with another.

Chapter Four

Prison Breaks: Modes of Escape in Auta de Souza's Poetics of Freedom

Numa cultura em que a mulher era idealizada como esteio da família e pilar moral da formação de "homens de bem" para a sociedade, a educação, a escritura e a autoria femininas foram tacitamente relegadas. Para transformarem-se em profissionais da escrita, essas mulheres tiveram de redefinir seu papel. Tiveram de ousar. No meu entendimento, Auta de Souza foi uma delas.
[In a culture in which the woman was idealized as the support for the family and moral pillar in the formation of "good men" for society, the education, writing, and authorship by women were tacitly relegated. In order to transform themselves into professional writers, these women had to redefine their role. They had to be daring. To my understanding, Auta de Souza was one of these such women.]

—Ana Laudelina Ferreira Gomes

No caso brasileiro, no tocante às mulheres negras, sabemos que no passado por força do regime escravista eram submetidas a todo tipo de exploração desumana, sexual, servil, despojadas de seus filhos, assassinadas, violentadas e perseguidas quando na tentativa de livrarem-se das opressões. Evidentemente este sistema não favorecia a alfabetização e muito menos a aquisição de conhecimentos intelectuais. Apesar disto, a participação da mulher negra na composição e resistência cultural é significativa em todos os setores. No tocante à literatura Auta de Souza chega até nós como exceção deste quadro de silêncio.
[In the Brazilian case, as far as black women are concerned, we know that in the past, due to the power of the institution of slavery, they were subject to all kinds of inhuman, sexual, servile exploitation, robbed of their children, murdered, raped, and persecuted when they tried to free

themselves from oppression. Clearly this system did not
favor literacy and even less the acquisition of intellectual
knowledge. In spite of this, the participation of the black
woman in writing and in cultural resistance is significant in
all sectors. With respect to Auta de Souza's literature, it
comes to us as an exception to this picture of silence.]

—Miriam Alves (2004, 9)

A noite não adormecerá
jamais nos olhos das fêmeas
pois do nosso sangue-mulher
do nosso líquido lembradiço
em cada gota que jorra
um fio invisível e tônico
pacientemente cose a rede
de nossa milenar resistência.
[The night will never sleep in the eyes of women for from
our woman blood from our liquid remembrance in each
drop that falls an invisible and tonic thread patiently weaves
the web of our millenary resistance.]

—Conceição Evarista (in Quilombhoje 1998, 43)

"Jesus, este vôo infindo / Há de amparar-me nos braços / Enquanto eu direi sorrindo: / Quebrei meus laços!" [My God, this infinite flight will raise me in its arms. While laughing I will say: "I have broken my chains!"]. A decade after a new constitution christened the República dos Estados Unidos do Brasil (Republic of the United States of Brazil), Brazilian poet Auta de Souza (1876–1901) wrote these lines that comprise the last stanza of a six-stanza poem titled "Fio Partido" (Broken Thread). Modeled after the U.S. Constitution, Brazil's constitution promised to protect its citizens' rights to "liberdade, à segurança individual e à propriedade" (freedom, safety, and property).

But Brazil was anything but free from its legacy of slavery. Ironically, masters and slaves relied on their experiences in slavery to help define freedom (Queirós Mattosso 1986, 166). In "Fio Partido" Auta explores freedom through a meditation on death; in "Minh'Alma e o Verso" (My Soul and Poetry), she explores freedom through the poet's relationship to language. By presenting escape from the body as a legitimate form of freedom, "Fio Partido" and "Minh'Alma e o Verso" inquire into the precarious and elusive freedom of a changing, postabolition nation. The poems interrogate the symbiotic relationship between slavery and freedom as they play out against the backdrop of personal reflection and the moment of creative inspiration. In both instances, Auta collapses the binary between freedom and slavery.[1] Furthermore, each poem reflects and reinterprets the language and symbols of freedom that circulated both nationally and transnationally in the Americas.

Ana Laudelina Ferreira Gomes begins the necessary task of rereading Auta's work to determine its relationship to contemporary literary canons. Ferreira Gomes suggests that biblical allusions and religious typology in Auta's poetry might function as double entendre as it bears meaning beyond the religious. She suggests that allusions to God, the figure of Christ, and the Virgin Mary can be read not only as indicators of Auta's Christian mysticism but also as "as forças psíquicas operantes no processo criador" (psychic forces operating in the creative process) (2001, 51). These possibilities challenge us to read Auta's work in a new context that goes beyond a simplistic assessment of authorial intent or biography. They challenge us to understand the poetic text as a body of signs engaged in a dialectic exchange with the tropes and signs that circulate nationally and transnationally and that manifest as ideas about slavery and abolition in and outside of Brazil.

Building on Ferreira Gomes's conjecture, I place Auta de Souza's poems "Fio Partido" and "Minh'alma e o Verso" in the historical moment of postabolition Brazil and consider the ways their formal and thematic elements engage it. In the case of "Fio Partido," enslaving the body to death permits the speaker's escape into an imagined realm of freedom. In "Minh'alma e o Verso," the speaker's enslaved soul, locked into marriage with poetry itself, ultimately frees itself to engage in the act of writing.

Freedom and the Literary Reimagining of Auta de Souza

Irrespective of the degree to which Auta de Souza herself conceived of her poetry in relationship to a hemispheric discourse about slavery and freedom, she uses the tools she was given—a literary tradition of French Symbolism and Catholicism primarily—to carve out a poetic space in which the rhetorical and political tensions coincide with the individual search for identity. Her precarious relationship to theories of Afro-Brazilian poetry takes us beyond debate about racial belonging and begin to ask how literary elements play a role in the history of national, racial, and gender identities.

Unlike Ayala and Harper, Auta makes no public claims as a nationally or racially inscribed voice. It would be overly simplistic, therefore, to impose a comparative reading of her poems with those of Harper or Ayala. Accordingly, I place Auta in contention with prior readings of her own work. I do so not from a political vantage point—I am not interested in debating her racial designation—but from a literary one.

The comparative dimension of my reading of Auta's work, therefore, is the comparison between a symbolist, text-based reading and a politicized, *con*textual reading. I focus on the interaction between these two readings and show how the national and transnational reading of a text transcends what is immediately "spoken" by the text and beyond what might bind the poetic text to a certain limited space (i.e., a single poet's or nation's experience). Auta de Souza's work, then, challenges us to consider ancestry itself as a textual phenomenon. It asks: how does an inheritance of historical narratives influence the composition, valences of meaning, and our reading of the poetic text?

Although aspects of Auta's poems certainly bear the signature of Symbolism—the predominate literary movement of late nineteenth-century Brazil—her widespread popularity and use of "common" language are just two characteristics that distinguish her from the poets of the "torre de marfim" (ivory tower) (Muzart 1991, 150). Nevertheless, Auta's poetry certainly does not conform to late modern and contemporary definitions of Afro-Brazilian poetry. Her work is not explicitly racial in content. In his comprehensive essay, "Survey of African-Brazilian Literature," Edimilson de Almeida Pereira maintains that Auta "did not treat themes relating to African-Brazilians" and that her "black ancestry" did not, therefore, "attract the attention of scholars" (1995, 879). Furthermore, her poems did not reflect any distinctive vernacular patterns reminiscent of African languages or speech patterns. Auta *does*, however, address themes related to Brazilians of African descent. The problem of freedom appears strongly in her work, and as we have seen in Harper and Ayala, it is ultimately bound to slavery.

I do not conflate the very complex understanding of ancestry and race in Brazil with that of the United States or Cuba—both of which differ in their own right. Nevertheless, I pose the same questions to Auta's texts that I posed to those of the other poets: what does her work suggest about the tension between slavery and freedom, and how does it contribute to constructions of nation and transnation? In this way, I abandon a purely symbolist or sentimental reading of her work. Focusing my analysis on two poems that are particularly bold in their assertions about the interdigitation of freedom and slavery, I argue that in "Fio Partido," freedom of imagination requires submission to death. In "Minh'alma e o Verso," freedom from slavery ultimately depends on enslavement to poetry. I suggest that a transhemispheric historical context provides fertile ground for reading new meanings in Auta de Souza's poetry.

The Dream and Flight: Modes of Escape in "Fio Partido"

> Fugir à mágoa terrena
> e ao sonho, que faz sofrer,
> Deixar o mundo sem pena
> Será morrer?
> [To flee this earthly sorrow and this dream that makes me suffer, to leave the world painlessly, could it be to die?]

Biblical notions of heaven and transcendence rely heavily on the concept of flight or escape: Christ's ascension to the Father, the promise of life after death, the idea of physical death as a passage into eternal life with God. In late nineteenth-century Brazil, however, *flight* had an additional set of connotations. Advertisements for fugitive slaves appeared in newspapers across the nation. From *Gazeta de Campinhas*: "Fugiu a Bernardo Teixeira Pinheiro um escravo de nome Ignacio, cor avermelhada, 15 a 16 annos de idade" (A slave named Ignacio, a reddish color, 15 or 16 years old, fled from Bernardo Teixeira Pinheiro) (287), "Fugiu no dia 7 de April da fazenda de Domingos Leite Penteado Junio, o escravo João" (Slave João fled from Domingos Leite Penteado Junio's farm on April 7th) (289), and "Ao barão d'Atibaia fugiu o pardo Ladisláu, de 18 annos de idade" (The 16 year old *pardo* Ladisláu fled from the Baron of Atibaia) (289). From *O Farol Paulistano*: "Pela pascoa fugiu um escravo de Dona Angela" (One of Dona Angela's slaves fled on Easter) (362) and "Fugiu em 24 de Dez da 1828 a João Luiz do Oliveira, fugiu o seu escravo Joaquim" (João Luiz do Oliveira's slave Joaquim fled on the 24th of Outubro, 1828) (289).

Other newspapers like *A Actualidade*, *O Constitucional*, or *Diario da Bahia* and *Bom Senso* also included daily listings beginning with phrases like "fugio um escravo" (a slave fled), "fugiu da fazenda" (fled from the farm), "fugido um escravo" (a slave has fled), and "escravo fugido" (fugitive slave). During the latter stages of the abolitionist movement, landowning slaveholders in the coffee regions of southern Brazil clamored for slaves from the north. Advertisements for fugitive slaves continued to voice slaveholder claims. Rio Grande do Norte, the region in which Auta was born, became a major haven for fugitive slaves (Conrad 1972, 137).

The notion of flight and escape appears in "Fio Partido." The speaker is driven by a desire to flee from early suffering, to escape the body and exist as an incorporeal "dream." This desire to escape the physical world leads the speaker to contemplate death.

> Fugir à mágoa terrena
> E ao sonho, que faz sofrer,
> Deixar o mundo sem pena
> Será morrer?
> Fugir neste anseio infindo
> À treva do anoitecer,
> Buscar a aurora sorrindo
> Será morrer?
> E ao grito que a dor arranca
> E o coração faz tremer,
> Voar uma pomba branca
> Será morrer? (Souza 2001, 272, ll. 1–12)

[To flee this earthly sorrow And this dream that makes me suffer, To leave the world painlessly Could it be to die? To flee from this infinite longing, To the darkness of nightfall, In search of the laughter of dawn Could it be to die? And from this cry that pries out pain And makes the heart tremble, A white dove soaring Could it be to die?]

Like an incantation, the repetition of the consonant phrase "será morrer" summons the dove. Consonance (namely, the repetition of the *r* sound) works further in this stanza to effect a certain sound texture that makes the word "pomba" more prominent when it appears in the third line of stanza 3; it stands out both visually and phonetically. The dove ascends and reappears through the repetition in stanza 4. The absence of the body from physical life suggests one form of escape from an Earth that is a "dream." Death is a means of flight. Auta inverts the relationship between physical reality and a surreal "dream" such that the Earth is in fact "the dream" and the place of suffering. The poem conflates reality with the surreality of the dream world. Unlike the symbolist ideal of the dream as a utopian space achieved through the imagination, the dream here is an earthly, unrealized ideal.

The second stanza progresses further into the pursuit of escape, a type of descent into darkness indicated by the "treva do anoitecer" (the darkness of nightfall). This darkness sets the stage for the opposing image of the *pomba branca* (white dove) as death presents a possible solution for the problem of an infinitely insatiable desire (*anseio infinido*). Freedom, symbolized by the white dove, first appears in the poem in physical proximity to death. Biblical iconography designates the dove as a symbol of the soul departing after death. At the baptism of Christ, the Holy Spirit descends on Earth in the form of a dove, thus foreshadowing Christ's death (see Mark 1:9–11, Matthew 3:16, Luke 3:21, 22). His death then releases the Holy Spirit onto the Earth.

In "Fio Partido," the dove indicates death as a passageway into a "space of freedom." On one hand, the speaker identifies with the dove. The dove emerges from a "grito" (cry), a violent, charged utterance outside of the realm of language.[2] The dove is an incorporeal spirit that, free from the body, can escape into the "amplidão"—an expansive, boundless space.

The speaker observes the dove in flight and identifies with it; the dove becomes a symbol of the speaker herself. The fifth stanza confuses the voices of the speaker and the dove. Is it the continuation of the dove's song or the speaker's response to the image? Ultimately, it is both. This merging of the speaker and the pomba occurs in the middle of the poem. By the final stanza, the speaker's appropriation of the dove is complete; it is sealed by the repetition of the dove's initial utterance. The repetition of the phrase, "Quebrei meus laços" (I broke my chains) affirms the dove's release and ultimately signals the speaker's freedom.

> Lá vai a pomba voando
> Livre, através do espaços . . .
> Sacode as asas cantando:
> "Quebrei meus laços!"
> Aqui na amplidão liberta,
> Quem pode deter-me os passos?
> Deixei a prisão deserta,
> "Quebrei meus laços!" (13–20)
> [There goes a dove flying Free, across spaces . . . It flutters its wings singing: "I have broken my chains!" Here, free in boundless space, Who can detain my steps? I have left the solitary prison "I have broken my chains!"][3]

But this freedom, though articulated in the past tense, is not complete in the present. Emphasized by the alliterative and consonant rhyme "La vai" and "Livre," freedom is at once here and there; it is both present and just beyond reach. The distance between the dove and the speaker, combined with their mirroring, reinforces this paradox.

End rhyme and internal ryhme reinforce the musical work of the lines. The end rhyme in stanza 4 (*voando* and *cantando*) link flight and freedom lyrically. The contrast of "amplidão" and "prisão" reinforces the tension between freedom and bondage in the same way that the resonance of "deixei and qeubrei" reinforce the act of breaking *away* (i.e., rupture) and breaking *out* (i.e., escape). The language of the text is inflected with the tension between freedom and bondage.

By the final stanza, the speaker is fully translated into the "voô infindo" (infinite flight).

> Jesus, este vôo infindo
> Há de amparar-me nos braços
> Enquanto eu direi sorrindo:
> "Quebrei meus laços!" (21–24)
> [My God, this infinite flight
> will raise me in its arms
> While smiling I will say:
> "I have broken my chains!"]

The speaker identifies with the dove's freedom through an utterance—"Quebrei meus laços." The repetition of this utterance not only creates a unifying pattern in both of the three-stanza sections of the poem, it also creates a rythmic pattern. This pattern emphasizes its musicality and the importance of the utterance itself.

The figure of Christ appears only once at a critical point. On one hand, the speaker's reference to Christ confirms her complete translation into the spiritual world through death. On the other hand, through identification with the dove, the speaker identifies with the physical death and spiritual resurrection of Christ. Biblically speaking, the practice of baptism itself is a symbolic affirmation of the death and resurrection of the believer who must die in body as Christ died to "live unto God."[4] We see this pattern of death and resurrection performed structurally in the poem. The desire for "flight" from the physical world is realized through a transgression of the physical body. This escape is performed first through a symbolic binding of the speaker and the pomba. In its flight, the dove achieves freedom. It is "free" because it has broken the "laços" that have bound it to the Earth. The broken thread suggests the rupture of death in the "thread" of life. The verb *partir* also infers a "breaking away"—both a physical break or tear as well as a shift or change in an established course. While the poem maintains its *abab* rhyme scheme, it performs this breakage with a change in the refrain from "Será morrer" (Could it be to die?) to "Quebrei meus laços" (I have broken my chains).

The symbol of the dove is the literal and figurative center of the poem. The speaker first observes the dove; she then identifies herself with it as a symbol of freedom; finally, she becomes free. In other words, a form of freedom is achieved through the interaction between the symbol and the self. The juxtaposition of a transient death and the breaking of binds establishes a stanzaic equilibrium that delineates the poem's cosmos—an "imagined" space. Freedom is achieved in this space through a symbolic reordering of the natural world through language. The poem is not just about freedom, it is a performance of it. Although the first half of the poem is a meditation on death, the second half affirms a new life of freedom. The "infinite flight" of the soul identifies the speaker with a form of spiritual resurrection: "Há de amparar-me nos braços" (Will raise me in its arms). Now reconfigured in the poem, the death of Christ for the collective freedom of humanity comes to signify the speaker's personal transcendence and individual freedom.

Is the symbolic freedom—represented by the ascent of the dove—enough to confirm the speaker's freedom? The symmetrical six-stanza structure—four lines each and a consistent *abab* rhyme scheme—establishes a balance between the longing for escape and actual exit from the prison of that longing. Bondage and freedom remain in undisturbed balance. The "space of freedom" is the poem itself, and yet, even within the poem, freedom is precarious. Death acts as a form of resolution invoked by repetition in the first half of the poem. Symbolizing the flight of the soul from the body after death, the flight of the dove transitions us into the breaking of the chains in part two. Yet the text is fraught with unresolved tensions between freedom and bondage, life and death.

The white dove not only represents a spiritual freedom in the biblical sense but also has meaning for ideas about national freedom and the freedom of African slaves. "Fio Partido" was written during a transitional period in the "free" modern nation of Brazil. This "modern nation" centered itself around an ideal of individual and collective *human* freedom (an ideological counterpart to a system of "free labor"). Auta de Souza problematizes this freedom in a way similar to that of her contemporary, Afro-Brazilian poet João da Cruz e Sousa (1861–1898). Cruz wrote in the poem "Livre," "Livre! Ser livre da matéria escrava, arrancar os grilhões que nos flagelam e livre penetrar nos Dons que selam a alma e lhe emprestam toda a etérea lava" (Free! To be free of slavish things, to tear off the shackles that lash us and free, to penetrate those Gifts that seal the soul). For both Cruz and Auta, freedom is more than ideological abstraction. It is to be free of anything that prevents a person from accessing a part of themselves. In another poem, "Cárcere das Almas" (Prison of Souls), Cruz locates the space of contention between slavery and freedom.

>Ah! Toda a alma num cárcere anda presa,
>Soluçando nas trevas, entre as grades
>Do calabouço olhando imensidades,
>Mares, estrelas, tardes, natureza.
>
>Tudo se veste de uma igual grandeza
>Quando a alma entre grilhões as liberdades
>Sonha e, sonhando, as imortalidades
>Rasga no etéreo o Espaço da Pureza.
>
>Ó almas presas, mudas e fechadas
>Nas prisões colossais e abandonadas,
>Da Dor no calabouço, atroz, funéreo!
>
>Nesses silêncios solitários, graves,
>que chaveiro do Céu possui as chaves
>para abrir-vos as portas do Mistério?! (1984, 12)
>
>[Ah! Every soul wanders captive in a prison cell, sobbing in the darkness, between the bars of the prison watching the boundless abyss, oceans, stars, noons, nature. Everything adorns itself in equal greatness as the soul dreams of freedoms among the shackles and, dreaming will pull forth immortality in the ethereal Space of the Pure. Oh imprisoned souls, mute and held up in colossal, abandoned prisons of Pain in horrid, funereal dungeons. In these, grave, solitary silences, which guard from Heaven holds the keys to open up the doors of Mystery?]

Like "Fio Partido," "Cárcere das Almas" presents the "open space" of freedom as a dream space. The experience of captivity *produces* the dream of freedom. Like the space "between the bars" in "Cárcere das Almas," freedom is imagined in the space between the lines in "Fio Partido."

Constructing a "Cidadão Brasileiro" (Brazilian citizen) in the postabolition era required a new understanding of freedom. The 1889 edition of the newspaper *O Philartista*—a special edition dedicated to abolition—featured a popular image of a white woman dressed in a frock of leaves with her hands uplifted, bearing the two halves of a pair of broken shackles. The abolition of slavery in 1888 had confirmed the new Brazilian republic, a "Brasil livre" (free Brazil) finally free from the stain of slavery. The physical body of the slave, freed from slavery by legal abolition, stood in metonymically for the body of the nation freed from the moral and economic degradation of slavery.[5] *A Tribuna*, a major abolitionist newspaper based in Recife and to which Auta de Souza contributed some of her poetry a decade later, featured the following line on the front cover of the May 13, 1888, edition: "Não ha mais escravos no Brasil" (There are no more slaves in Brazil). This refrain appeared repeatedly in abolitionist newspapers across the nation. Brazilian abolitionists and politicians alike heralded the abolition of slavery as a major milestone in Brazil's progress toward true nationhood. One writer wrote:

> Era preciso que de uma vez para sempre fosse *arrancado de teu seio* o negro cancro que corroia as tuas instituições, leis e costumes. A familia brazileira, que tantos males devia a essa creação ante-natural, a que até o dia 13 deu-se o nome de escravidão, *quebrou os laços infamantes* que a prendiam, ergueu-se nobre e altiva ante o mundo civilisado para dizer-lhe: <<No sólo desta patria querida não existe mais um escravo.>> (Diniz Barreto 1988, 2)
>
> [It was necessary that the black cancer that corroded its institutions, laws, and customs be one and for all torn from its breast. The Brazilian family, which owes many of its evils to this unnatural invention, that, until *o dia 13*, bore the name of slavery, has broken the infamous chains that bound and risen noble and proud before the civilized world to say: In this beloved country there no longer exists even one slave.]

The vying between abolitionism and proslavery sentiments in the second half of the nineteenth century brought the question of freedom to the forefront of Brazilian national consciousness. It also fueled an ideological, political, and economic battle between a firm legacy of slavery and emerging ideals of democracy and capitalism.

Although abolitionism had achieved one aspect of its goal by the turn of the century, namely, the legal emancipation of all slaves, it remained to be seen how this legislative "freedom" would play out socially, economically, or politically. Abolition in Brazil was preceded by a period of precarious "freedoms" for slaves. A legacy of legal manumission had established a system of degrees of freedom that resembled slavery. According to scholar of Brazilian slavery Katia M. de Queirós Mattoso, "The liberated slave was not entirely a free man" (1986, 156; 177). The 1871 "law of the free womb" made freedom for some within reach and yet not absolute (1986, 155–56). The lack of economic provision forced many *emancipados* to remain on plantations in de facto slavery. Many "liberated" sons and daughters of slaves were indebted to their parents' masters and forced to earn their freedom through a form of indentured servitude, thus perpetuating the economic and social hierarchies of slavery.[6] Ultimately, legal processes established to confer the freedom of slaves in Brazil reinforced their status as commodities (Queirós Mattoso 1986, 164).

Expanding on the biblical idea of death as an escape from earthly suffering, "Fio Partido" exhibits both a textual and formal ambivalence about freedom.[7] This ambivalence reflects the precarious state of freedom in Brazil. The poem's central image—the biblical symbol of the dove—walks the line between life and death and delimits the elusiveness of "freedom" itself. "Fio Partido" posits an elusive freedom attainable in death. The desire for freedom as escape from the physical world and from the body culminates in a symbolic escape performed in the poem. "Fio Partido" forms a poetic critique of what Queirós Mattoso refers to as the "dreamlike period" (1986, 182) after abolition, highlighting what Saidiya Hartman calls the "contestation over the meaning of abolition and emancipation" (1997, 14) in the Americas during the abolition era.

> *O poeta negro sonhava mais do que vivia, e isso porque, na oposição entre o sonho e a realidade, repousava toda a sua existência.*
> [The black poet dreamed more than he lived, and this is because his entire existence rests in the opposition between dream and reality.]
>
> —Abelardo F. Montenegro (1998, 61)

> *Não acordeis o escravo que dorme, ele sonha talvez que é livre.*
> [Don't wake a sleeping slave, he may be dreaming he is free.]
>
> —Abolitionist saying (Nabuco 1988, 43)

Poetic Reimagining and the Dream in "Minh'alma e o Verso"

A woman stands among rosebuds. She is dressed in white with a blue ribbon wrapped around her waist. Her hands are pressed together, poised for prayer. Her head tilts slightly and her gaze is averted outward. A subtle smile traces her lips, and she looks out toward an unseen onlooker. Rays of light bend outward from her veiled head.

This idyllic image describes an artistic rendition of Our Lady of Lourdes, the apparition of the Virgin Mary in the French town of Lourdes (Calamari and DiPasqua 2004, 68). Images of the Virgin Mary like this one permeate nineteenth-century Western art. Mother of the Catholic faith, Mary appears as the quintessential virginal woman. Marian iconography highlights the Brazilian nineteenth-century feminine ideal—the mother and bride.[8]

Similar to "Fio Partido," the twelve-stanza poem "Minh'alma e o Verso" (My Soul and Poetry) posits the poem as a space in which to renegotiate the relationships between images, symbols, and—in this case—genders. Auta disturbs the master–slave and husband–wife paradigms. The bride, wed to her verse, becomes poet; the enslaved soul becomes free to imagine through the portal of a dream state achieved through an encounter with poetry itself.

"Minh'alma e o Verso" begins with the speaker's explicit rejection of a male lover.

> Não me olhes mais assim . . . Eu fico triste
> Quando a fitar-me o teu olhar persiste
> Choroso e suplicante . . .
> Já não possuo a crença que conforta.
> Vai bater, meu amigo, a uma outra porta
> Em terra mais distante. (Souza 2001, 223, ll. 1–6)

[Don't look at me anymore as you do . . . it saddens me when your gaze fixes on me, tearful and supplicant . . . I no longer possess the faith that comforts. Go knock, my friend, on some other door in a more distant land.]

The speaker rejects the lover's gaze, thus refusing to be caste into a Marian mold. She rejects the gaze that would fix her as the idyllic symbol of faith. The "choroso" (tearful) and "suplicante" (supplicant) gaze demands "a crença que conforta" (faith that comforts) a "crença" that the speaker claims to have lost. After refusing the lover's gaze, the speaker describes her own gaze onto him.

> Cuidavas que era amor o que eu sentia
> Quando meus olhos, loucos de alegria,
> Sem nuvem de desgosto,
> Cheios de luz e cheios de esperança,
> Numa carícia ingenuamente mansa,
> Pousavam no teu rosto?
> Cuidavas que era amor? Ah! se assim fosse!
> Se eu conhecesse esta palavra doce,
> Este queixume amado!
> Talvez minh'alma mesmo a ti voasse
> E num berço de flor ela embalasse
> Um riso abençoado.
> Mas, não, escuta bem: eu não te amava,
> *Minh'alma era, como agora, escrava . . .*
> *Meu sonho é tão diverso!*
> Tenho alguém a quem amo mais que a vida,
> Deus abençoa esta paixão querida:
> *Eu sou noiva do Verso.* (7–24; emphasis added)

[Did you think it was love that I felt when my eyes, drunk with happiness, without a cloud of displeasure, full of light and full of hopes, rested on your face in ingenuous gentle caress? Did you think it was love? Ah! if it were so! If I knew this sweet word, this beloved complaint! Perhaps my very soul would fly to you and it would rock in a cradle of flowers a consecrated smile. But, no, listen well: *I didn't love you, my soul was, as [it is] now, a slave . . . My dream is so different!* I have someone whom I love more than life, God blesses this beloved passion: *I am the bride of Poetry.*]

What the penitent sinner or the anonymous male lover has mistaken for love, the speaker identifies as her intimate relationship with and passion for Poetry. She claims not to "know" the kind of love the anonymous lover requires of her. She rejects that ideal in favor of Poetry. By identifying herself as a slave and affirming a love for poetry, the speaker disrupts the idyllic Marian image. The personification of "Verso" (Poetry) as her lover finalizes the rupture between the speaker and the lover who desires to fix her with his gaze. The speaker ultimately chooses to *enslave* her soul to poetry: "eu não te amava . . . [m]inh'alma era, como agora, escrava" (I didn't love you, my soul was, as [it is] now, a slave).

The tense of the narrative switches for the first time in this line from past to present; it is our first glimpse into the present state of the speaker. For the first time, she asserts "eu sou" (I am). Bound up in a relationship with poetry, Love then becomes "mais que a vida" (more than life). It is redefined. It transcends the socially defined relationship of husband and wife. Once enslaved, her soul is then free to dream a different kind of dream ("sonho . . . tão diverso"). The speaker is free to engage with poetry, referring to it as a "paixão querida" (beloved passion) blessed by God. Further rejecting any identification with the idyllic Marian figure, the speaker defines herself not as the bride of Christ but as "noiva do Verso" (the bride of Poetry). Her soul is not linked symbolically to the white dove fixed above Mary's head, but is rather linked metaphorically to the figure of the slave.

> E foi assim . . . Num dia muito frio.
> Achei meu seio de ilusões vazio
> E o coração chorando . . .
> Era o meu ideal que se ia embora,
> E eu soluçava, enquanto alguém lá fora
> Baixinho ia cantando. (27–30)
> [It was like this . . . One very cold day. I found my soul empty of illusions and my heart weeping . . . It was my ideal that was taking leave and I wept, while someone outside was whispering in song.]

The poem momentarily shifts away from the sestet and introduces a new voice with a four-quatrain ballad. This lyric poem within the poem begins at the center of the narrative (i.e., the sixth of twelve stanzas), thereby drawing attention structurally to narrative itself as a theme.

> "Eu sou o orvalho sagrado
> Que dá vida e alento às flores;
> Eu sou o bálsamo amado
> Que sara todas as dores.
> Eu sou o pequeno cofre
> Que guarda os risos da Aurora;
> Perto de mim ninguém sofre,
> Perto de mim ninguém chora.
> Todos os dias bem cedo
> Eu saio a procurar lírios

Para enfeitar em segredo
A negra cruz dos martírios.
Vem para mim, alma triste
Que soluça de agonía;
No meu seio o Amor existe,
Eu sou filho da Poesia." (35–46)

["I am the sacred dew that gives life and strength to the flowers; I am the beloved balm that heals all wounds. I am the small coffer that holds the laughter of Aurora; close to me no one suffers, close to me no one weeps. Everyday very early I go out in search of lilies to decorate in secret the black cross of suffering. Come to me, sorrowful soul that weeps from agony; in my breast is Love, I am the child of Poetry."]

Here the poem moves into the realm of the archetypal. It describes the perennial search for the lyric impulse to "decorate" or pay secret homage to those who have died suffering. It conjures an unspoken history of suffering that transcends the speaker's individual experience. The maternal figure has a love affair with the child of poetry, a Christic figure. The poem therefore contrasts a mystical encounter with the Son of God with a transcendent experience with poetry. The repetition of "Eu sou" in stanzas six and seven echoes the voice of God in Exodus who asserts "I am that I am" (Exodus 3:14). The admonition to "Come to me, sorrowful soul / That weeps from agony" echoes Christ's call to sinners: "Come unto me all ye that are heavy laden and I will give you rest" (Matthew 11:28). As the poem continues, the call to Christian discipleship is reconfigured and becomes a call to an encounter with the poetic imagination.

Meu coração despiu toda a amargura,
Embalado na mística doçura
Da voz que ressoava . . .
Presa do Amor na delirante calma.
Eu fui abrir as portas de minh'alma
Ao Verso que passava. . . .
Desde esse dia, nunca mais deixei-o;
Ele vive cantando no meu seio,
Numa algazarra louca!
Que seria de mim se ele fugisse,
Que seria de mim se não ouvisse
A voz de sua boca!
Não posso dar-te amor, bem vês. Meus sonhos
São da Poesia os ideais risonhos,
Em lagos de ouro imersos . . .
Não sabias dourar os meus abrolhos,
E eu procurava apenas nos teus olhos,
Assunto para versos. (46–64)

[My heart, stripped bare of all its bitterness, entangled in the mystic sweetness of the resounding voice . . . a prisoner of Love in the delirious calm. I went to open the doors of my soul to the verse passing by . . . Since that day, I never left it again, it lives singing in my soul, in a dissonant clamor. What would become of me if it escaped? What would become of me if I had not heard its voice. I cannot give you love, as you can see. My dreams are of poetry, the raptured ideals, immersed in lakes of gold . . . You did not know how to polish my roughness and in your eyes I only sought out a subject for poetry.]

The suffering soul ultimately discovers a mysterious freedom in poetry. As "o verso" enters the soul, it then defines the speaker: "Que seria de mim se ele fugisse, / Que seria de mim se não ouvisse / A voz de sua boca" (What would become of me if it escaped? What would become of me if I had not heard its voice?). A surreality delineated by a dream world of imagination and linguistic play determines the speaker's reality. The subtle introduction of a sexual element in the encounter—the soul stripped bare and open for the penetration of poetry—further challenges the asexual maternality of the ideal woman.

The tension between bondage and freedom in "Fio Partido" resurfaces in "Minh'alma e o Verso" in the image of a prisoner opening the doors of the soul. The pivotal line "Minh'alma era, como agora, escrava" (My soul was, as it is now, a slave) not only shifts the poem into the present tense and the present state of the speaker's mind but also suggests that being enslaved alters one's perception of love by changing the object of desire.

Completely emptied of illusions and stripped of ideals, the speaker "finds herself" a slave to poetry. The state of being enslaved transforms the nature or content of the dream and thereby alters the "ideal." Redeemed not by a Christ figure or "the Son of God," she is healed instead by the "child of Poetry." As the silent antonym to slavery, freedom becomes a goal to be reached through and by poetry. A creative act of language, poetry emerges as a means of reversing subjectivity and redefining the self. Describing her soul as "a slave," the speaker rejects the role of wife or lover in favor of a spiritual union with poetry. Ultimately, her rejection of this anonymous lover serves as the impetus and subject for poetry.

Auta establishes a link between the identity of the poet and language itself. After the heart is "stripped bare," poetry penetrates the speaker and the moment of climax is the speaker's personal transformation. The erotic is the poetic. The sight of the lover inspires the creative impulse, resolving ultimately in the act of writing poetry.

Plagued by the impulse to resolve a viable tension between slavery and freedom during the nineteenth century, Brazil sought an identity independent of Europe. Attempting to define a distinctly Brazilian "type," Euclides da Cunha postulated the *sertanejo* in *Os Sertões* (1902). The ideal of Brazilian nationhood relied heavily on a romanticized image of the Brazilian woman.[9] Women were expected to mend the fabric of society both literally and figuratively. In the formula for national progress in a "Brasil livre" (free Brazil), the ideal woman served at the center of the family and from there would transform the nation. She would do so by maintaining her commitment to the role of wife and mother and not involving herself in the public arena of politics.[10] Any education a woman received was for the sole purpose of raising children. Girls were generally forced to marry young. Consequently, most young girls were taken out of school by the age of fourteen (Hahner 1990, 14).[11] A popular saying was:

> Menina que sabe muito
> É menina atrapalhada
> Para ser mãe de família
> Saiba pouco ou saiba nada. (quoted in Hahner 1990, 230)
> [A girl who knows a lot is a girl who is much confused. To be a mother with a family, she should know little or nothing at all.]

Toward the end of the nineteenth century, women's rights activists began to link the cause of women's emancipation with women's suffrage, a clear indication of a changed idea of women's relationship to politics.[12] Nevertheless, as Hahner notes, the "emphasis remained on the needle not the pen" (1990, 22).

The particular way that women fit into abolitionism in Brazil, for instance, reflected the country's patriarchal hierarchy. On the whole (with few exceptions), Brazilian abolitionism was a male movement. Women were not mentioned at all in the constitution of 1891. However, the symbolic "woman" played a major role in Brazilian abolition movements during the 1870s and 1880s. As Roger A. Kittleson articulates well, women were as much symbolically present as well as physically present in Brazilian abolitionism. Both women abolitionists and the movement's male leadership made use of constructions of elite womanhood, as well as campaigning by women, in their efforts to build an antislavery consensus. Linking their cause to qualities deemed natural to "decent" women in nineteenth-century Brazil—particularly morality, sentimentality, and charity—abolitionists in effect heeded the great activist José Patrocínio's admonition to "make the weakness of woman into the strongest of forces" (1996, 99). Kittleson goes on to emphasize the fact that women were incorporated into the movement as "nonpolitical, moral agents" (2005, 100). Problematizing the male–female relationship, "Minh'alma e o Verso" highlights the question of gender in relation to slavery. In doing so, Auta de Souza implicitly links the struggle of the female poet with that of women in general negotiating their political and social restrictions in the nineteenth century. She also links this struggle to the history of slavery in Brazil.

Reading Auta de Souza's "Minh'alma e o Verso" in the shadow of Princess Isabel allows us to furtherunderstand how the poem engages a discourse of gender in nineteenth-century Brazil. During Auta de Souza's childhood years, Princess Isabel governed Brazil three times as regent in her father's stead. When she signed the A Lei Áurea (The Golden Law), it was the third time that she had been left to rule. A few months after enacting the law, Princess Isabel reflected on her decision in her journal.

> How did the abolitionist viewpoint gain ground so quickly in me? The concept, already innate within me, was intrinsically humanitarian, moral, generous, great, and supported by the Church. Slavery was essentially an imposition . . . *the idea of the injustice of slavery* and the excessive time that the owners had exploited their slaves *could not fail to influence my spirit.* My children, should you later on read this paper, please realize that if your mother acted thus in the great question of abolition,

it was out of a conviction that it would be best for the nation, which she had a duty to watch over, and for you all, to whom she would leave her reputation as a mother and *the throne free of any blemish of egotism or weakness*, God aided me, my children, in acting entirely in accord with my conscience. (quoted in Barman 2002, 183–84)

During a period in which many hailed the established monarchal patriarchy as ordained by God (Barman 2002, 5), Princess Isabel's political agency disputed constructs of traditional femininity. Although she was exiled with the imperial family in 1889 when the monarchy was overthrown, by then she had already left an indelible imprint on the landscape of Brazilian political and social history.

In the year Auta de Souza was born, Princess Isabel took on temporary headship of the Brazilian regency. She faced the challenge of governing a nation that was sustaining economic hardship and general popular discontent about its progress (Barman 2002, 140). Isabel was valued both as a symbol of Brazilian "redemption" from slavery and a quintessentially feminine figure. An article published by the Comissão Executiva Permanente do Professorado Publica Primario da Corte (Permanent Executive Commission of the Court's Primary Professorship) in 1888 read:

Toda esta grande revolução social (. . .) foi feita por um coração e esse coração aninha-se no peito de uma senhora, que é filha, que é esposa, que é mãe, reunindo as três fases sublimes da mulher na humanidade! Filha, que aureolar o reinado de seu pai; esposa, reabilitou o lar doméstico, reabilitando o trabalho que é a consolidação e a moralização da família; mãe, não quis que seus filhos corasem algum dia ao lembrarem-se de que eram filhos de uma terra de escravos. (quoted in Daibert Junior 2004, 136)

[This entire great social revolution (. . .) was accomplished through one heart and this heart is housed in the breast of a woman, who is a daughter, wife, and mother, joining together the three sublime aspects of woman! Daughter, who illumines the reign of her father; as wife, she revitalized the domestic space of the home, revitalizing the work and the establishing and moralizing of the family; as mother, she did not want her children to be ashamed one day when they remember that they were children of a land of slaves.]

The feminization of abolition communicated the idea that abolishing slavery would virginize Brazil, thereby laying the foundation for a new, progressive nation.

As redeemer of the Brazilian nation through her efforts to free the country from the blight of slavery on its history, Isabel was also popularized as a messianic figure.

A Princesa passou a ser considerada "Redentora" da "raça" africana. Como Cristo, proporcionara a libertação dos cativos e os incorporava como filhos de uma mesma família. A salvação dos perdidos estava consumada por um ato de entrega e amor incondicional. Na formação da imagem de Isabel como "Redentora" dos escravos e libertadora de um povo são associados aspectos da religiosidade e cultura africana com a concepção cristã de salvação. A imagem de Isabel é composta, assim, de duas matrizes de discursos distintos, ressignificadas na construção que buscava também construir uma nacionalidade a partir da integração das diferenças entre os povos formadores da nação. A idéia de ruptura entre dois tempos tinha assim a intenção de apagar a lembrança de um passado marcado pela violência e pela exploração de brancos sobre negros. (quoted in Daibert Junior 2004, 224)

[The Princess came to be considered "Redeemer" of the African "race." Like Christ, she gave liberty to the captives and took them in as children of the same family. The salvation of the lost was realized by an act of surrender and unconditional love. Through the formation of Isabel as "Redeemer" of the slaves and liberator of a nation, aspects of African religiosity and culture are connected with the Christian concept of salvation. As such, the image of Isabel is composed of two forms of distinct discourses, redefined in the act of construction that also sought to build a nationality from the integration of the differences between peoples comprising the nation. The idea of rupture between two eras had, in that sense, the intention of wiping out the memory of a past marked by violence and by the exploitation of blacks by whites.]

Robert Daibert Junior argues that abolition in Brazil was in fact a dynamic process in which slaves and their descendants actively maintained the myth of Isabel as *redentora* (2004, 18).

A expectativa em relação à extinção da escravidão era grande. Ao assumir a Regência pela terceira vez em 1887, Isabel já havia se tornado alvo das esperanças abolicionistas. Já era vista como o messias que trazia a boa nova da abolição. (2004, 120)

[There was great anticipation regarding the end of slavery. Upon assuming regency for the third time in 1887, Isabel had already become the object of abolitionist hope. She was already seen as the Messiah that was bringing the good news of abolition.]

Many abolitionists believed that abolition in Brazil would effectively project the nation to new heights of development and redefine its position on an international scale (Daibert Junior 2004, 112).

Princess Isabel, as an icon of Brazilian abolition, demonstrates the relationship between the construction of gender and the abolition of slavery in Brazil. Auta's poetics engage this intersection. Isabel's construction as a feminine figure did not rely solely on political power, of which she had a limited amount. It relied on the way she was constructed through and by language. This construction combined Christic typology and a political use of symbolism (one if not *the* major tenet of poetic language).

According to contemporary Brazilian poet and member of Quilombhoje Miriam Alves, Auta de Souza's work counters a tradition of racial and gender oppression in Brazil. Alves refers to Auta de Souza an "exeção deste quadro de silêncio" (exception to this portrait of silence) (1994, 9) that characterized women's voice in Brazil. A strong culture of patriarchy was still alive and well in Brazil when Auta de Souza depicted a female figure who rejects her lover and instead identifies herself as a *novia* (bride) and *escrava* (slave) to Poetry. Auta's double metaphor works both as a challenge to patriarchal hierarchy *and* an assertion about the use of language and poetry to enact such opposition.

Drawing parallels between the "naturalization of racial inequalities" and the definition of true womanhood during the nineteenth century, Elisa Nascimento argues that the "project" of womanhood in Brazil was linked to the subhumanization of both women broadly and of *afrodescendente* peoples (2007, 27). Pamela Scully and Diane Paton argue that gender "both helped to construct and was itself constructed through class and racial categories." Furthermore, as it had with "African-ness," "scientific discourse and European colonial cultures came to see femininity as pathological. Ideas about women as both marginal and threatening mirrored and came to enhance emergent racist ideologies about people of African descent" (Scully and Paton 2005, 2). Auta examines this intersection of race and gender poetically; in "Minh'alma e o Verso," a single voice collaborates freedom, slavery, and gender identity.

Auta de Souza's "Fio Partido" and "Minh'alma e o Verso" call into question the meaning of freedom in the context of slavery and gender relationships. The tension between freedom and bondage characterizes these two poems. The suggestion that they are in fact in an interdependent and unresolved relationship introduces a critique of postabolition Brazil. In both, Auta focuses on the intimate world of dreams and desire. She is not explicitly transhemispheric in her sensibility, but her way of reconfiguring biblical tropes and her treatment of freedom and slavery connects her work to that of Harper (who was explicitly transhemispheric in her poetics) and Ayala (who was explicitly national). The way Auta reconfigures or riffs on biblical allusions and tropes aligns her literary strategy with that of Ayala and Harper. Like Ayala and Harper, Auta reconfigures biblical tropes to speak to the interlocking concepts of slavery, freedom, and nationhood.[13] The thematic and formal elements of the poems create a space in which to realize freedom, effect personal transformation, and reimagine identity.Auta's work is of particular importance to our understanding of Afro-Brazilian canon formation. Her work prompts us to further investigate what constitutes an Afro-Brazilian early literary tradition.

Conclusion

Where Do We Go from Here? The Implications of Textual Migrations

The slave population, it could be and was assumed, offered itself up as surrogate selves for meditation on problems of human freedom, its lure and its elusiveness . . . this slave population was understood to have offered itself up for reflections on human freedom in terms other than the abstractions of human potential and the rights of man.

—Toni Morrison (1993, 37–38)

As a literature of the Americas, nineteenth-century *afrodescendente* poetry has evolved in the shadow of New World slavery. During "the nadir" in particular, African descendants in Brazil, Cuba, and the United States faced the challenge of defining freedom for themselves. The process of defining freedom was not just political; it was also literary. It called for a culling of metaphors, symbols, and tropes to create the stories afrodescendentes would tell about their individual and collective lives. In its various forms and modalities, nineteenth-century afrodescendente literature problematized freedom and examined the relationship between freedom and slavery. It recognized the literary aspect of history and identity and the ways in which language could be used as a tool to construct it. As a literary space, language was a "loophole of retreat" (Hartman 1997, 9)—a contested space where freedom and slavery coexist and where new histories and identities are generated.

The transnationalism of afrodescendente poetics demonstrates this fact. Certainly, not all afrodescendente literature is explicitly transnational; nor do all afrodescendente writers engage liberationist themes. Transnationalism remains, however, the basic condition out of which afrodescentente literature has evolved. Transhemispheric study of afrodescendente poetics challenges us to engage in a certain kind of reading. It demands a reading reflective of the movement of ideas and tropes across hemispheres. The transatlantic and transhemispheric movement of Africans and their descendants models not only a kind of reading but also a kind of textuality. The text itself takes on the qualities of this migration. It resists totalizing readings that override difference and yet opens up to new kinds of identities.

Between the Lines demonstrates the kind of readings that can evolve out of this context. It traces the connection between poetic theory and transnationalism through the specific analysis of afrodescendente women's poetry. This denomination of poetry is just one possible lens, but it is particularly helpful for us because it stands at the crossroad of ancestry-based symbology (i.e., racially influenced symbology) and gender-based symbology, both of which rely heavily on biblical tropes and figures. These texts prompt us to a new level of inquiry regarding textuality and literary history, particularly as it reflects the literary process of individual and group identity formation.

Through a combination of hermeneutical approaches that combine structuralist and historicist readings of the literary text, we can read the forms and mediums of this transhemispheric exchange—symbolic allusions, tensions, and binary oppositions that are ultimately collapsed. Although there is no singular or monolithic "black aesthetic" either across national lines or within them, the thematic and typological commonalties we see in Harper, Ayala, and Auta de Souza are the footprints that verify these figurative territorial transgressions. Harper's work speaks to the transhemispheric aspect of American nationalism and the internal hypocrisies of the United States. Ayala's work shows us an early Cuban nation viewed through the lens of racial slavery and exposes the dark underside of Cuban nationalism—its exploitation of women and codependence on slavery. Auta de Souza's work highlights the intersection of spiritual and social strivings for freedom and the symbiotic relationship between imaginative freedom and physical slavery.

Any comparative project runs the risk of reinforcing the very boundaries it claims to deconstruct. Afrodescendente literature does not stand in opposition to "other" literatures, but represents variant attempts to use language poetically to reconstruct history and, in doing so, to impose a vision of how the future should be. Auta's, Ayala's, and Harper's engagement with language goes beyond specific formal or thematic considerations, ultimately placing language itself under the microscope. In doing so, these poets help us see how poetics play a role in the construction of historical memory. During the critical years leading up to the turn of the twentieth century, the project of nation-building called on the resources of intellectuals and poets alike. Auta's, Ayala's, and Harper's poetry actively destabilized myths about afrodescendente peoples. Their poetry also provided a foundation for a viable tradition of afrodescendente poetry by women and demonstrated the influence of poetry on the process of nation-building and the construction of gender and race at the turn of the century.

At times convergent and at times divergent but always interlocking, Harper's "Deliverance" and Ayala's "Redención" tell the redemption stories of peoples of African descent in the New World. In their message and choice of language, both poets respond to a range of discourse—the language of law, New World slavery, and the biblical language of the Old Testament. Harper and Ayala use the Bible—perhaps the most transnational of all texts—to theorize the lives and history of African descendants in the New World. Harper's "Deliverance" recalls North American slavery through the Exodus narrative and, in doing so, challenges African Americans to both see themselves as contemporary Israelites and understand their legal emancipation as a part of a continuing struggle for freedom. Harper challenges the American nation to both recall and revise the ideals on which it has based its concept of nationhood.

Similarly, Ayala urges black Cubans to recall their recent legal emancipation, admonishing them to know their history but to also recognize the role they play in formulating an independent Cuban nation of the future. Analysis of her poetry promises not only to restore a missing piece of Cuban literary history but also to shed light on how afrodescendente poets imagined a "free" Cuba. Though Harper is already established as a canonical figure in the African American literary canon, placing her work in a transnational context challenges the defining lines of African American literature as a national literature.

Auta de Souza also uses the Bible in a way that signals the interdependence of freedom and slavery in postabolition Brazil. "Minh'alma e o Verso" provides a metadiscourse on poetry as a space in which to renegotiate identity. Using the language of abolitionist rhetoric, "Fio Partido" dramatizes an individual's pursuit of freedom in the face of death. Auta de Souza does not explicitly refer to race in her poetry, but she wrote during the period following abolition in Brazil now criticized for its failure to ensure the full emancipation of enslaved Brazilians. Her affiliation with the history of slavery in the Americas through the metaphor of ancestry invites us to consider the implications of her work in this context. Furthermore, her work challenges us to reconsider what constitutes "Afro-Brazilian" literature. Auta's revision and reconfiguration of predominant symbols, tropes, and themes reflect a tension between slavery and freedom on national and transnational levels. In doing so, it helps lay the symbolic, tropological, and thematic groundwork for contemporary Afro-Brazilian poetry.

Auta's Marian Catholicism distinguishes her from Harper, whose Anglo-Protestantism infuses much of her poetry. The reconfiguration of the Virgin as the "bride" of Poetry in "Minh'alma e o Verso" follows the speaker's loss of a lover and submission to a form of slavery (i.e., the enslavement of the soul). The female speaker's explicit rejection of a male lover in "Minh'alma e o Verso" offers a critique of Brazilian patriarchy. Catholicism, not Protestantism, permeated Cuban nineteenth-century culture, but Ayala's allusion to Christ in "Redención" also leads to a heroic climax—the realization of "Libertad" in a new vision of Cuba. In "Fio Partido" the declaration of freedom is not that of a nation's independence—as in Ayala's "Redención"—or the collective freedom of a race—as in Harper's "Deliverance." Instead, freedom in "Fio Partido" signifies the individual freedom of the poet, a freedom whose realization depends on the specter of the slave.

Harper's Anglo-Protestant elements express the heroic victory of freedom. Maceo rises victorious over death through his linkage with the figure of Christ. Eliza Harris secures her child's freedom. African Americans recollect victory over slavery through the biblical exodus of the Israelites. Ultimately, Harper moves us further toward a less nationally based African (North) American literary theory by recalling the transnational context by which African (North) Americans defined and conceptualized freedom. Harper reminds us that peoples of African descent have a *tradition*—both intellectual and literary—from the very early stages of their presence in the New World of which twentieth- and twenty-first-century black literary transnationalism is a major part. When Harper describes the demise of a community of escaped slaves in Brazil, she makes no reference to race or nation, but—placed in its historical context—"Death of Zombi" resonates strongly with an "imagined" racial community in the United States. Though literally set in Brazil, the poem opens up and moves across that imagined national space, ultimately becoming meaningful in the context of North American slavery. Harper's use of the Exodus narrative in "Deliverance" writes an important counternarrative to an evolving American nativism rooted in a biblically based white supremacy.

Ayala's work represented in this study demonstrates most clearly a range of poetic styles and forms within a repertoire of afrodescendente Cuban literature. In "A mi raza," she uses the didactic form to convey a political message of racial uplift, writing a succinct recipie for racial uplift. In "El Arroyuelo y la flor," she explores the specific relationship between the construction of nation and the construction of gender. Ayala makes the act of creating allegory a structural and topical aspect of the poem. In doing so, the poem highlights the very process of framing national history in poetic allegory. In "Redención," Ayala inquires into racial slavery in Cuba as a precedent for national independence. She demonstrates the interdependence of racial slavery and subsequent conceptions of Cuban freedom. Her literal references to race refer to both an imagined racial community and an imagined national community. In fact, through the interplay of these referents, the poem opens up, evolving into a critique of Cuban nationhood, the role of slavery in Cuba's collective memory, and the role of the *raza negra* in Cuba's future. Furthermore, these literal references to race and nation do not limit the extent to which the text can stand in metonymically for racial and national freedoms in the Americas at large.

In his introduction to a recent anthology of contemporary Cuban poetry, Francisco Morán refers to the afrodescendente poet Ángel Escobar's treatment of messianic myths in Cuban history. Escobar's poem "Paráfrasis sencilla" (Simple Paraphrase) reads:

> Yo pienso, cuando me aterro,
> como un Escobar sencillo,
> en aquel blanco cuchillo
> que me matará: soy negro.
> Rojo, como en el desierto,
> salió el sol al horizonte:
> y alumbró a Escobar, ya muerto,
> colgado, ausencia del monte.
> Un niño me vio: tembló
> de pasión por los que gimen:
> y, ante mi muerte, juró
> lavar con su vida el crimen. (in Morán 2007, 104)

[When I'm afraid I think like a simple Escobar of the white knife that will kill me: I am black. Crimson as the desert, a sun rose to the horizon, illuminated the already cold Escobar hanging, blank wilderness. A child saw me. And shuddered ardently for the afflicted. As witness to my death, he swore to erase the crime with his life.] (trans. Barbara Jamison; 104–5)

Erasure promises redemption through the "blank wilderness" of the blank page. According to Morán, "from the perspective of black flesh fated for the white knife, the voice rewrites with mordant irony all of the movements for personal and social redemption, including the Cuban" (2007, 14). The preoccupation with renaming and historical revision evident in Ayala, as well as Harper, surfaces also in Escobar's speculation on messianic myths.

Like Ayala, however, Auta examines the recent aftermath of legal abolition and the relationship of the female voice to patriarchy. Like Harper, Auta interrogates the relationship between freedom and death as a way of deconstructing the binary between slavery and freedom. The forced migrations of Africans in the Americas not only informed the stories nations told about themselves, but also informed the stories Africans in diaspora told about themselves as problematic participants in a series of national projects in the Americas.

In addition to a preoccupation with naming and revision, comparative readings of Harper, Ayala, and Auta de Souza also lead us to question whether religious or secular rhetoric permitted more possibilities for envisioning freedom during the abolition eras. As we see most clearly in Auta's "Fio Partido" and Harper's "Maceo," the secular accounts that allude to religious tropes are the most effective at textually and literarily addressing the specific political predicaments of the nation. "Fio Partido" converses with print culture, yet still fosters a fertile symbolic space within the poem to present a duly complex representation of freedom. By presenting Maceo as a Christic figure, Harper creates a larger-than-life symbol of redemptive freedom while still addressing the "real-life" problem of war and colonial oppression in the Americas.

Harper's poetic treatment of Maceo lends to further comparative endeavors involving Cuban and African (North) American literatures. We might consider, for instance, the fact that, about fourteen years after Harper, Ayala also wrote a poem about Maceo titled "Antonio Maceo." Ayala published the poem in a special volume of *Minerva* dedicated to Maceo in 1910.[1]

> Cual el bravo Le[ó]nidas en su famoso *Paso*,
> este egregio Caudillo, que en patrio amor ardiendo
> sus hu[e]stes condujera del Naciente al Ocaso
> para luchar heroico y morir combatiendo.
> Ha grabado en la historia de su patria adorada
> página tan brillante, que la vista deslumbra;
> y esa invasión sublime, por ninguna igualada,
> ¡nimbada por la gloria ha dejado su tumba! . . .
> [É]l, desde el sacro Empíreo donde los buenos moran,
> [a] los firmes patriotas que su memoria adoran
> contemplará con ojos do brille la ternura;
> ¡Pero también, los rayos de su pupila ardiente
> —si las almas las tienenvcalcinarán la frente
> de aquellos que [a] la Patria suman en desventura!
> —Güines, Diciembre de 1910[2]
> [Like the valiant Leonidas in his famous *Paso*, this eminent *Caudillo*, who, burning with love for his native land, drove his hosts from East to West to fight heroically and

to die waging war. He has recorded such a brilliant page in the history of his beloved country that the sight of it astonishes; and that sublime invasion, equal to none, has left his grave wreathed in glory. From the sacred Celestial Empire where the good men dwell, he will, with eyes that shine with tenderness, gaze down on the unyielding patriots who worship his memory. But also, the rays of his flaming eyes will reduce to ashes the faces of those who—if they even have souls—bury the Motherland in misfortune. —Güines, December 1910]

In this elegy to Maceo, Ayala inverts the structure of the traditional English sonnet. Harper's "Maceo" and Ayala's "Antonio Maceo" eulogize Maceo in a way that links his life and his death to the present condition and the future evolution of the nation. The poems certainly differ in at least as many ways as they are alike in thematic content and poetic elements. Nevertheless, Ayala's and Harper's literary prowess lies partly in their ability to walk the line between a black and nonblack elite while at the same time developing theories about the relationship between literary aesthetic and the social status of black Cubans.

Both Ayala and Harper seem to cater to an elite audience that in their minds very consciously includes a nonblack audience. They understood racial uplift, at least in part, as an effort to prove to a larger society that black peoples had the sophistication and virtuosity necessary to participate in national citizenship. Poetry not only took on an aesthetic "burden" but also a sociopolitical one. Much has been written about the burden on the black writer in the United States to actually represent the race and embody proof of the capabilities of blacks, but less has been written about the way this burden influenced the literary corpus of black literatures in Cuba.

Ayala addressed the "amables lectoras" (beloved readers) of *Minerva* in the essay "Me adhiero" (I Believe) (1889, 3).

> Pero, á pesar de todo esto, nosotros, los menos responsables, tenemos, por dignidad propia, que echar sobre nuestros débiles hombros, la pesada carga de cubrir una responsabilidad que hace tres siglos pesa sobre todo un pueblo. Mas no debemos arredrarnos ante la idea de tamaño sacrificio, porque éste será una prueba más de abnegación, que tendremos que añadir á las muchas que nuestra raza ha dejado consignadas en su largo período de cautiverio . . . tratemos de demostrarles que un corazón donde tengan cabida nobles aspiraciones, no puede mostrarse sordo á la voz que le indique el camino del deber y la virtud. Sigamos esas leales inspiraciones, y, no tengáis duda de ello, el porvenir será nuestro.
>
> [However, in spite of all of this, we, the least responsible, we, for the sake of our own dignity must thrust on our weary shoulders the heavy burden of taking responsibility that for three centuries has burdened an entire people. But we ought not retreat from the idea of such sizable sacrifice, for this will be even more a test of self-denial that we will have to add to the many [i.e., many tests] which our race has been assigned during its long season of captivity . . . let us try to show them [i.e., members of society] that a heart where noble aspirations are fitted cannot show itself deaf to the voice heralding the path to duty and virtue. Let us follow these trustworthy inspirations, and, the future will be ours, have no doubt.]

Writing to a community of women writers, Ayala conjoins the black poet's literary endeavor with the moral and political imperative of racial uplift.[3] Furthermore, she characterizes black writers as harbingers of postabolition national ideals.

A publication that stood at the epicenter of Cuban literary and political thought during the abolition era, *Minerva* is a fertile source for further study on literary transnationalism in Cuba. An international and multilingual project—including translations of poems and essays by or about Lord Byron, Alexander Pushkin, Sor Juana Inés de la Cruz and others—*Minerva* is a critically important collection of texts worthy of continued scholarly attention as a landmark of women's literary and political history and the literary and political history of African descendants in the New World. Ayala was one of the few women whose involvement in the magazine extended to its second phase in the early twentieth century. Her longevity and wide range of style, form, and theme make her stand out among her peers. Her poetry and essays and the influence of her work both in and outside of Cuba merit further investigation. Her longevity as a poet-intellectual who demonstrates in her essays an ability to ingratiate a wide audience through a combination of rhetoric and poeticism, makes her an essential figure in the canon of Cuban and African American literary studies.

As the United States continues to reexamine its own history in the twenty-first century, a global perspective will be paramount. Afrodescendente literature offers a means to do just that. Robin D. G. Kelley's essay highlighted the extent to which "a diasporic vision or sensibility" characterized nineteenth- and twentieth-century "black intellectual and historical traditions" and maintained that these scholars did not allow "national boundaries to define their field of vision" but instead were informed by an "international context and ultimately defined themselves as part of a larger international community" (1999, 1047).

Almost a decade later, in an era of rapid globalization, Kelley's observations of early black intellectualism are even more relevant. The comparative framework established by the transnationalism of early black intellectualism must also inform our contemporary reading of early African American writing. When faced with what George B. Handley identifies as the "challenge of postnational readings" posed by various writers in the Americas, he calls for a more "diasporic approach to African American studies" (2000, 2). Frances Harper's early poetic gestures toward Cuba and Brazil heighten the urgency of Handley's call. They suggest that a diasporic approach to African American literature is necessary not only for postnational readings but for nineteenth-century readings as well. Future studies will need to consider how this fact reconfigures literary canons constructed on national lines.

Creating a viable literary tradition has been a major part of the contemporary literary project in Afro-Brazilian literature, provoking a retrospective rereading of texts written by writers of African descent in Brazil.[4] In her discussion of *Cadernos Negros* (Black Notebooks), a literary series established in 1978 by a group of Afro-Brazilian poets and writers, Florentina da Silva Souza suggests a "possivel linha imaginaria" (possible imaginary line) between early Brazilian afrodescendente writers and contemporary Afro-Brazilian writers that links "suas produções e aquelas produzidas por outros escritores negros que, desde os séculos passados, vêm fazendo uso da palavra escrita para combater a escravidão, o racismo e a exclusão de vida socio-cultural e política do país" (their work and the work of other black writers that, from centuries ago, have been using the written word to fight against slavery, racism and exclusion from the socio-cultural and political life of the country) (2005, 71).

The "literatura negra" we speak of in the nineteenth century, however, requires a different type of reading than that of the twentieth. This difference is critical. We cannot assume poets of African descent conceived of themselves or their art as a part of a canon of Afro-Brazilian poetry, nor can we presume any unifying aesthetic or distinctly Afro-Brazilian way of writing in the nineteenth century. Some might argue, for instance, that Auta de Souza cannot be legitimately included in a canon of Afro-Brazilian literature because of the idiosyncratic system of racial classification in Brazil. We can see elements of ambiguity in Harper and Ayala as well, however. Ayala composed a wide range of poems that differ formally and thematically, in spite of her explicit involvement in nineteenth-century racial politics. Many of her poems did not address race at all and even went as far as to laud the Spanish influence on Cuban literary and cultural heritage. Harper's class and social circles and her sentimentalism could be said to make her more closely aligned with her white abolitionist counterparts than with black slaves. Auta's relationship to a canon of afrodescendente literature in Brazil, for instance, depends on more than just the extent to which she meets the criteria determined by twentieth-century racial concepts. The suggestion of her ancestry prompts questions that extend beyond Brazilian national borders and into the transhemispheric history of the Americas at large. The *significance* of these poets in a tradition of literature by afrodescendente women, then, is gained from the efforts on the part of contemporary poets and scholars to *re-member* them as a part of a retrospectively constructed tradition of poets of African descent. To re-member is to (1) recall to one's own or another's remembrance as a deliberate act of will, or (2) rearrange the "members" or parts of a whole, to revise an established structure. Inevitably, any categorization of a body of literary works must be re-membered by way of deliberate interpretive acts and extratextual organizing narratives.

The Americas comprise a space of discursive exchange among afrodescendente peoples that appears in the thematic content and dialectical tensions of their literatures. The existence of transnational interchanges refutes the idea that we should *read* cultures, traditions, or even texts in isolation to get to their "truth." Face-to-face dialogue is only one form of transnational exchange. As a site of "boundary-crossing"[5]—in the sense of my first definition of "between the lines"—writing by afrodescendente women allows us to develop theories about the textual and extratextual implications of comparative readings that cross over the implied boundaries of national literatures and languages. These "particular" communities are not fixed, immutable, geopolitically determined categories but are rather in constant flux and characterized by contingencies. Dialogue among black populations transnationally characterizes what J. Lorand Matory refers to as the "history of African culture around the Atlantic perimeter" (2005, 15).[6] For Matory, this "Afro-Atlantic dialogue" also suggests that afrodescendente peoples "never simply embraced nation-states as sufficient indicies of their collective identities. Nor did they suddenly find liberation from them amid a thirty-year-old transnationalism" (2005, 35). Instead, peoples of African descent in the Americas actively engaged in constructing their vision of the world and their place in the Americas. Considered side by side, Harper's, Ayala's, and Auta de Souza's poetics help us understand how slavery informed conceptions of national freedom in Brazil, Cuba, and the United States.

I hope this book will generate further interest in the literary aspects of history and the historical aspects of literature. In various ways, the poetry of Harper, Ayala, and Auta de Souza grapples with and ultimately decodes for us the literary aspects of racial and national bodies. Furthermore, these poets allow us to explore gender as a significant factor in the literary reimagining of race and nation. Their work challenges us today to mark the poets of this generation that are engaging in this kind of visionary poetics, those who are composing an imagined world out of lexicon of the past, those who are about the business of rebuilding the very language we use to speak of it.

Further exploration of the Orwellian "historical impulse" in the poetics of historically marginalized groups will require a comparative, transnational approach to literary history. Such an approach acknowledges the precariousness of national boundaries and recognizes the fertility of meaning located in the space between national lines.

My strategies for reading these poetic texts have sampled from formalist, structuralist, and poststructuralist literary theories. Simultaneously, I ask how afrodescendente writers have often challenged some of the fundamental premises of what language can and should achieve. I ask how these writers conceive of the relationship between the individual and the collective and the purpose of poetic expression. Ultimately, further studies in languages and literatures will need to consider the various ways differing literary and poetic uses of language in mainstream arenas influence contemporary conceptions of freedom and even morality.

Additionally, future studies will require a more nuanced comparative literature of the African diaspora, one not wholly based on comparative theories of racial formation or on cultural studies that focus on competing definitions of "blackness" inevitably bound to specific moments in time and specific places in geographical space. I hope instead that further studies will parse the various literary transnationalisms—thematic, typological, structural, and even semantic—at work in the writings of African descendants in the Americas. In doing so, they will more truly reflect the polyphonic nature of afrodescendente literatures in the New World.

Epilogue

Afrodescendente History As/And Transnational Poetics

By the second half of the nineteenth century, Africans had been enslaved in the Americas for over 400 years. In the cases of Brazil, Cuba, and the United States, the second half of the nineteenth century was characterized by evolving theories about race and gender and vigorous attempts to reconcile them with an emergent national identity. It was also during this period that abolitionism emerged as a discursive and political critique that opposed slavery in favor of a socially and economically progressive nation.

The "africanization" of Brazil, prominent abolitionist Joaquim Nabuco (1849–1910) and many other abolitionists claimed, was at the very root of Brazil's problems. He writes in *O Abolicionismo*:

> Quando mesmo essa esperança nos parecesse irrealizável não seria perversidade fazer penetrar no cárcere do escravo, onde reina noite perpétua, um raio de luz . . . Mas a esperança não nos parece irrealizável, graças a Deus, e nós não a afagamos só pelo escravo, afagamo-la por nós mesmos também, porque o mesmo dia que dér a liberdade àquele—e esse somente—há de dar-nos uma dignidade, que hoje não o é—a de Cidadão Brasileiro. (1988, 41)
>
> [Even if this hope seemed unattainable, it would not be perverse to penetrate with a ray of light the prison cell of slavery where perpetual darkness reigns . . . But hope does not seem unattainable, thank God, and we will not comfort the slave only, but we also comfort ourselves, because the moment we impart freedom to the slave—and only this—we will also give ourselves an honor which we do not have today—that of being a Brazilian citizen.]

Ironically, while Nabuco championed the idea of abolition as a means of achieving nationhood, he also advocated for a strict divide between "the slave" and the "Brazilian citizen."

Abolition and a failed Reconstruction in the South tilted North America's imperialist gaze toward Brazil and Cuba. In the second half of the nineteenth century in particular, news of the wars of independence in Cuba spoke of the large numbers of *negro* troops in the Liberation Army and expressed fear of a "race war" like that of Haiti in 1791.[1] Numerous articles appeared in newspapers like *Frederick Douglass' Paper* and *The North Star* with accounts of slavery in Brazil and Cuba. After the Civil War in the United States, thousands of Southerners, lamenting the loss of the Confederacy, saw in Brazil and Cuba new territories where they could sustain slavery and the ideals and mores of the Old South. Many Confederate leaders and their families migrated to Cuba and Brazil (Griggs 1995, 53). As one settler put it, Brazil was an "empire of freedom and plenty" (Griggs 1995, 51–52). Between 1866 and 1868, approximately 3,000 Southerners immigrated to Brazil, carrying with them an image of Brazil promulgated by Protestant missionaries in the United States: a nation with fertile land, legal slavery, and religious freedom (Gussi 1997, 86).[2]

As legal slavery disappeared from the face of the Americas, its absence further fueled ideological anxieties about what constituted national, racial, and gender identities in the Americas and what defined freedom. Dawn Duke suggests that by "exploring beneath the veneer of *de jure* abolition" we can see that abolition was "but one point in a protracted transitional era in the Afro-Atlantic world during which patterns of hegemony established under slavery were transposed into the new conditions of post-emancipation societies" (2007, 23). During this period, the United States, then Cuba, and finally Brazil effected the complete abolition of slavery in the Western Hemisphere. Saidiya Hartman challenges us, however, not to conceive of abolition as a "static historical event but, rather, as a dynamic process in which conflicting objectives were negotiated" (1997, 24). Hartman describes this process as a "transdiasporan phenomenon in which individual abolitions had repercussions affecting the entire Afro-Atlantic world beginning with the start of the Haitian Revolution of 1791 and ending with Brazilian abolition in 1888" (1997, 24). The institution, practice, and abolition of slavery in the Americas helped shape ideas about national, racial, and individual freedom.

Debate about slavery and its abolition proved to be a transnational phenomenon. Paul Gilroy's *The Black Atlantic* (1993) is one of the most influential texts addressing modern black internationalism. His analysis of black Britons and what he calls "modern black political culture" provided one of the first treatments of black internationalism in the Western Hemisphere. Through his reading of Martin Delany's *Blake; or, The Huts of America*, a story about a black slave in the United States who escapes to Cuba and plans a rebellion, Gilroy suggests an alternative vision of what he calls an "intercultural" and "transnational" process of categorization.

> [*Blake*] locates the black Atlantic world in a webbed network, between the local and the global, challenges the coherence of all narrow nationalist perspectives and points to the spurious invocation of ethnic particularity to enforce them and to ensure the tidy flow of cultural output into neat, symmetrical units. I should add that this applies whether this impulse comes from the oppressors or the oppressed. (1993, 29)

Afrodescendente writing in the history of the Western Hemisphere has confronted, directly or indirectly, the history of slavery in the Americas. It constitutes a tradition of literary resistance to the integrity of national boundaries.

In the essay "Free to be a Slave" (2007) J. Lorand Matory draws a distinction between Afro-Latin and Anglo-African American views of slavery. He suggests that the tropic value of slavery differs significantly in the two contexts. The term *slavery* has what Matory calls "temporal and interregional vacillation in meaning" and yet was and is a metaphor "through which the descendants of Africans throughout the New World regularly (and at their most serious moments of self-fashioning) understand themselves and act upon their worlds" (2007, 399). Matory rightfully highlights the variability of interpretations of slavery and its history in the New World. "Just as 'freedom' is defined and made salient by the visible co-presence of the slave," he maintains, "so has citizenship in the American republics been defined and made salient by the visible co-presence of groups whose race or gender defined them as the opposite and as worthy victims of theft, exploitation, murder and other forms of expiatory violence" (2007, 418). By virtue of their gender and—to varying degrees—their race, Harper, Ayala, and Auta de Souza represent a segment of these "opposite" and "worthy victims."

As historian Anthony W. Marx contends, the elements that become salient in a culture are designated as legitimate ways to see the past or, as he suggests, interpretations. In his comparative analysis of the "race" histories of the United States, Brazil, and South Africa, Marx argues that the interpretations of the past determine the "racial orderings" of the present.

> Colonialism, religious tradition, slavery, and miscegenation were later interpreted in particular ways to fit the political situations in each of the three cases under consideration. These interpretations were widespread in each culture, shaping perceptions of what and how post-abolition racial order could be and was constructed. (1988, 29)

Afrodescendente writing offers a range of interpretations of transatlantic history that disavow any strict allegiance to national boundaries.

Comparative studies that cross national lines help us think more broadly about ways to organize literature. Recognizing the history of a global view of "African American studies" as established by early scholars in the United States, Michael Hanchard rightly cautions against African American studies practices that "betray [its] global legacy" by succumbing to a "preoccupation with United States African American perspectives on Africa and African descended peoples without first interrogating 'African American' as a settled category of racial and cultural identification" (2004, 147). Hanchard challenges the idea that national difference preoccupies distinctions between African American, Latin American, and American studies, noting that, in fact, "literatures, peoples, territories, languages, influences and ideologies rarely line up in the way that area studies paradigms do" (2004, 150). Frances Harper's transnational allusions to black icons in Brazil and Cuba, for instance, elicit a kind of African American poetics that acquires its meaning (at least partially) from "other" nations. Harper's poems not only employ the allusions, they engage and rewrite the narrative that has already been composed for them.

The theoretical framework for literary studies up until the late twentieth century has been characterized by a binary between Western and non-Western texts. As a result, much scholarship has focused on the generative interplay between "the (white) West" and "minority literatures." In *Between the Lines* I have used the theoretical framework of an imagined transhemispheric space of "the Americas," to place these minority literatures in conversation with one another. I build on the work of scholars such as Caroline F. Levander, Anna Brickhouse, Amy Kaplan, and Homi Bhabha, who have noted the transnational character of apparently national American literatures.

In the literature of the African diaspora during the formative years of national narratives, we see traces of a struggle to define racial and national freedom during the nineteenth century. The metaphor of diaspora—combined with the physical movement of Africans throughout the Western Hemisphere—informs this literature. Henry Louis Gates Jr. maintains that due to "the experience of diaspora," the fragments "embody aspects of a theory of critical principles around which the discrete texts of the tradition configure, in the critic's reading of the textual past. To reassemble fragments, of course, is to engage in an act of speculation, to attempt to weave a fiction of origins and subgeneration. It is to render the implicit as explicit, and at times to imagine the whole from the part" (1988, xxiv). Here, Gates refers to the process of creating a "whole" history out of the fragments that the diaspora experience produces. To do so, one must not only "imagine" a point of origin but also determine an imagined space to occupy. In this book I posit the African diaspora in the Americas as a theoretical point of origin *and* a theoretical space occupied by a literary tradition of African descendants in the New World. Their literatures are not separate from the verdant landscape of New World literatures, but they elicit a particular history of transatlantic slavery and precipitate new ways of reading the history of the Americas.

Presenting afrodescendente literature as a category and context within which to read Harper, Ayala, and Auta de Souza does not pigeonhole these writers into a single tradition of writing, nor does it conflate the texts into a single canon. On the contrary, it demonstrates what is true of all writers and their texts: that they are in simultaneous conversation not only with multiple sociohistorical contexts but also with other writers and other texts. Accordingly, the poems discussed in *Between the Lines* have indicated a series of similar textual anxieties (i.e., unresolved binary oppositions), typological usages, and themes that are meaningful on a transnational scale.

Of course, not all writing by afrodescendente writers is racially nationalist or liberationist. The formal and stylistic differences even among this small selection of poets, as well as the disparate degree to which they are explicit about a racial message, clearly demonstrates the polyphonic character of afrodescendente literature. As a result, the moments at which this polyphony sounds in unison demand our attention.

> *Victor Hugo has spoken of the nineteenth century as being the women's era, and among the most noticeable epochs in this era is the uprising of women against the twin evils of slavery and intemperance, which had foisted themselves like leeches upon the civilization of the present age.*
>
> — Harper (1990d)

The Political Work of Afrodescendente Women's Writing

Over twenty-five years ago, Edward Said challenged the idea that "good" literature and literary scholarship were apolitical in nature. In his critique of the West's relationship to the Orient in *Orientalism* (1978), Said debunked the notion of nonpolitical knowledge, which he defined as a knowledge disconnected from the power structures imposed by imperialism, colonialism and racism. He argued that this "pretended suprapolitical objectivity" (1978, 76) masked a much messier complex that placed the individual, inescapably, in the web of her surroundings.

The political nature of afrodescendente women's writing stems from its position at the intersection of race and gender in New World history. As Evelyn Brooks Higginbotham notes in the essay "African-American Women's History and the Metalanguage of Race," gender identity is "inextricably linked to and even determined by racial identity," particularly in "societies where racial demarcation is endemic to their sociocultural fabric and heritage—to their laws and economy, to their institutionalized structures and discourses, and to their epistemologies and everyday customs" (1992, 254). The specific sociohistorical contexts of Harper, Ayala, and Auta de Souza's work differs. Nevertheless, the "sociocultural fabric" and collective historical heritage of the nineteenth-century Americas is circumscribed by a history of racial slavery.

Understanding the political implications of these poets' work relies on a broad definition of "the political." David Easton expands the scope of "the political" by diversifying the types of activities that constitute political life. For Easton, "political life" involves "all those varieties of activity that influence significantly the kind of authoritative policy adopted for a society and the way it is put into practice" (1981, 128). While Easton's definition of political life requires that the end result of the activity be policy, Jane Mansbridge takes a difference stance. For Mansbridge individuals can act politically without having the power necessary to translate their actions into policy. Any speech act, then, that aims to persuade the public by engaging in public *deliberation* is political.[3] Like Mansbridge, my use of political extends beyond Easton's theory to incorporate the literary. My formulation of the political as it relates to afrodescendente women's writing combines Easton's broad scope with Mansbridge's emphasis on persuasion through deliberation and the political nature of the (poetic) speech act. I suggest that poetry is in fact a form of deliberation with an imagined individual or collective audience.

As Lyde Sizer notes, nineteenth-century women writers did "political work" (2000, 8) as they aimed to write alternative histories and narratives (11). In the essay, "Why I Write," George Orwell gives four reasons why a writer writes: sheer egoism, aesthetic enthusiasm, historical impulse, and political purpose (1984, 4–5). He defines political purpose in a simple way—the "desire to push the world in a certain direction, to alter people's ideas of the kind of society that they should strive after" (1984, 5). Orwell's notion of political purpose resonates with Mansbridge's notion of the speech act as persuasive deliberation. To take Orwell's idea of political purpose a step further and apply it to this study, I suggest that the text itself can exert "political purpose" through its internal "strivings." By *strivings* I mean (1) the ways in which its language, themes, or poetic voice struggle against its sociohistorical context; and (2) the way the poem exhibits internal struggles through unresolved or, in the Derridean sense, "disseminated" binary oppositions. This process takes place "between the lines" of the text. Language does political work in a poem through two kinds of deliberation—deliberation between the elements within the text and deliberation between the poet-text and the imagined reader-audience. By initiating a form of deliberation, Harper, Ayala, and Auta de Souza's poetry challenges prominent belief systems about gender and race.

The phenomenon of modern racial slavery has had a distinct impact on myths about women of African descent in the Americas. While slavery still thrived in the Americas, subjecting most black women to a life of labor, concepts of white femininity emphasized white female domesticity. The white woman was exempt from the work reserved for her breadwinning husband. As bell hooks maintains, in its insistence on the physical labor of enslaved women, the system of slavery masculinized black women and effectively disqualified them from national standards of womanhood.

The ideal of the chaste, genteel white woman was a major European export to the Americas during the nineteenth century. As part of an effort to designate white women as the ideal representation of womanhood, English planters in the late seventeenth century implemented a new policy regarding plantation work. It stipulated that no white woman, of any class or status, was to work in plantation labor gangs. Hilary M. Beckles identifies this gesture as the moment in which English planters began to think through gender in terms of race. Labor divisions based on race served "the social need of patriarchy to idealize the white women as a symbol of white supremacy, moral authority and sexual purity" (2000, 168). One year after the Fifteenth Amendment franchised black men in the United States, Anna Julia Cooper observed the peculiar way in which race intersected with gender in the United States. She wrote that the black woman's "unnamable burden" was the burden of not being recognized as a woman (1990, 90). Representations of the black woman varied from Aunt Jemima—the seasoned, loyal "mammy" figure, to Harriet Beecher Stowe's Topsy—the young, witless, and animalistic child. The figure of the "tragic mulatto" was often a female character torn between the burden of "black blood" and her desire to pass for white.

Throughout the Reconstruction era, the myth of white female purity continued to service the ideal of Southern white nationalism. hooks observes a shift in the mythology surrounding the Euro-descended woman. She was no longer the sexual temptress or "Eve" persona, but the pure, innocent goddess, the "nobler half of humanity" who embodied the feminine ideal of delicateness and chastity (1981, 31). This myth stood in counterdistinction to major myths about black women. Frances S. Foster condenses some of these myths into three major types. The first type is Topsy—the black black child in Stowe's *Uncle Tom's Cabin*; she is "black with big eyes . . . more imp than human" (1973, 433). Completely detached from memory, Topsy lacks origin or ancestry. Peaches, Foster's second type, is the promiscuous seductress. By tempting white men, she threatens the very foundation of the ideal white Protestant family unit. Caldonia, the matriarch, not only masculine in her aggressiveness but also emasculating, disturbs the "natural" order of gender relations.

She is anomalous in her brutish *a*sexuality (1973, 433). Each of these caricatures equated black women with immorality and sexual aberrance and opposed a tradition of white female idealization as a moral, sexually pure, maternal figure.

In her analysis of gender paradigms in the Caribbean and throughout the Atlantic, Beckles discusses how the figure of the slave woman played a central role in abolitionism in the Caribbean

> Abolitionists also centered the slave woman with respect to their campaign strategies, propaganda and analytical critiques. The slave woman was placed at the core of a contradictory discourse that sought on one hand to protect and prolong slavery, and on the other to undermine and destroy it. The discourse was transatlantic in nature. . . . In Europe the slave woman was depicted as the tragic and principal victim of the worst system of masculine tyranny known to the modern world. The debate was part of a wider gender discourse that sharpened opinion on both sides of the Atlantic, and focused attention on the nature of slavery as a particular kind of gendered power. (2000, 223–24)

Placed in the colonial context, the slave woman stood in for the exotic and available landscape of the racialized and gendered identities of the New World. The symbology of national bodies relied heavily on the figure of the woman. Adriana Méndez Ródenas maintains that the nineteenth-century "literary imagination" in Latin America, "established a poetic correspondence between nation and womanhood, so that the emerging sense of national cohesion was figured largely through a female protagonist, who came to embody the core values of the nation" (1998, 3). What Méndez Ródenas refers to as the "symbolic process of inventing identity" relied heavily on images of women (1998, 4).

Debra Castillo goes on to maintain that the role of woman as a bearer of the symbolic weight of Latin American national imaginaries made her body the "primordial site for the metaphorical generation of discourse" and embodied the "unchanging, pristine values of permanence, privacy, immobility, and purity as the essential core of national identity" (1992, 16). Late nineteenth- and early twentieth-century political propaganda and iconography in Cuba heralded the white woman as an aesthetic ideal and symbol of the nation. Cartoons appeared in Cuban newspapers like *El Triunfo* and *La Lucha* in the early 1900s featuring representations of Cuba as a white woman often threatened by a black male figure.

Reflecting on the colonial history of Brazil, Brazilian intellectual and psychiatrist Raimundo Nina Rodrigues (1862–1906) held the black woman responsible for the sexual corruption of Brazil's "young masters." Rodrigues claimed that due to their African ancestry, *negras* and *mulattas* were sexually abnormal because they were more prone to sexual excitation. In turn, this hypersexuality gave them a desire to corrupt their male masters. He claimed to observe a tendency among black women to commit violent crimes against their children stemming from the "sobrevivencia psíquica na criminalidade dos negros no Brasil" (psychic survival of criminality of Brazilian blacks) (1982, 273). Rodrigues justified his characterization of black women with a larger argument about the underdeveloped morality and inherent criminality of Brazilians of African descent. This belief fell in line with the eugenics and positivist theories circulating throughout Europe and crossing over into the Americas. The critique of such theories relied on a reconstruction of the enslaved female figure.

Elisa Larkin Nascimento identifies the "entwinement of patriarchy and racism" as an "integral part of the critique of western ethnocentrism" (2007, 28). Auta's particular experience and poetry makes an interesting test case for this theory. Although Auta came from a slave-owning family, the female speaker in "Minha'alma e o Verso" (My Soul and Poetry) explicitly identifies with the slave in the process of rejecting of a male lover. Auta also address the role of women vis-à-vis a "free" nation. In "Minh'alma e o Verso," the poet frees her female speaker from the male gaze, thus challenging the idea that women were ideal symbols of the nation. Auta's speaker collapses the dichotomy between slave (one lacking femininity, corrupting) and the ideal female figure (depicted through the allusion to Marian iconography) by having the speaker reject this ideal and identifying her soul with the slave.

Ayala and Harper make similar poetic interventions. In the poem "A mi raza" (To My Race), Ayala specifically addresses the role of afrodescendente women in postabolition Cuba. Both Ayala and Harper challenge a tradition of male-oriented nationalism in "El arroyuelo y la flor" and "Deliverance." Harper presents a complex figure of a slave woman in "Eliza Harris," through which she confronts the contradiction of national freedom and the practice of slavery. In "Deliverance," Harper highlights the woman's role in the realization of freedom in and outside of the United States.

The last decade of the nineteenth century in Cuba marked an increase in women's involvement in the movement against Spain. For example, they were often involved in fund-raising and pamphlet-writing and worked as nurses at standing hospitals during the war (Prados-Torreira 2005, 3). Ayala's "A mi raza" contributes to this appeal to the populous through didactic forms of expression. She directly addresses black Cubans as citizens of the Cuban nation and specifically urges black Cuban women to act in line with a sense of *duty*. A poet who identified with a distinct afrodescendente population in Cuba and also aligned herself with her Spanish progenitors, Ayala crafted a counterhistory that featured the heroic divinity of the slave in "Redención." Depicting the black woman as moral agent and mother, Harper's "Eliza Harris" portrays a female figure actively challenging the role imposed on her by slave society.

As Harper, Ayala, and Auta de Souza engage the question of women's role in the politics and symbology of the nation, each challenges us to consider the role gender plays in conceptualizing national and individual identities. Their poetic strategy ranges from aggressive didacticism to subtle symbolism, instigating a form of deliberation with a readership for which gender greatly determined the extent (or limitations) of their social and political freedoms.

It is the Negro's tragedy I feel
Which binds me like a heavy chain,
It is the Negro's wounds I want to heal
Because I know the keenness of his pain.
Only a thorn-crowned Negro and no white

Can penetrate into the Negro's ken,
Or feel the thickness of the shroud of night
Which hides and buries him from other men.
So what I write is urged out of my blood.
There is not white man who could write my book,
Though many think their story should be told
Of what the Negro people ought to brook.
Our statesmen roam the world to set things right.
This Negro laughs and prays to God for Light!
—"The Negro's Tragedy" (McKay 1953, 50)

Crossing Space and Time: Transnational Movements in Afrodescendente Poetry of the Americas

As a form of literary play, transnationalism appears in the very semantics of Claude McKay's "The Negro's Tragedy." The word *negro*, around which the entire poem is built, is imported etymologically from the Spanish and Portuguese word *negro*, meaning black. Europeans applied this term to peoples of African ancestry as early as the thirteenth century. Although it is highly unlikely that McKay was thinking of the etymological roots of this term which had been, by the time of his writing, fully inducted into American English, the fact remains that the word signals a form of linguistic crossing and highlights the fluidity of language even in its application to identity. The specter of slavery, signaled by the "heavy chain," binds slavery and "the Negro" together and ultimately informs the writing of the poem ("So what I write is urged out of my blood"). The speaker is at once "the negro" ("It is the Negro's tragedy I feel") and *not* "the negro" (the speaker is *I*, while "the Negro" is *him*). The dual natures share what is hidden from others ("the thickness of the shroud of night / Which hides and buries him from other men"). Ultimately, the ambiguity of the referent allows for the coming together of the speaker and "the Negro" while at the same time maintaining a degree of ambivalence.

The poem retells a story that has been tragically miswritten. This rewriting or setting things right occurs in a global space ("Our statesmen roam the world to set things right"). By incorporating an allusion to Christ ("a thorn-crowned Negro"), "The Negro Tragedy" follows various instances in which African Americans have identified with the suffering of Christ and expressed this identification through the literary appropriation of Christic typology. McKay's poem teaches a kind of reading of a transnational literary imaginary. "The Negro Tragedy" is one example of the way transnationalism as boundary crossing plays out in a poetic meditation on race and the legacy of slavery. Similar poetic meditations characterize much of afrodescendente poetry in the New World.

A number of journals and anthological projects have performed a kind of comparative literature by bringing together writers and scholars in the Americas and continental Africa to theorize about race and writing. *Présence Africaine* in Paris aimed to provide a forum in which to theorize about what constituted a Pan-African space, to demonstrate the "*présence* of Africa by continuously recalling the conflictual context in which this presence finds itself placed because of its historical relationship to Europe" (Mouralis 1992, 6). Founder Alioune Diop emphasized the importance of a "dialogue of cultures" within the African context, recognizing that "complete and living cultures must enter into a dialogue. A full-fledged, civilized community must know how to appreciate, through the individual members of its body, the wealth and the meaning of that which it borrows from over civilizations" (Diop 1992, xv). The dialogic aspect of the journal and its ideological exchanges concerned an Africa in opposition to Europe and sought to negotiate its own definition through this opposition. Anthological projects like Rosey Pool's *Beyond the Blues: New Poems by American Negros* (1962) offer another form of comparative work that collaborates thematically and formally varied poetry from nineteenth- and twentieth-century writers in the United States including W. E. B. Du Bois, Claude McKay, and Gwendolyn Brooks. More specifically, in the United States, African American literature features a well-documented tradition of poetics varying in style and subject matter. My work, however, aims to give attention to the contingency of a transhemispheric sensibility on these poetics. The idea that such a prominent and prolific nineteenth-century poet like Frances Harper had such a transhemispheric sensibility opens up the canon for further inquiries of this kind regarding African (North) American literature(s).

As we see in the triangulation of Brazil, Cuba, and the United States, the *idea* of a transnational imaginary—a symbolic "New World" space traced by the transatlantic slave trade—necessarily influences any conceptualization of afrodescendente literature. Furthermore, this transnational imaginary provides a context for rereading afrodescendente writers who wrote during the "abolition eras" of the nineteenth century. My readings of Harper, Ayala, and Auta de Souza represent one such effort.[4] A precedent was set during this period for the type of transnational discourse that we see in the twentieth and twenty-first centuries. To elaborate on the connection between contemporary afrodescendente poetics and its nineteenth-century counterpart, I include a sampling of poetic works that speak to the transnational character of afrodescendente poetry. These readings do double work: they provide a broader context within which to situate my readings of Harper, Ayala, and Auta de Souza in the previous chapters, and they suggest a way of conducting other comparative readings of afrodescendente poetry across national and linguistic lines.

Cuban poet Nancy Morejón's "Mujer Negra" (Black Woman) features an anonymous female speaker who traverses both space *and* time.

> Todavía huelo la espuma del mar que me hicieron atravesar.
> La noche, no puedo recordarla.
> Ni el mismo océano podría recordarla.
> Pero no he olvidado el primer alcatraz que divisé.
> Altas, las nubes, como inocentes testigos presenciales.
> Acaso no he olvidado ni mi costa perdida, ni mi lengua ancestral
> Me dejaron aquí y aquí he vivido.
> Y porque trabajé como una bestia,
> aquí volví a nacer. (Morejón 2002b, 115, ll. 1–9)
> [I still smell the foam of the sea they made me cross. The night, I cannot remember it. Not even the ocean itself would be able to remember it. But I haven't forgotten the

first *alcatraz* I saw. The clouds, high in the sky, like innocent eyewitnesses. Though I have not forgotten my abandoned seashore, nor my ancestral tongue They left me here and here I have lived. And because I worked like a beast, here I am born again.]

In these first nine lines of a forty-nine-line poem in free verse, the speaker crosses the Atlantic and is born again. In Morejón's own words, the speaker speaks in the first person but is not autobiographical; it is rather "an 'I' which is at the same time a 'we,' as the great American poet Walt Whitman suggested." "So, when I talk about 'me,' it is 'us,'" Morejón continues, "and it is the story of an epic vision. It is an epic poem. It is the history of a fundamental chapter of humanity: the uprooting of African slaves from the West African coast mainly to America, seen from a woman's perspective" (2002b, 39). This speaker, at once collective and individual, follows a trajectory from the shore of Africa, to Cuba, tracing the contours of an imagined space that stretches across the Atlantic to the Caribbean. Slave castles on the coast of Africa are an "alcatraz" ("Pero no he olvidado el primer alcatraz que divisé"), a temporary prison for those sentenced to the journey across the Atlantic. The clouds serve as silent witnesses to this translation from one imaginary space to another ("Altas, las nubes, como inocentes testigos presenciales").

The speaker walks the line between remembering and forgetting (lines 1–6). The tension between memory and loss (of memory) stands at the entrance of this poetic space; it delineates the "path" from Africa, across the Atlantic, and into to the "New World." This imaginary path is also a type of birth canal; the speaker is reborn in the "New World" space. This (re)birth takes place in language. It is located at the intersection of a lost language-homeland accessible only tentatively through memory ("Acaso no he olvidado ni mi costa perdida, ni mi lengua ancestral") and "aquí" ("Me dejaron aquí and aquí he vivido") where the speaker is enslaved.

Afrodescendente Cuban poet Excilia Saldaña also addresses the question of memory and movement across a transatlantic space. In Saldaña's prose poem, the entrance into memory through the poetic reconstitution of the body, links literary process and identity.

Y entro en el recuerdo y hago que tus manos entren en la fiesta que es mía y tuya. Y entro en el recuerdo y tus manos recorren mis pies de cañadonga, mis calcañales cachazudos: mis pies de montunos y mis piernas de ceiba suntuosa, y mis curvas de azúcar cruda, y mis muslos de jutía conga, y mis nalgas de turrón de caimito y mi espalda agónica, y mi pecho de trapiche, y mis pulmones envejecidos, y mis bronquios de yute agujereado, y mis hombros de raspadura, y mi nuca de palma de corojo, y mis orejas de melado, y mi pelo de yagruma, y mi frente preñada de aparecidos y espectros, y mis ojos equivocados, y mi nariz de sijú platanero, y mi boca de mamey, y mi garganta de tabaco salvaje, y mis caderas de cazuela freidora, y mi vientre de calabaza panuda, y mi cintura de trapo multicolor, y mi ombligo de güiracimarrona, y el triángulo de las prestidigitaciones y el vello manigüero, y el reverso de la concha hacendosa con su perla negra e iridiscente, y la crisma sápida en su crismero de bronce y mis senos de miel, canela y anís. (2002, 72–73)

[And I enter into memory and make your hands enter into the feast that is mine and yours. And I enter into memory and your hands traverse my Angolan sugar cane feet, my sluggish heels, my ordinary feet. And my untamed ankles and my sumptuous silk-cotton tree legs, and my crude sugar curves, and my Conga jutía thighs, and my star apple nougat buttocks, and my gunnysack bronchia, and my raw sugar shoulders, and my nape of cohune palm, and my thick cane syrup ears, and my trumpet-wood hair, and my forehead pregnant with specters and apparitions, and my mistaken eyes, and my banana tree gnome owl nose, and my mamey mouth, and my wild tobacco throat, and my frying pan hips, and my bread fruit belly, and my multicolored rag waist, and my runaway calabash bellybutton, and the triangle of prestidigitation and jungle hair, and the reverse of the diligent conch shell with its black and iridescent pearl, and the savory consecrated oil in its bronze oil maker and my breasts of honey and cinnamon and anise.] (translation by González Mandri and Rosenmeier)

Like Morejón's, Saldaña's speaker is at once one and many. She has no specific place but is a composite. As the *I* enters into memory, she addresses the Cuban nation: a personified, androgynous lover. She is an intensely corporeal being, and the symbolic elements are literally a part of her body. As readers, we experience the corporeality of this woman through a series of metaphors alluding to slave experience in the Americas: the mammy, the domestic, the hot mulatta. Saldaña presents the black female body as an articulation of a collective afrodescendente history and identity. Language, history, and corporeality intersect in the poetic space. "Blackness" is corporeal only in as much as it is constructed historically and literarily and then grafted onto the physical and psychic body.

"Excilia Saldaña logró encontrar" (Saldaña was able to find), writes Morejón in the prologue to *In the Vortex of the Cyclone*:

> la voz histórica de la mujer cubana buscando su origen en los barcos negreros, en esa amarga travesía que data del siglo XVI y que subió a las montañas durante las dos guerras necesarias del siglo XIX. Buscó por fuera una herencia de opresión y la puso ante el espejo para revelarnos cuán endeudados estamos todos con ese pasado de despojo y depredación nacido en las plantaciones no sólo cubanas sino de todo el Caribe y de las Américas negras. (2002c, x–xi)
> [the historical voice of the Cuban woman looking for her origin in slave ships, in those bitter crossings dating back to the sixteenth century, and who climbed the mountains during the necessary ways in the nineteenth century. Out in the world she looked for an inheritance of oppression and she placed it before a mirror to show us how indebted we are to that past of plundering and depredation, born in the plantations not only of Cuba but of the entire Caribbean and the black Americas.] (translation by González Mandri)

As Saldaña composes the black female body, she simultaneously composes a collective narrative history of afrodescendente peoples in Cuba and in the Americas. This process, recorded in the poem, requires a type of crossing that rewrites history across national lines. The idea of "Américas negras" (black Americas) emerges out of the metaphorical crossing manifested in the lyrical composition of this black female speaker.

Similarly, the female subject of an untitled poem by Afro-Brazilian poet Esmerelda Ribeiro, is the "mulher do hemisfério negro" (a woman from the black hemisphere). She is a "mulher sem definição sem limitação" (woman without definition and without limitations), and she represents a "força guerreira na luta africana" (warrior strength in the African struggle) (Ribeiro 1986, 98). This transhemispheric female figure transcends time and place; she is delimited by an imagined space of the African diaspora. In "Branca História" (White History), Afro-Brazilian poet Sonia Fátima da Conceição recognizes the poem as a politico-literary space where identity can be aggressively recomposed.

> Hoje num esforço sobre humano
> lutamos pela integridade do Ser
> que a branca história
> covardemente esfacelou. (Coneição 1986, 18).
> [Today, with superhuman strength we fight for the integrity of Being that white history, in its cowardice, disintegrated.]

This emphasis on the centrality of language to identity informs two major black literary movements in the Americas—the Black Arts Movement (BAM) in the United States and *Quilombhoje* in Brazil. Both of these movements feature the literary manifestation of a transnational sensibility evident in the physical border-crossing of afrodescendente poets as well as in the internal workings of their poetry.

If Cheryl Sterling is right to say that the "common demand" of BAM and Quilombhoje was in fact "the entelechy of the Black subject" (2007, 45), then what happens when the implied monolithism of the "black subject" is pluralized by the concept of literary transnationalism? When we confront black subjecthood with literary transnationalism, we come to better understand the plurality of subjecthood and the literary efforts to construct it.

The racially charged political turbulence of the late 1960s and '70s in the United States created an environment that challenged the definitions of literary art.[5] The BAM, perhaps the most prominent black artistic movement in the United States, aimed to reimagine black identity and its relationship to black art. In his seminal essay "The Black Arts Movement," Larry Neal defined this burgeoning literary, artistic, and musical renaissance of "Black Art" as the "aesthetic and spiritual sister of the Black Power concept" (1968, 29). Central to this aesthetic project was the "radical reordering of the western cultural aesthetic" partly through a heightened awareness of the interrelationship of art and politics as well as between the social conditions of black peoples and their artistic expression.

In a personal interview (August 14, 2006), BAM poet Sonia Sanchez spoke with me about the role of a transhemispheric space in determining the scope of her work, particularly during the Black Power movement.[6] "With the advent of the turbulence in the South, and also with the advent of Malcolm and all the things that were going on in this country," Sanchez observed, "my poetry began to meld with those issues . . . in the country . . . in our personal lives that affected how we were seen and viewed not only by the country but by the world . . . as I began to travel outside the country I began to understand how our work affected other people . . . younger people in the Caribbean." In the poem "blk/rhetoric," Sanchez interrogates the use of language and poetic space to construct identity. She asks fundamental questions about the production of meaning itself as it applied to language and what was a burgeoning black literary and cultural aesthetic in the United States.

> who's gonna make all
> this beautiful blk/rhetoric
> mean something.
> like
> i mean
> who's gonna take
> the words
> blk/is/beautiful
> and make more of it
> than blk/capitalism? (Sanchez 1985, 19, ll. 1–10)

The question of "meaning" stands at the structural and topical center of the stanza. "I mean" stands alone on the line as a reflexive statement linking identity (*I* mean) and the linguistic acquisition of meaning (I *mean*). The speaker asks "who's gonna take / these words" and make them *mean* something, to become "more" than fuel for an economic system. Sanchez alludes to a certain economy of language. Through the elision and compression of letters and words, she demonstrates the malleability of words and syntax. She inquires about the production of meaning itself, particularly as applied to "blackness." The poem asks, quite simply: what is to be done with words?

James Brown popularized the phrase "Say it Loud, I'm Black and I'm Proud," with his famous 1968 release. The phrase "black is beautiful" served as an ideological currency for the "economy" of a new black political and cultural movement. The mandate for black art was to translate what was considered aesthetically unbeautiful into a beauty defined on its own terms. Sanchez's speaker calls on the poet to "make more of it than blk," that is, to extend beyond the black-white binary to gain a more nuanced understanding of a burgeoning black aesthetic.

"High art," writes BAM poet Amiri Baraka in "The Myth of 'Negro Literature,'" "must reflect the experiences of the human being, the emotional predicament of the man, as he exists, in the defined world of his being. It must be produced from the legitimate emotional resources of the soul in the world" (1994, 167). Just as art was inseparable from the physical world, and therefore the political world of "the people," the poem was intimately connected to the existential (not to be confused with the essential) and the human in BAM poetry. The poem came to stand for the "collective conscious and unconscious of Black America—the real impulse in back of the Black Power movement, which is the will toward self-determination and nationhood, a radical reordering of the nature and function of both art and the artist" (Neal 1968, 32).

In "I am," Baraka redefines "the West" by constructing a transhemispheric space of "the Americas":

> The West is
> The New World
> not Europe
> The West is
> El Mundo Nuevo
> The Pan American

> Complexity
> As diversity as the routes
> & history
> of our collection
> The West is The Americas
> not Europe. (1996, 40. ll. 8-19)

Baraka evokes the idea of a pan-American space of "the Americas" that is at once one and many. Using the lens of the Cuban revolution, Baraka envisioned new possibilities for African Americans in the United States. In the essay "Cuba Libre," Baraka reflects on his trip to Cuba in 1960, claiming that the Cuban people were one of the many "new" peoples of the world who, for him, made the notion of revolution take on a degree of tangibility that it did not have in the United States. "The idea of 'a revolution' had been foreign to me," writes Baraka. "It was one of those inconceivably 'romantic' and/or hopeless ideas that we Norteamericanos had been taught since public school to hold up to the cold light of 'reason'" (1991, 160).

Phillip Brian Harper's readings of poetry by Sanchez, Madhubuti, and other BAM poets indicate the "*intra*racial distinctions" (emphasis mine) that actually "solidify the meaning of the Black Aesthetic" (1993, 240). For Harper, BAM poetry highlighted internal contradictions of black nationalist ideology, not a monolithic blackness (1993, 255, 239). David Lionel Smith criticizes BAM critics for overstating the "polemics and excesses" of BAM while overshadowing its nuances (1991, 108). James Edward Smethurst (2005) gives attention to the regional, ideological, and political variants within BAM and its players, showing how it was not a singular impulse of black nationalism.

Scholars like Smith, Smethurst, and Harper have duly complicated our reading of BAM as a nationalist and literary project. Less attention has been given to the movement's *trans*national character and how this aspect of its theory works to pluralize its aesthetic. BAM was not only an aesthetic movement, it was also an "ethical movement"; to the extent that it was "an ethical movement," it was a transnational movement encompassing "most of the useable elements of Third World culture" (Neal 1968, 30).

BAM proposed its own form of global redemption. It claimed to "redeem" the world from a Western postulation of what was human and pursue its own universal concept. The movement claimed to "reorder" the oppressive and "antihuman" sensibility of a Western aesthetic that had effectively "run its course" (Neal 1968, 29). Haki Madhubuti (1994) emphasized the importance of this "third world ethos" to the emergent black literary aesthetic.

In the poem "Resgate" (Ransom), Afro-Brazilian poet and activist Alzira Rufino (1949–), like Sanchez does in "blk/rhetoric," examines language as a medium by which to (re)negotiate black identity.

> Sou negra ponto final
> devolva-me a identidade
> rasgue minha certidão
> sou negra sem reticências

sem vírgulas e sem ausências
não quero mais meio-termo
sou negra balacobaco
sou negra noite cansaço
sou negra ponto final. (in Alves and Durham 1994, 34)
[I am black period give me back my identity tear up my birth certificate I am black without ellipses without commas and without absences I no longer want in-betweens I am black *balacobaco*[7] I am black weary night I am black period]

Rufino refutes the phenomenon of *mulatez* or *mestizaje*. Peter Wade characterizes the terms as terms that refer to "the notion of racial and cultural mixture" (2005, 239) and that contain "tensions between sameness and difference" (240). As the "site of heterogeneous cultural identities" (Martínez-Echazabal 1998, 23), the concept of mestizaje has been a major factor in the intellectual formation of "Afro"-Latin America, especially in the latter half of the nineteenth century and the early twentieth (22).

"Resgate" also explicitly refutes the cultural projects of *branqueamento*. As the end of slavery grew more imminent, intellectual leaders like Joaquim Nabuco stood in favor of *whitening* to detract from the detrimental effect of the black and Asian presence in Brazil (Augusto dos Santos and Hallewell 2002, 66; Telles 2004, 29–31). They successfully advocated for government-subsidized European immigration to Brazil. Many wanted to consolidate the nation through this immigration as a means of preventing the Africanization of Brazil (Augusto dos Santos and Hallewell 2002, 68). The government went as far as to prohibit a group of African Americans from the United States who wanted to form a community in Mato Grosso (Augusto dos Santos and Hallewell 2002, 71).

Rufino's deliberate omission of punctuation highlights the raw material of language itself, which—unchecked—determines the syntactical shape and delineating boundary lines of the poem. The racial and gender identity of the speaker is theorized literally through a series of references to the grammatical elements of language and its cadences. The demand for identity ("devolva-me a identidade") precedes the destruction of the "certidão"—the externally imposed inscription of identity. The title term "resgate" (ransom) derives from the verb *resgatar*, which means to free from captivity, to redeem (livrar de cativeiro; remir). The verb contains within its denotation both *to recapture* (i.e., to reclaim ownership of something or someone) and *to free* (i.e., to redeem a person or an object). A dialogic between freedom and slavery appears at the semantic level of the poem. This dialogic correlates language and identity.[8]

Itself a "ransom," the poem demands its own self-contained space, enclosed within the beginning and ending phrase: "Sou negra ponto final." Between these repeated lines, Rufino develops a tension between affirmation, or *presence* ("sou negra"), and *absence* ("*sem* reticencias"; "*sem* virgulas"; "*sem* ausências"). She does not use the plethora of terms referring to racial identity that, as a practice, are written on the Brazilian "certidão." Instead, she favors the small lexical economy of nine lines and uses the identity marker, negra. Ultimately, the speaker rejects these "in-betweens" ("não quero mais meio-termo"). She expresses her demand for the restitution of a stolen identity by abandoning syntactical devices that might similarly compartmentalize the body of the poem. Rufino links language and identity here through the use of metaphors that connect "being" to the physical environment ("weary night"). "Resgate" articulates identity through a dialogic encounter with language and its structural elements in the space between these repeated lines.

Although the speaker actively rejects absences and in-betweens, the poetic structure draws attention to the absences and in-betweens of language. It mimics the way language constantly reaches for metaphor to achieve meaning. Identity materializes between the lines. Ultimately, Rufino posits the poem as a linguistic space that can create a new "self."

With the "sweetness of sugar from Pernambuco," BAM poet Jayne Cortez takes us to northeastern Brazil in "The Guitars I Used to Know."

Guitars
with excavated rhythms
with maps and bridges
and the sweetness of sugar from
Pernambuco
from Nacogdoches
from Itta Bena
from Chituguiza
Guitars. (Cortez 2002, 79–81, ll. 1–9)

Pernambuco is also the region of one of the most famous escaped slave society—the Republic of Palmares. The rhythms of the guitar are "excavated rhythms," unearthed through a poetic invocation. "Maps and bridges" refer to defined territory and the crossing-over or transgressions of that territory. Maps designate borders and name blank spaces; bridges cross over and connect the spaces.

What Cheryl Sterling calls the "artistic arm" of the Movimento Negro in Brazil (2007, 53), began in the early 1970s among middle-class blacks primarily in the urban areas of Brazil. In 1980, a group of Afro-Brazilian writers formed what became known as Quilombhoje, a writers' collective of Afro-Brazilian poets and writers whose writings attested to the reality of racial problems in Brazil (Castellón 2007, 82). They challenged the salient myth of "racial democracy" put forth by Brazilian cultural anthropologist Gilberto Freyre. Part of this political and aesthetic movement has involved a reevaluation of the lexicon of racial signifiers. A number of Afro-Brazilian poets, especially those affiliated with Quilombhoje, have adopted the term "Negro" to define themselves.[9] Asserting a similar stance to the BAM poets who were also greatly influenced by a political impetus (namely, the Black Power movement) many Afro-Brazilian poets made a conscious effort to redefine the term in their work.

Abdias do Nascimento introduced "Quilombismo" or what he called "an Afro-Brazilian political alternative" (1980, 141). The term *quilombismo* derives from *quilombo*, a term designating the various groups of escaped slaves that developed over the course of Brazil's slave history. These quilombos effectively created "free" societies alongside a very prominent and thriving system of African slavery. For Nascimento, Quilombismo was a political project that first involved "redeeming" the memory of slavery with a specific appeal to a preslave African history and a transnational sensibility (1980, 143).[10] Nascimento's seminal essay appeared in the United States in the *Journal of Black Studies*, in which he defined quilombismo as a "scientific and historiocultural concept" (1980, 174). His was a transnational vision. "Estamos conscientes," Nascimento wrote, "de que nossa luta transcende os limites dos nossos respectivas países: o sofrimento da criança, da mulher e do homem negros é um fenômeno internacional" (We are conscious of the fact that our struggle transcends the limits of our respective countries: the suffering of black children, women and men is an international phenomenon) (1980, 17). Nascimento further commented that "black Brazilian memory is only a part and particle in this gigantic project of reconstruction of a larger past to which all Afro-Brazilians are connected. To redeem this past is to have a consequent responsibility in the destinies and futures of the Black African nation worldwide, still preserving our quality as edifiers and genuine citizens of Brazil" (1980, 143).

The Quilombhoje poets capitalized on the metaphor of the quilombo as a "free" space where Africans and their descendants could live freely. The term *quilombhoje* represented the words *quilombo* and *hoje* (today). Poet Jônatas Conceição de Sílva describes the quilombo as follows:

> Extinto em 1695, o Quilombo de Palmares, símbolo maior do quilombismo nacional, revelou-se marco exemplar para a luta dos negros brasileiros depois da Abolição. O quilombo foi o espaço onde africanos e brasileiros puderam reinventar a cultura Africana e reafirmar um modo de ser e viver que se opunha radicalmente ao discurso colonial. (2004, 39)
>
> [Wiped out in 1695, the *Quilombo de Palmares*, the greatest symbol of national quilombismo, became an exemplary sign for the struggle of black Brazilians after abolition. The quilombo was a space where Africans and Brazilians could reinvent African culture and reaffirm a way of being and living that radically opposed colonial discourse.]

The group soon began producing the serialized publication *Cadernos Negros* (Black Notebooks), featuring poems and short stories written by a growing cadre of Afro-Brazilian writers.[11] This concept of the quilombo framed the aesthetic and political context for *Cadernos Negros*. Quilombhoje poet Benedita Delazaria's "Homenagem ao 'Quilombhoje'" (Homage to "Quilombhoje") illustrates this fact.

> *Quilombhoje* quilombando
> quilomba seu bando
> na roda de poemas
> no grito de protesto
> na voz do poeta
> cadernos negros
> semeando . . .
> estrelas no dedo
> no batuque de tocaia
> teclas de ébano
> despertando . . .

a cor da pele
o banzo
no despacho poético
um homem tenta ser anjo
da consciência adormecida. (in *Cadernos Negros*, no. 9 [1986]: 136).
[*Quilomhhoje quilombando quilomba* your *bando* in the circle of poems in the cry of protest in the voice of the poet *cadernos negros* spreading into your fingers in the *batuque de tocaia*[12] ebony keys awakening . . . the color of the skin *o banzo* in the sorcery of poetry a man seeks to be angel of an unawakened consciousness.]

In Delezaria's poem, the voice of the poet and the collection of poems expressed in *Cadernos Negros* create a space like the quilombo, a free space that can generate new forms of consciousness. Quilombo becomes a noun and a verb, a figurative place and a way of actively engaging with an African-derived culture and a new consciousness.

In his introduction to a 1998 anthology of *Cadernos Negros*, poet and co-founder of Quilombhoje Luiz Silva "Cuti" describes the artistic imperative that drives *Cadernos Negros*.

A poesia, por meio do ritmo, tem sua ligação ancestral com as próprias funções do corpo e as atividades elementares do ser humano: a respiração, o fluxo sangüíneo, a cadência de uma caminhada, o ato sexual, o piscar dos olhos, a mastigação, etc. Neste sentido, os poemas dos afro-descendentes brasileiros partilham de uma corpo histórico, em essência articulado no diapasão do verso de Solano Trindade: "O meu canto é o grito de uma raça em plena luta pela liberdade." (1998, 20)
[Poetry, though its rhythm, has the same ancestral roots as the fundamental function of the body and the primary activities of the human being: the act of breathing, the flow of blood, the cadence of a walk, the sexual act, the blinking of the eyes, chewing, etc. In this sense, poems by Brazilians of African descent share a historical body articulated, in its essence, in the diapason of Solano Trindade's lines: "My song is the cry of a race in absolute struggle for freedom."]

This "historical body" is not an essencialized racial body preoccupied with its biological integrity, but rather a metaphor for the body of history that contextualizes the collective history of African descendants in Brazil and throughout the Americas. This historical body is circumscribed within a history of racial slavery. This body becomes tangible in the poetics of *Cadernos Negros* writers. Manuel Castellón compares the "negritud" evident in Cuti's work to that of Wole Soyinka in that he rejects the notion that the black writer must write to proclaim his blackness, while at the same time Cuti adopts attitudes similar to those of Martin Luther King Jr., Malcolm X, and James Baldwin in his efforts to "recusar con firmeza y coraje la arrogencia de los blancos o su pretensión de querer constituirse en modelos para el pueblo negro" (to reject firmly and confidently white arrogance and its desire to set itself up as a model for black people) (87).

In her preface to the fourth edition of the volume, Thereza Santos suggested that *Cadernos Negros* effected a necessary transformation by presenting literature as a "forma de uma ação que transforma" (form of action that transforms) that induces change and that imposes its own revision of the world around it (1981, 5). Santos went on to say that

> o choro do negro não será elimindado . . . São conscientes já o disse; como negros, como homens, fazem parte desta maioria-minoria sem nenhuma parcela do "NADA" neste país . . . É exatamente isto o que estes negros fazem: criam, a cada hora, a cada momento, sabem do compromisso que assumiram frente à comunidade afro-brasileira e para ela criam, por ela avançam no caminho da liberdade. (1981, 5)
>
> [the cry of the *negro* writes will not be silenced . . . As has already been said, they are conscious; as *negros*, as humans, they comprise a part of this majority-minority having no part of 'NOTHINGNESS' in this country . . . It is precisely this that these *Negros* do: they create, every hour, every moment, they understand the obligation that they have to the Afro-Brazilian community and for it they create, so that it can progress along freedom's road.]

Informed by a distinctive Afro-Brazilian cultural nationalism, Elisa Lucinda's "Constatação" (Proof) is a performance of identity as a transnational phenomenon.

> Pareço Cabo-verdiana
> pareço Antilhana
> pareço Martiniquenha
> pareço Jamaicana
> pareço Brasileira
> pareço Capixaba
> pareço Baiana
> pareço Carioca
> pareço Cubana
> pareço Americana
> pareço Senegalesa
> em toda parte
> pareço
> com o mundo inteiro
> de meu povo
> pareço
> sempre o fundo de tudo
> a conga, o tambor
> é o que nos leva adiante
> pareço todos
> porque pareço semelhante. (Lucinda 2007, 86)
>
> [I look Cape Verdean I look Antillean I look Martinican I look Jamaican I look Brazilian I look *Capixaba* I look Bahian I look *Carioca* I look Cuban I look American I look Senegalese all over I look like the whole world of my people I look always like the essence of everything the *conga*, the *tambor* is what carries us forward I look like all of this because I look the same.]

Lucinda's use of simple diction with an emphasis on repetition informs the structure of the piece by creating a symmetry in the poem. This symmetry reinforces the tension between sameness and difference as the speaker is one and many at the same time. The geographical references evoke the notion of an imagined space that extends across Brazil and beyond in both transhemispheric and transatlantic space. The poem enacts the project of re-collecting the fragments of an African diaspora in one speaker who is at the same time all of them and none of them.

For poet and scholar Edimilson de Almeida Pereira, the Quilombhoje project emphasizes a critical, rather than sentimental, return to an African past and the recreation of Afro-Brazilian identity through a revision of the "imaginario nacional" (national imaginary) (2007, 173). Pereira suggests that the "poética de vários autores afrodescendentes procura dar forma a um projeto de fundação estética, psicológica e política do sujeito que se reconhece e que é reconhecido como afro-brasileiro" (poetry of many afrodescendente writers aims to give form to a project that is fundamentally aesthetic, psychological and political belonging to the individual who recognizes him or herself and is recognized as an Afro-Brazilian) (2007, 172).

In Adão Ventura's "Desencontro," the speaker seeks identity in the "mirror" of an imagined black community.

> Procuro
> no espelho desses rostos negros
> nessa pele marcada
> nesse ombro curvado,
> ainda que forte
> nessas mãos atadas
> ainda que vazias
> o desejo de luta
> que ... sucumbo ante a espera
> e encontro o medo
> e sob ele
> ainda perceptível
> o grito quase inaudível
> sufocado pelo próprio riso
> que retesa o pranto
> contido
> guardado
> o coração pulsando
> como que cronometrando
> os segundos que restam para
> a inevitável explosão. (in *Cadernos Negros*, no. 1. [1978])
> [I seek in the mirror of these black faces in this branded skin in this bowed shoulder still so strong in these bound hands still so empty the desire to struggle that ... before the mirror I diminish and I face fear and beneath it still perceiving an almost inaudible cry choked by its own laughter that quells the waiting contained protected the heart beats like the ticking of the seconds that remain before the inevitable explosion.]

In the mirror of "rostros negros" (black faces)—an imagined community of people whose skin is also "marked"—and the physical posture indicating a history of slavery ("nesse hombro curvado," "nessas mãos atadas"), the speaker seeks the "desejo de luta" (desire to struggle). The self is constructed through the symbolic act of linking the marked body to its mirror image within the poetic space. Yielding before the mirror, the *I* accepts the mark (ancestry) and the posture (history) that will inform her present struggle. The tension between laughter and crying—a juxtaposition of the pleasure and the pain of receiving this "mark"—propels the poem to its inevitable "explosion."

In this particular sampling of modern and contemporary afrodescendente poetry, transnationalism surfaces in the thematic and structural elements of the poems. They are characterized by topical, thematic, and structural heterogeneity, by transatlantic and transhemispheric movement, by the voicings of individual and collective identities, and finally, by the representation of marked or named bodies. The inquiries represented by this small selection of texts also suggest that afrodescendente writers endeavored, through a literary use of language, to understand and rewrite the inscriptions on their histories and identities.

> *National consciousness, which is not nationalism,*
> *is the only thing that will give us an international dimension.*
> —Fanon (1963, 247)
>
> *The idea of beginning, indeed the act of beginning,*
> *necessarily involves an act of delimitation by which*
> *something is cut out of a great mass of material,*
> *separated from the mass, and made to stand for,*
> *as well as be, a starting point, a beginning . . .*
> —Said (2000, 82)
>
> [The nation is] . . . the home of specific mythical powers, gods, demons, and traditions. It is home to these powers in the sense that it is the dwelling wherein they need not account for themselves, where they are accepted without judgment, and are ultimately beyond question . . . [a nation is not] geographical in the sense of objective space. It is determined by the scope of the mythico-practical norm-style. . . . It is a "community-horizon" within which ultimate questions about who I am and what the world is are referred to a coherent matrix of myths.
>
> —Knies (2006, 100)

The Myth of (the) Nation: Territorial Transgressions and Their Canons

In the introduction to *Nation and Narration*, Homi Bhahba points to the dark underside beneath the veneer of a seemingly whole, coherent nation. He argues that the nation—a veritable form of narration—is in fact characterized not by continuity or ideological stability but by ambivalence.

> The 'locality' of national culture is neither unified nor unitary in relation to itself, nor must it be seen simply as 'other' in relation to what is outside or beyond it. The

boundary is Janus-faced and the problem of outside/inside must always itself be a process of hybridity, incorporating new 'people' in relation to the body politic, generating other sites of meaning and, inevitably, in the political process, producing unmanned sites of political antagonism and unpredictable forces for political representation. (1990, 4)

In this tug-of-war between coherence and ambivalence, homogeneity and hybridity, questions of racial, gender, and national identity come to the forefront.

In her assessment of postrevolutionary American literature, Gabriel Pisarz-Ramírez notes that American national identity played a crucial role in the "processes of inventing and negotiating a national identity that was still far from being coherent" (2009, 97). Pisarz-Ramírez focuses on 1780s–1830s, maintaining that for revolutionary writers in the United Sates, Latin America, and the Caribbean were "discursive reference points both as potential spheres of influence for the young nation and as sites of projection for the negotiation of national and group identities" (2009, 98). Pisarz-Ramírez also maintains that, particularly evident in the first African American newspaper *Freedom's Journal*, free African Americans looked toward Haiti and South America to conceive of "alternative visions of community and identity that diverge[d] from dominant national narratives" (2009, 99).

After abolition in Cuba and the battle for independence won twelve years later, debates about the role of race in Cuba's future vacillated between two ideological polarities: (1) complete disassociation from Africa and blackness, and (2) Afro-Cuban solidarity and separatism. Black Cuban involvement in the War for Independence raised the level of expectation among black Cubans in the postwar period. The white Cuban elite confronted this expectation with the equally salient myth of racial equality and oppressive racial ideology (Helg 1995, 3).

Influenced by his contemporary the poet Walt Whitman's anti-imperialism and poetic treatment of a liberal American democracy, Cuban poet, intellectual, and revolutionary José Martí began to imagine an "America" for himself (Grandin 2006, par. 6).[13] Two years later, Martí presented his recipe for "American" (or Latin American) national ideology, which he publicized in the seminal essay "Nuestra América" (Our America) (1889). In it, Martí stated firmly, "No hay odio de razas, porque no hay razas" (There is no race hatred, because there are no races) (2001, 27). Martí's argued against racial classification. The rise of social Darwinism and the eugenics movement reinforced categories of racial difference and belief in the inherent inferiority of Africans and their descendants. Alternatively, Martí espoused the idea of cubanidad (Cuban-ness) encapsulated in the emerging term *mestizo*. He advocated for the elimination of terms like *negro, moreno, pardo, mulato* and the residue of a European racial discourse that had dominated nineteenth-century Cuban thought (Fuente 2001, 31).

Martí and his contemporary and fellow leader of the Cuban wars of independence General Antonio Maceo (1848–1896) used a rhetoric of *aracialism* to confront the salience (rather than the absence) of a binary racial ideology among Cubans. Martí feared the potential conflict between Cubans *de color* and the white descendants of the European elite. On many occasions during the years leading up to the Spanish-American War, Maceo was accused of trying to create a "Negro republic" in

Cuba. He had to walk the thin line between his own racial self-designation as a black man—which he expressed most directly in a letter from Haiti to General José Lamothe—and his nationally unified, anti-oppression stance in favor of Cuban "libertad" (2002, 46). Martí led the Liberation Army into war against Spain proclaiming the idea that Cubans were more than white and more than black. They were simply *Cuban*.

Six years before slavery was formally abolished in Cuba, Cuban novelist Cirilio Villaverde wrote the novel *Cecilia Valdés* (1882). The protagonist in the novel is a *mulata*, whom Villaverde posits as a symbol for a virginal Cuban nation faced with the challenge of its own hybridity. Throughout the novel, Cecilia struggles to reconcile her mother's "odioso color" (hateful color), the "causa aparente y principal" (principal and evident cause) of her "inacabable esclavitud" (unending slavery) (1995, 125) and Cecilia's desire for acceptance by a rich, white lover. As the wars of independence became increasingly "black," Villaverde's novel dramatizes the tension between black power and white privilege in Cuba. Cecilia is the "colonial subject," whose personal tragedy—torn between blackness and whiteness, between subservience and the desire for independence—ultimately becomes "emblematic of nineteenth-century Cuban nationalism, torn as it was between its ideals of independence rooted in the emancipation of slaves and the capitalist interest of the slave trade"(González Mandri 2006, 15).[14]

In a comparative analysis of race and the nation-state in the United States and Brazil, historian Anthony Marx perceives a distinct difference between the nation-concept in Brazil and in the United States.

> The flag of the United States included a stripe for each of the original thirteen colonies and a star added for each state, symbolizing the federal unity of localized authority and allegiance. By contrast, the Brazilian flag bore no such references to divided powers or loyalties. Instead, Brazil's banner projected the immutable unity of the post-colonial nation, symbolized by the central motif of the constellation of southern stars at the moment of the founding of the republic. The Brazilian nation was thus projected not as an emerging political compromise, but as a fixed part of the natural order. . . . The issue of how to construct a racial order was central to the historical process of nation-state consolidation, as symbolized by the respective flags. (1998, 82)

Marx explains the differences in constructions of racial identifies in the project of nation building by the relative presence or absence of "intrawhite conflict." Marx rightly identifies a major difference in the racial climate of Brazil and that of the United States during the later half of the nineteenth century. Especially after the close of the Reconstruction Era in the South, nostalgic whites of the planter class employed anti-black rhetoric to forge commonality with Northern whites. D. W. Griffith's *The Birth of a Nation* (1915) depicted this phenomena with frightening clarity as in its final scenes the Ku Klux Klan cavalry swooped in to "redeem" the South (symbolized by the white female character Elise) from the new black aristocracy, declaring "the former enemies of the North and South are *united again in common defense* of their Aryan birthright" (emphasis mine).

In Brazil, prominent intellectuals like Authur de Gobineau, the representative of France in Brazil from 1869 to 1870, and leading Brazilian psychiatrist Raimundo Nina Rodrigues wrote vehemently about the deleterious effects of racial miscegenation.[15] Brazil's essence rested either in its northeastern colonial past or the interior (or backwoods) of Brazil, but certainly not with Africans.[16] Furthermore, Brazil's transition from colony to independent republic was far from a clear break from the preeminence of a firmly established elite. The desire for national authenticity was coupled with a desire on the part of many to sustain an oligarchic hierarchy. Elite white Brazilians aligned national progress with whiteness. Anxiety about the future of ex-slaves was major caveat of Brazilian nationalism. According to Celia Maria Marinho de Azevedo:

> Era, sim, o negro, elemento considerado de raça inferior porque descendente de africanos, viciado, imoral, incapaz para o trabalho livre, criminoso em potencial, inimigo de civilização e do progresso, que os discursos imigrantistas repudiavam abertamente, em uma época que as teorias raciais ainda estavam longe de cair em desuso. (1987, 156)
> [The Negro was considered to be of an inferior race because he descended from depraved, immoral Africans who were incapable of free labor, potentially criminal, an enemy to civilization and progress and whom discourse about immigration openly repudiated in an era in which racial theories were far from falling into disuse.]

To solidify their position, Marx maintains, European descendants "established early legacies of racial discrimination against African descendants, despite dramatic differences in population mix and mixing" (1998, 178). Marx gives us an extensive comparative analysis; his focus on "the state" and the white elite as active nation builders, however, inevitably focuses on only one side of the coin. Afrodescendente poetry helps us see another. Comparative study of afrodescendente poetics provokes inquiry into the poetic use of language in public discourse as well as the private invention of new forms of national, racial, and gender freedoms.

NOTES

Introduction

1. Terry Eagleton provides the following useful summary of Russian linguist Roman Jakobson's assessment of the poetic use of language:

> What he [Jakobson] contributed in particular to poetics, which he regarded as part of the field of linguistics, was the idea that the "poetic" consisted above all in language's being placed in a certain kind of self-conscious relationship to itself. The poetic functioning of language "promotes the palpability of signs," draws attention to their material qualities rather than simply using them as counters in communication. In the "poetic," the sign is dislocated from its object: the usual relation between sign and referent is disturbed, which allows the sign a certain independence as an object of value in itself. (1996, 85)

2. This historical figure is most commonly referred to as Zumbi in both Brazil and the United States. Some historical documents transcribe the name Zombi. In this book, I use "Zumbi" to refer broadly to the historical figure and "Zombi" to refer to Harper's character in "Death of Zombi."

3. Carpentier does seem to exoticize the "idea" of "el negro" as an importation of vibrance and culture onto a "New World" canvas. He writes:

> la aportación del negro al mundo a donde fue llevado, muy a pesar suyo, no consiste en lo que ha dado en llamarse erróneamente "negritud" (¿por qué no hablar, en tal caso, de una "blanquitud"?), sino en algo mucho más trascendental: una sensibilidad que vino a enriquecer la de los hombres con quienes se le había obligado a convivir, comunicándole una nueva energía para manifestarse en dimensión mayor, tanto en lo artístico como en lo histórico, puesto que el

criollo de indio y europeo no alcanzó la edad adulta, en América, mientras no contó con la sensibilidad del negro. (Carpentier 1999, 148)

[the contribution of the Negro to the world to which he was taken, much to his dismay, does not consist of what has erroneously been called "negritud" (in that case, why don't we talk about "whiteness?"), but rather something much more transcendental: a sensibility that came to enrich the sensibility of those persons with whom it had to live, expressing a new energy to manifest itself in a greater dimension, as much in Art as in History, such that the Indian or European *criollo* could not reach adulthood in America without relying on the sensibility of the Negro.]

As poetic and historical texts, Ayala's poems duly complicate this portrayal. This project resists a narrative history that would posit the presence of Africans in the New World as an exotic literary presence rather than an actual presence. At the same time, it recognizes that the ideology of freedom was very much influenced by both the romanticization and the enslavement of Africans and their descendants in the New World. This fact must inflect our reading of the texts because it inflected the political and social climate in which they were composed and read.

4. My claims about the implications of "race" on the contemporary debate landscape do not disregard the particular aspects of Brazilian, Cuban, and U.S. history(ies), nor do I concede an oversimplified reading of history that would suggest that there is an objective historical "truth" advocated by one interest group or another. I do maintain, however, that these differences emerged out of a need to account for a legacy of slavery and the presence of Africans that challenged myths about cultural, national, and racial homogeneity.

5. My formulation of "imagined" communities borrows from Benedict Anderson's definition of an *imagined* national community. Anderson (1991) defines "the nation" as an "imagined political community." According to Anderson, this community is "imagined" because "the members of even the smallest nation will never know most of their fellow-members, meet them, or even hear of them, yet in the minds of each lives the image of their communion.... Communities are to be distinguished, not by their falsity/genuineness, but by the style in which they are imagined" (1991, 6).

6. In "Dissemination: Time, Narrative and the Margins of the Modern Nation," Homi K. Bhabha posits "nation" as a "narrative strategy" and an ambivalent category whose margins are challenged by "a continual slippage categories" that heterogenize the "imagined" unit (2004, 201).

7. A number of factors were working concurrently to link burgeoning nations in the Americas during the nineteenth century, slavery being one of the most salient. As Katia M. de Queirós Mattosso affirms, the "international marketplace and common concerns made the slave systems of the Atlantic world a unity in the nineteenth century, and probably before that" (1986, vii).

8. In an attempt to denormalize the use of "American" to refer only to the United States, I make specific reference at times to "(North) Americans" and even "African (North) Americans," to reference a specific nation-based imagined community.

9. Considered by many to be a virtual guru of historical and ontological theory, philosopher Georg Wilhelm Friedrich Hegel (1770–1831) argued in *Lectures on the Philosophy of World History* (1837; 1975), a collection of his lectures, that development is not

just a harmless and peaceful process of growth like that of organic life, but a hard and obstinate struggle with itself. Besides, it contains not just the purely formal aspect of development itself, but involves the realisation of an end whose content is determinate. And we have made it clear from the outset what this end is: it is the spirit in its essential nature; i.e. as the concept of freedom. (1975, 127)

Hegel concluded that the history of the world "accordingly represents the successive stages in the development of that principle whose substantial content is the consciousness of freedom" (1975, 130–31). By citing Hegel I do not mean to imply that the poetic texts in this book conceive of freedom in the same way he does. I draw attention to Hegel instead to consider his formulation of the connection between the conception of history and the conception of freedom.

10. To date, there is no known parallel figure in the lusophone context. It is my hope that my discussion of Auta de Souza in this book will suggest a way of conceiving of a tradition of such writing.

11. Wheatley traveled to England, sponsored by Susanna Wheatley, and published poetry there.

12. In the poem "Contestación," Ayala claims that in fact the poets Plácido, Manzano, and Antonio Medina, "en el tiempo del látigo inhumano" (during the time of the inhumane whip), "nuestra Cuba nos dió / que en medio de tamaña desventura / llegaron a cantar con tal dulzura / que el mundo se asombró" (in the midst of such great misfortune, they came to sing with such sweetness that the world was amazed). That is to say they gave "Cuba" to the Cubans and placed it on the world stage poetically.

13. A comprehensive collection of Harper's poetry and letters can be found in Frances Smith Foster's *A Brighter Coming Day* (1990); this collection includes all of Harper's poems from extant volumes, poems published in periodicals, and an unpublished manuscript.

14. Using empathy as a persuasive strategy, abolitionist literature often emphasized the common humanity of enslaved blacks and their white masters through an appeal to human emotion. We can look the Stowe's concluding remarks in *Uncle Tom's Cabin* for an example of such an appeal. She writes

> To you, generous, noble-minded men and women, of the South,—you, whose virtue, and magnanimity and purity of character, are the greater for the severer trial it has encountered,—to you is her appeal. Have you not, in your own secret souls, in your own private conversings, felt that there are woes and evils, in this accursed system, far beyond what are here shadowed, or can be shadowed? Can it be otherwise? Is man ever a creature to be trusted with wholly irresponsible power? And does not the slave system, by denying the slave all legal right of testimony, make every individual owner an irresponsible despot? Can anybody fail to make the inference what the practical result will be? If there is, as we admit, a public sentiment among you, men of honor, justice and humanity, is there not also another kind of public sentiment among the ruffian, the brutal and debased? (1851, 622)

Stowe bridges the gap between the powerful master and the "debased" slave by suggesting that they both have a kind of "public sentiment."

15. See Carmen Montejo Arrechea's article on Minerva in Lisa Brock and Digna Castañeda Fuertes (eds.), *Between Race and Empire* (1998). Montejo Arrechea documents some of Ayala's regular contributions to the magazine during its early period (1888–1889) in particular.

16. *Minerva: Revista Universal Ilustrada* Tomo III (Número 20) (Octubre 1911): 14.

17. I discuss Gualberto Gómez's ideology and its relationship to Ayala's work in chapter 2. For a more extensive discussion of his political life and ideology see Philip Howard, *Changing History: Afro Cuban Cabildos and Societies of Color in the Nineteenth Century* (1998).

18. Chapter 2 examines how these two aspects of Ayala's work play out in the poem "Redención."

19. French Symbolism played a major role in the evolution of Brazilian Symbolist and Romantic poetry—the idea that observable objects in nature could represent aspects of human experience or nature to produce a moral truth or to reflect religious belief. Commenting on major nineteenth-century writer Antônio Gonçalves Teixeira e Sousa (1812–1861)—who also used a great deal of Christian mythology in his poetry—Roger Bastide notes that Gonçalves "afirma a sua igualidade com o branco, no movimento de libertação política e de construção de uma nova pátria. Mas não quer ser ao mesmo tempo confundido com o negro escravo" (1943, 28).

20. Jorge O'Grady de Paiva argued that in fact to read Auta from the context of the "preconceito racial" was a critical error made by scholars of such writers as Gonçalves Dias and Machado de Assis who formed a part of the "aristocracia intellectual" of Brazil independent of the "pigmentação da pele" (1972, 28). Although Auta's poetry has been repeatedly tied critically to autobiographical truths, the fact that (1) she was raised by a grandmother of African descent, (2) members of her family owned slaves and were involved in the cotton and sugar business that demanded slave labor (Cascudo 1961, 29); and (3) the garden at the center of the *fazenda* her family owned was tended by slaves (Cascudo 1961, 30) is often completely ignored.

21. Ferreira Gomes writes in the introduction to the fifth edition of *Horto*, "[A]pesar de sua tez escura, pouco se falou até hoje sobre as origens africanas de Auta de Souza. Pode-se mesmo dizer que, no plano imaginário, ocorreu uma espécie de "embranquecimento" da poeta" (In spite of her dark complexion, until now little has been said about Auta de Souza's African origins. One could even say that, on the level of imagination, there took place a type of "whitening" of the poet) (2001, 31).

22. Anna Brickhouse notes that the nineteenth century, even before the Civil War, would "largely define the canonical US literary tradition—a tradition we have since come to understand and receive as primarily nationalist, monolingual, and geographically centered in the northeast—rested on a considerable network of transnational literary practices and affiliations that shaped some of this tradition's central texts as well as the self-understanding of a number of its most influential writers" (2004, 23).

23. *Ofrendas Mayabequinas* (Ayala 1926) demonstrates formal, stylistic, and thematic range, from the popular *décima* to the didactic poem. In the context of African literary traditions, didacticism not only constitutes an aspect of the performance of a certain moral teaching, but also forms a part of the poetic aesthetic. What Catherine Atherton refers to as a "popularising form," (1997, 88) the didactic poem not only proposes a moral but also consciously and formally embraces the language of popular rhetoric. In the didactic poem, the importance of communicating meaning to a collectivity influences the poetic style (Ojaide 1996, 23).

Chapter 1

1. Hanchard argues that "viewed historically, Africana and African American studies provides an opportunity to connect contemporary globalization to its antecedents in global history. The middle passage and racial slavery generated two distinct but deeply intertwined modes of globalization affecting African and African-derived populations: the circulation and dissemination of ideologies of race and racism, and the scattering of various African peoples, technologies, cosmological systems, and cultural practices throughout the world" (2004, 151).

2. In his discussion of Paul Laurence Dunbar, Johnson also refers to other "outstanding" figures among "the Aframericans of the whole Western world." He continues: "There are Plácido and Manzano in Cuba; Vieux and Durand in Haiti; Machado de Assis in Brazil, and others that might be mentioned, who stand on a plane with or even above Dunbar. Plácido and Machado de Assis rank as great in the literatures of their respective countries without any

qualifications whatever. They are world figures in the literature of the Latin languages. Machado de Assis is somewhat handicapped in this respect by having as his tongue and medium the lesser known Portuguese, but Plácido, writing in the language of Spain, Mexico, Cuba and almost the whole of South America, is universally known. His works have been republished in the original in Spain, Mexico and in most of the Latin-American countries; several editions have been published in the United States; translations of his works have been made into French and German" (1958, 7). In addition to being one of the earliest known Afro-Cuban poets, Juan Francisco Manzano (1797–1854) wrote the only known slave narrative in the Spanish-speaking world. Machado de Assis (1839–1908) was a Brazilian novelist, poet, short story writer, and one of the most well-known and highly acclaimed writers of his time. Although Johnson mentions Harper, he does so only briefly and in the context of Dunbar's use of dialect. Analysis of Harper in the larger context of Johnson's Aframerican "world" allows us to consider the role of African American women poets in this hemispheric vision.

3. This historical figure is most commonly referred to as Zumbi both in Brazil and in the United States. Some historical documents transcribe the name Zombi. In this book, I use Zumbi to refer broadly to the historical figure and Zombi to refer to Harper's character in "Death of Zombi."

4. In *The Talking Book: African Americans and the Bible* (2006), Callahan argues that in fact African American literature does not "properly begin with writing" but rather that "it begins with religion" and, more specifically, Christianity. He argues that African American interpretation of the Bible and symbolic use of the Christ figure has permeated African American culture and, at a fundamental level, informed African American artistic production. He further maintains that "African Americans read their own collective experience into the agony and exaltation of Jesus. The story of the Christ child, blessed by God yet born in the shadow of poverty and violence, was their story. Jesus' humble birth in antiquity signified the humble origins of African peoples in modernity. In his impoverished entry into the world, Jesus turned the tables on earthly valuations" (2006, 236).

5. My use of the term *sign* here and discussion of Maceo as a figure "signifying" a symbolic redemption draws on Ferdinand de Saussure's theory of "the sign" as described in his *Course in General Linguistics* (1974). Saussure maintained that language is comprised of a series of linkages between sound and thought which ultimately constructs a system of language made up of pairings between signifier (form) and signified (concept). The *signifier* and the *signified* combine to produce the *sign*. We can understand this poem's process in the same way. Harper employs the figure of Maceo as a signifier, signifying the concept of freedom and nationhood. The poem is structured around this process of signification; Maceo as a historical figure is semiologically linked to the African American racial and U.S. national contexts. Ultimately, Maceo becomes a *sign* for the African American struggle for freedom during the post-Reconstruction era in United States.

Chapter 2

1. The history of "race" as a concept in the U.S. and Cuban contexts diverges in the nineteenth century and, even more drastically, in the twentieth. After a failed attempt to "reform" the South, the Reconstruction era ended in the final decades of the nineteenth century and a class of "redeemers" emerged, restoring the rule of a white elite in the South nostalgic for the old caste hierarchy of the plantation system (Fireside 2004, 57–87). They fought avidly to reverse Reconstruction legislation in an effort to reestablish their hegemony and resist biological and social miscegenation. In 1896, the U.S. Supreme Court decided *Plessy v. Ferguson*, thereby legalizing racial segregation and further defining the boundary lines of racial segregation

in the South. Indeed, the symbolic appropriation of "blood" and racial purity prevailed in North American political and social "mythology." Throughout the colonial period and up until 1878, the "blood code" in Cuba prevented Cubans of African descent (and others who could not verify Catholic Christian ancestry) from pursuing higher education (Lane 2005, 145; Montejo Arrechea 1998, 39). Similarly, "black codes" in the Southern United States limited blacks' access to political power and reinforced racial hierarchies established during slavery. Although different fractional and biologically based definitions of race governed law in the United States, Cuban leaders like José Martí and Antonio Maceo sought to downplay racial difference in an effort to unite Cubans against the Spanish Crown.

2. As the United States moved into what became known as the Reconstruction period following the Civil War, so began a wave of North American immigration to Cuba and Cuban immigration to major cities in the United States, which extended into the close of the nineteenth century and into the twentieth. In "Telling Silences and Making Community: Afro-Cubans and African Americans in Ybor City and Tampa, 1899–1915," Nancy Raquel Mirabal (1998) discusses the immigration of Afro-Cubans to Florida. Nancy Hewitt's *Southern Discomfort: Women's Activism in Tampa, Florida, 1880* (2001) provides an extensive discussion the Afro-Cuban community in late nineteenth-century Cuba. In "Encounters in the African Atlantic World: the African Methodist Episcopal Church in Cuba," Jualynne E. Dodson (1998) documents the presence of African Americans in Cuba who were affiliated with an increasingly global African Methodist Episcopal (AME) church. According to Dodson, the relationship between the AME church and Afro-Cubans—particularly as a function of Bishop Henry McNeal Turner's "nationalistic vision"—was "problematic" but "founded on a shared racial consciousness developed through common historical experiences with social oppression" (1998, 89). Carmen Montejo Arrechea shows how the magazine *Minerva*, first published in 1888, represented a literary and intellectual exchange between Afro-Cubans and African Americans and linked black Cubans living in the United States in places like Tampa and New York (1998, 35–36). In 1869, a continually growing number of Cuban tobacco workers began immigrating to Key West, Florida, and later to other major cities in the United States (Castillo Téllez 2003, 10–11).

3. The ramifications of this geographic difference are extensive and complex and merit attention, and although these differences inform my analysis, I do not attempt a comprehensive macro-analysis of comparative Cuban and U.S. history. Instead, I use a close reading of two specific poems to suggest that their resonances might be indicative of a larger web of interlocking histories and poetics.

4. Throughout the Old Testament, particularly in the Pentateuch, God required the sacrifice of live animals for redemption for the sins of the Israelites.

5. I am referring again to Benedict Anderson's notion of "imagined" communities. See introduction, note 5.

6. The "deserts" of black life in the South had yet to sing during Harper's lifetime. By the mid-1890s, incidents of lynching in the South had reached an all-time high (Hahn 2003, 427). Organized violence against blacks especially threatened literate, financially independent, or openly opinionated black men (Hahn 2003, 425). Frederick Douglass's essay "Lynch Law in the South" appeared in *North American Reviews* in July 1892 (Douglass 2000). The "revival of lynch law," Douglas wrote, "shows that prejudice and hatred have increased in bitterness with the increasing interval between the time of slavery and now.... When the negro is degraded and ignorant he conforms to a popular standard of what he should be. When he shakes off his rags and wretchedness and presumes to be a man, and a man among men, he contradicts this popular standard and becomes an offence to his surroundings" (2000, 223–24). As a result of antiblack sentiment and the strategic attack on the black male population in the South, public protest was largely up to educated African Americans outside of the South (Hahn

2003, 428) who, like Harper, sympathized with the cause but were not the immediate targets of white violence.

7. From the time Christians fleeing persecution in England perceived America as a "promised land," a Canaan of religious freedom, the exodus narrative has informed American national identity. According to Sacvan Bercovitch, early American Puritans perceived America as a "New World Canaan" (142) that they would enter as a "new chosen people" (136). In *Beyond Ethnicity*, Werner Sollors identifies the exodus as one of "America's central themes" and maintains that its use in American literature has placed a "typological hold on the American imagination" (44). Michael Walzer argues that the exodus story became "a part of the cultural consciousness of the West" such that a number of events and political relationships could be told through it (7). For Walzer, the exodus is not a narrative of divine intervention alone, but also of human striving against oppression. It tells a political history of a people moving from a figurative wilderness to Canaan, from slavery to freedom. The exodus can be seen then, according to Walzer, as a "model for messianic and millenarian thought, and it is also a standing alternative to it-a secular and historical account of "redemption," an account that does not require the miraculous transformation of the material world but sets God's people marching through the world toward a better place within it . . . The Exodus is not a lucky escape from misfortune. Rather, the misfortune has a moral character, and the escape has a world-historical meaning" (17; 21).

8. Also published later as a part of the *Ofrendas Mayabequinas* volume, "Redención" first appeared in *Minerva* on February 15, 1889.

9. Cuba officially abolished slavery in 1886, three years before the publication of "Redención."

10. In a later poem titled "Plegaria ante Cristo Crucificado" (Prayer Before [the] Crucified Christ) (1920), Ayala draws a direct link between Christ's suffering and that of the poem's speaker. "¡No sean pérdidas para mí! ¡Dios Mío! / yo te imploro postrada ante la cruz, / y en tu sagrado corazón confío / ¡Oyeme buen Jesús! / Tú, que sabes los duelos de mi alma, / que ves mi lucha con el mundo impío; / del conturbado corazón, la calma / vuélveme Cristo mío" [Be not prostrate before the cross, I beg you, and in your sacred heart I trust. Hear me well, Jesus! You, who know the pains of my soul, who sees my struggle with this godless world; come back to me my Lord, the calm for my troubled heart] (Ayala 1926, 227–28).

11. In his seminal work *Contrapunto cubano del tobaco y el azúcar* (Cuban Counterpoint of Tobacco and Sugar) (1940), Fernando Ortiz discusses the pervasiveness of biblical justifications for Cuban slavery. According to him, "la esclavitud de los negros y luego la de los indios, como fatalidad de raza, tenían un remancha reglioso especial, sacado arbitrariamente de las Sagradas Escrituras" (the enslavement of the Negros and later of the Indians, as a consequence of race, have a particular religious mark, taken arbitrarily from the Holy Scriptures) (1987, 349). The idea that "los nietos de Cam fueron los negros y esclavos" (blacks and slaves were the descendants of Ham)—which Ortiz called the "pérfida tesis del racismo bíblico" (treacherous thesis of biblical racism)—was still used against black Cubans and the *independentistas* even up to the end of the nineteenth century.

One Spanish priest writing in 1896 validated "Noah's curse" as a rationalization for slavery in Cuba and characterized the involvement of the "raza negra" in the struggle for independence as a blatant abuse of its freedom, writing, "En cuanto a los motivos que aleguen los negros para contra España, opinamos que no tienen ninguno fundado. La raza negra sufre las consecuencias de un castigo y de una maldición que el Pentateuco nos refiere al hablar de Noé y de sus hijos; su inferioriad viene perpetuándose a través de los siglos. La redención de Jesucristo comprende a todos los hombres según nos enseña el dogma católico; pero las naciones y los individuos de dicha raza negra han abusado de su libertad, negándose a participar de los beneficios que el Salvador nos mereció, derramando su divina sangre por todos los hombres ... El continente negro rehusó la libertad cristiana, y es víctima de la esclavitud del demonio y de las pasiones de los hombres malos" [As for the reasons that Negroes alleged against Spain, we believe them to be unfounded. The black race suffers the consequences of a punishment and a curse that we are referred to by the Pentateuch when it speaks of Noah and his sons; its inferiority continues to perpetuate itself over the centuries. As Catholic dogma teaches us, the redemption of Jesus Christ includes all men; but the nations and individuals of the aforementioned black race have abused their liberty, neglecting to take part in the benefits that the Savior deserves from us, shedding his divine blood for all men ... The black Continent refused Christian freedom, and is the victim of slavery and of the demon and the passions of evil men] (Casas 1896, 30–31).

12. See Aline Helg's *Our Rightful Share* (1995) for an extensive discussion of black Cubans' involvement in the War for Independence in Cuba. Helg argues that "Afro-Cubans" saw their wars for independence as a way of ensuring equal rights and opportunities in postwar Cuba. According to Helg, these hopes were disappointed and the reality after the war was not one of racial equality.

13. Calixto Castillo Téllez characterizes this period preceding the Spanish-American War as a "reposo turbulento" (turbulent repose). According to Castillo Téllez, during this "reposo turbulento ... o sea, en la etapa preparatoria de la 'guerra necesaria' preconizada por José Martí, fue aumentando la solidaridad de la Iglesia Protestante con la causa cubana. Esto se hizo más evidente y en la población nordente y tomó mayor fuerza política en la población norteamericana al producirse el estallido patriótico del 24 de febrero de 1895. Entonces, la Iglesia Protestante tuvo una notable participación en la defensa de los ideales independentistas de los cubanos" [turbulent repose ... or rather, during the preparatory period of the 'necessary war' advocated for by José Martí, the solidarity grew between the Protestant Church with the Cuban cause. This became most evident among the population in the northeast and had the most political force in the North American population, producing the patriotic explosion of February 24, 1895. Therefore, the Protestant church played a significant role in the defense of independentista ideals of the Cubans] (2003, 44).

14. According to Fernando Ortiz, beliefs about "las razas" in Cuba reflected ideas circulating outside of Cuba and throughout the Americas. "El vulgo," writes Ortiz, "creía en la existencia de razas inferiores y superiores, como siglos atrás creyó en la sangre azul de la nobleza y la sangre sucua [i.e., sucia] de la plebeyez, y aceptaba la predestinación de unas *razas selectas* llamadas a dominar siempre sobre otras, fatalmente condenadas a servidumbre" [The common people believed in the existence of inferior and superior races, just as centuries before they believed in the blue blood of the noble classes and the dirty blood of the lower classes, and accepted the predestination of a few *chosen races*, called forever to dominate over others (who were) fatally condemned to servitude] (1953, 8).

15. Ayala's subtle allusion to the Israelites is not as extensive as Harper's allegorical use of the Exodus. One possible explanation for this difference is the fact that the system of *coartación* in Cuba—by which slaves manumitted themselves gradually (literally, piece by piece)—had existed in Cuba since the slave code of 1842. According to Philip A. Howard, the system of coartación allowed a large number of Cuban slaves to earn their own freedom prior to abolition (1998, 6).

Chapter 3

1. The author notes in *Ofrendas Mayabequinas* that says that this line "Se refiere a un folleto que se titulaba 'Cuba y su gente' donde se denigraba a la raza de color y sobre todo a la mujer" (1926, 17).

2. José Martí's theory of race in Cuba informed the independence movement. Writing about this particular period, during the Cuban struggle for independence, Fernando Ortiz claimed that Martí's "misión histórica" (historic mission) was to "elaborar y darle al pueblo cubano la ideología que debía capacitarlo para ganar sus libertades, constituirse y sostenerse como república democrática y progresista" (prepare and give to the Cuban people the ideology that would enable it to gain its liberty, to establish itself and sustain itself as a democratic and progressive republic) (Ortiz 1953 7 8). To do so he was forced to "considerar el problema de las razas como uno de los más fundamentales e ineludibles de la formación de Cuba" (to consider the problem of the races as one of the most fundamental and unavoidable in the formation of Cuba) (1953, 8). José Martí's ideological response to such ideas came to characterize Cuban twentieth-century nationalism in that it supplanted a categorization of "race" with that of *cubanidad* (Cuban-ness).

3. Gualberto Gómez wrote in "Programa" in 1890:

> Durante tres centurias, cultura y riqueza, monopolizadas fueron por el blanco . . . Al negro, en cambio, se le trajo para que viviera como esclavo. . . . Vino ignorante de las selvas africanas y en el latifundio donde se le encerró, más que nada fué preciso que se procurara la atrofia de su inteligencia; cultura y esclavitud son términos antagónicos. Esclavo e ignorante, claro se está que la riqueza y el poder resultaban cosas vedadas para el negro. (1954b, 231)
>
> [For three centuries, el blanco monopolized culture and wealth . . . El negro on the other hand, was brought to live as a slave. . . . He came ignorant from the African jungles and, confined to the plantation, it was necessary more than ever to dull his intelligence; culture and slavery are antagonistic terms. A slave and ignorant, it is evident that wealth and power were prohibited for el negro.]

4. Morúa Delgado identified education as the primary means of social and economic elevation of black Cubans, also a strategy of assimilation and integration (Howard 1998, 166). He believed that an "immoral people, a perverted people [could] never be free" (quoted in Howard 1998, 167) and posited education "from our nebulous past" (quoted in Howard 1998, 166) and societies for moral instruction. "How can we condemn ourselves to be victims when we can easily be heroes?" he claimed. "Our societies are responsible for perfecting men who lack principles . . . [and] from the centers they will leave as citizens who will gloriously carry the title of 'freemen,' a new name for all of them" (quoted in Howard 1998, 166). According to Morúa Delgado, schools were like "mother[s] who take our children from our homes only to return them later with nourishing intelligence, which in the end immediately strengthens society" (quoted in Howard 1998, 166). He wrote "Instrucción, Solo Instrucción," which appeared in *El Ciudadano*—a decidedly pro-Spanish newspaper—and claimed that "the increase in the number of schools for blacks was the best step toward acquiring liberty for the race" (quoted in Howard 1998, 166).

5. The idea of racial uplift and trying to lift the stain: Harper has a similar sentiment in "The Rallying Cry" (1891) published in *The Christian Recorder*, where she admonishes blacks to "Dream not of ease nor pleasure, / Nor honor, wealth nor fame, / Till from the dust you've lifted / Our long dishonored name. / And crown that name with glory / By deeds of holy worth." In Foster (1990, 265–66).

6. The poem "Defence of Fort McHenry" written by Francis Scott Key in 1814 later became the lyrics for the "Star-Spangled Banner," which in 1931 was official declared the national anthem of the United States.

7. "So God created man in his own image, in the image of God created he him; male and female created he them" (Genesis 1:27).

Chapter 4

1. As Joaquim Nabuco suggests in the following excerpt from *O Abolicionismo*, one of the goals of abolitionism in Brazil was to challenge the opposition of master and slave:

> No Brasil a questão não é, como nas colônias européias, um movimento de generosidade em favor de uma classe de homens vítimas de uma opressão injusta a grande distância das nossas praias. A raça negra não tão pouco, para nós, uma raça inferior ... Para nós, a raça negra é um elemento de considerável importância nacional, estreitamente ligada por infinitas relações orgânicas à nossa contituição, parte integrante do povo brasileiro. Por outro lado, a emancipação não significa tão somente o termo da injustiça de que o escravo é martir, mas também a eliminação simultânea dos dois tipos contrários, e no fundo de mesmos: o escravo e o *senhor*. (1998, 36)

> [In Brazil the situation is not, as it is in European colonies, a motion of generosity in favor of a class of men who are victims of unjust oppression far away from our shores. Nor is the black race an inferior race ... For us, the black race is an element of considerable national importance, closely linked through countless organic linkages to our continuation, an integral part of the Brazilian people. On the other hand, emancipation does not only mean the end of injustice for the slave and martyr, but also the simultaneous elimination of other kind of oppositions, and at the base of these: the slave and the master.]

2. The verb *arrancar* denotes a separation achieved by force or violence, to extract or liberate by force.

3. The Portuguese word *laço* refers to a forced binding that is not easily undone. I use the English word *chain* here because it most accurately maintains the poem's system of metaphors, providing the appropriate opposition to flight and extending the metaphor of the prison.

4. The full text of Romans 6:3–10 (King James version) reads "Know ye not, that so many of us as were baptized into Jesus Christ were baptized into his death? Therefore we are buried with him by baptism into death: that like as Christ was raised up from the dead by the glory of the Father, even so we also should walk in newness of life. For if we have been planted together in the likeness of his death, we shall be also in the likeness of his resurrection: Knowing this, that our old man is crucified with him, that the body of sin might be destroyed, that henceforth we should not serve sin. For he that is dead is freed from sin. Now if we be dead with Christ, we believe that we shall also live with him: Knowing that Christ being raised from the dead dieth no more; death hath no more dominion over him. For in that he died, he died unto sin once: but in that he liveth, he liveth unto God."

5. Although the actual process of abolition in Brazil was gradual and approximately 90 percent of slaves were legally free by 1887 (Hasenbalg 164), the legal abolition of slavery inaugurated the *idea* of a new Brazil—one free from slavery, free to progress as a modern nation. Newspapers and magazines played a major role in circulating this idea of a free Brazilian republic.

6. A stipulation of the Free Womb Law (1871) stated that slaveholders could choose between the labor of "free-born" children until they reached the age of twenty-one or monetary indemnification from the government.

7. Though Protestant clergy in the United States made up a large portion of the Abolitionists, religion in Brazil did not have an antislavery mission.

8. The Cult of the Virgin Mary, a movement that began in 1854 and continued to gain stature during the second half of the nineteenth century, challenged male domination of the institutional structure of the Catholic and Protestant church (Barman 2002, 125).

9. My discussion of gender and conceptions of womanhood here is an unavoidable problematic due to the fact that the terms "woman" and "mother" referred to elite women of distinguishable European ancestry exclusively. The term "mãe" (mother) was used exclusively to refer to the white woman who bore her own children as distinct from the "mãe preta" or "ama-de-leite" used to describe enslaved black women charged to nurse and care for white children of a *senhora* (Giacomini 1988, 34). Essentially, being a woman in Brazil at this time meant rejecting the very duties that characterized enslaved women of African descent—namely, manual labor and the daily business of marketing and childrearing.

10. See Roger A. Kittleso(2005) for a more extensive discussion of how women functioned as a symbolic presence in the abolition movement. According to Kittleson, they were incorporated as nonpolitical, moral agents, particularly during the new phase of abolitionism that began in the 1870s where activists "put moralized, feminized visions of abolitionism at the service of an emerging social movement" (2005, 105). As a result, Brazilian abolitionism both "moved women's activities toward the center of public politics" and "embraced dominant notions about women's roles" (2005, 106).

11. I am referring here generally to the free population to describe the climate of gender stipulations according to general Brazilian society. Part of that was the exclusion of enslaved girls of African descent from such a consideration.

12. Also during the second half of the nineteenth century there emerged a viable women's movement. A number of publications emerged dedicated explicitly to women and the question of women's emancipation, including *O Sexo Feminino*, *O Jornal das Senhoras*, and *O Bello Sexo*. Born in the same region as Auta de Souza, Nísia Floresta Brasileria Augusta (1809–1885) became a major intellectual and one of the first women's rights activists. In addition to providing a translation of Mary Wollstonecraft's *A Vindication of the Rights of Women*, Augusta advocated the increased education of women, the higher social status of women, freedom of religion and the abolition of slavery (Hahner 1990, 14). At the same time, according to Brazil's constitution of 1891, "active citizenship" was only open to literate males twenty-one years of age or older (Scully and Paton 2005, 18).

13. I allude here to how Auta's work resonates with Cristina Ayala's and Frances Harper's work as I argue in chapter 3. In the case of these three poets, *race*—that is, their racial affiliation by way of their African ancestry—does not represent an uncontested mark of sameness, but pulls together disparate parts in a common narrative of transatlantic slavery and creates a space in which to construct theories of reading that facilitate the process of relating language and identity. Race conjures a set of historical landmarks, symbols, and themes that, in coming together, produce meaning for the text. This process goes beyond authorial intent, beyond biographical analysis, and allows us to think about the texts as a space in which these symbols and themes come together in organic ways to produce meanings that both create and challenge the concepts that form collective and individual identities. These meanings not only become relevant for the period in which they are produced but are also critical to retrospective readings, particularly as related to canon formation.

Conclusion

1. By this time, the magazine was in its second phase of publication and was called *Minerva: Revista Universal Ilustrada*.

2. *Minerva: Revista Universal Ilustrada* 8: [3?].

3. We should not take for granted Ayala's bold stance here. *Minerva* was a major literary and political platform for female and male writers that confronted racial concerns as well as promoted literary aspiration. Ayala recognized that a bold poetic voice might threaten her

position in society. She expressed her initial ambivalence about being involved with the magazine in a letter to the editor:

> Y ¿cuál es el m[ó]vil que me ha impulsado [a] escribir hoy en MINERVA? Os lo manifestaré, hallando muy lógicos los razonamientos del artículo que he citado de "La Antorcha," que me han servido de gran estímulo. Estando yo sosteniendo una lucha en mi interior con el deseo de cooperar y el temor que abrigaba, ha sido vencido éste, por las alentadoras frases de ese artículo que nos dice: <<*Que la prensa ilustrada sabe que la clase de color viene con sus propios esfuerzos trabajando por la emancipación de la ignorancia, de aquí que con justicia tiene que ser indulgente con nosotras en todo aquello que se relacione con las bellas letras y el buen gusto.*>> Esas frases son las que me han estimulado, y me han animado, porque doy fe [a] la veracidad de esas apreciaciones, quizás sin ese estímulo no me hubiese atrevido nunca, señor Director, distraer vuestra ocupada atención, pues si alguna merece indulgencia soy yo, y espero me la dispenséis. (1889, 4)
>
> [And what motive has driven me to write today in *Minerva*? Finding the arguments in the article that I have cited by "La Antorcha" very logical and that have given me much motivation, I will make [my motive] clear. [I was] enduring an internal struggle with the desire to collaborate and the fear that enveloped me, this fear has been overcome by the inspiring words of this article that tells us: *"The elite press knows that the colored class comes by its own efforts working towards emancipation from ignorance, from this it justly must be gracious with us in everything related to elegant poetics and good taste."* These words have motivated me, they have animated me, because I believe these assessments are true, and perhaps without this motivation I would have never dared, Mr. Director, draw your attention, but if anyone merits grace I do and I hope you will give it to me.]

4. The idea of a "literatura negra" characterized by a rejection of the use of language and literary models of *os brancos* (Barbosa 2002), evolved alongside a rise in racial consciousness in Brazil facilitated primarily by the Movimento Negro Unificado and the Frente Negra Brasileira in the 1930s and 1940s. Although poets like Castro Alves included the themes of slavery and black figures in their work, twentieth-century scholars and writers distinguish literatura negra by its use of distinctly African cultural referents, language, speech patterns and rhythms (Bastide 1943, 36; Bernd 1992, 13). As a result, most scholars begin the canon of Afro-Brazilian literature with Domingos Caldas Barbosa (1739–1800), whose poetry was heavily influenced by *lundu*—dance music derived from Afro-Brazilian "*batuque* round dances" (Crook 2005, 64). Other major figures include Luís Gama—the poet most closely affiliated with black Brazilian abolitionism and widely celebrated in late nineteenth and early twentieth century by the black Brazilian press—and João da Cruz e Sousa (1861–1898), poet and son of freed slaves.

5. In the essay "Black Women Writing Worlds: Textual Production, Domination, and the Critical Voice," Carole Boyce Davies argues that black women's writing is a "series of boundary-crossing literatures, not a fixed geographically, ethnically, or nationally bound literature" (1994, 1).

6. In his study of Candomblé in the "black Atlantic," for instance, Matory argues that the development of Afro-Brazilian Candomblé is proof that transnational networks existed even during the transatlantic slave trade, predating our contemporary use of the term "transnational" by hundreds of years (2005, 3). Matory emphasizes the transnational nature of so-called national cultures, arguing that in fact "diasporas create their homelands" (2005, 3). He

continues, "Something greater than 'collective memory,' the endurance of African 'logical principles,' white-dominated local contexts, or the passive reception of ideas from the 'dominant' race or class has shaped black Atlantic religion"—that is, a transnational, Afro-Atlantic dialogue (2005, 16).

Epilogue

1. As early as the sixteenth century, the Spanish empire had imported Africans in to Cuba to work the sugar mills and, later, coffee fields. Likewise, enslaved Africans worked cotton and tobacco fields in the Southern colonies of North America. After the Haitian revolution in 1791 destroyed the system of slavery in what had been the world's largest sugar supplier, Cuba became even more central to the European colonial economy. Africans were shipped to Cuba in such numbers that the Spanish creole elite began to worry about the potential for a similar slave rebellion in Cuba.

2. A poem in the March 18, 1866, edition of the *New Orleans Picayune* read:
>Oh, give me a ship with sail and with wheel
>And let me be off to happy Brazil
>Home of the sunbeam—great kingdom of heat,
>With woods evergreen and snake forty feet~
>Land of the diamond—bright nation of pearls,
>With monkey's aplenty, and Portuguese girls!
>Oh give me a ship with sail and with wheel,
>And let me be off to happy Brazil!
>I yearn to feel her perpetual spring,
>And shake by the hand Dom Pedro her king.
>Kneel at his feet—call him, "My Royal Boss!"
>And receive in return, "Welcome old Hoss!" (Harter 1985, 39)

3. Mansbridge argues for the politics of "everyday talk," defining the political as "that which the public ought to discuss" (1999, 214). In her essay "Everyday Talk in the Deliberative System," she expands on Easton's expansion of the scope of what is deemed "political" and defines the political as "that which the public ought to discuss." Using this definition, Mansbridge includes "talk" that is persuasive or that challenges the status quo in the category of political. She makes permeable and arbitrary the boundaries drawn between formal and informal politics, so-called political talk and what she calls "everyday talk." Drawing on her theory, I suggest that poetry functions in this deliberative system as an impetus for and instigator of deliberation, as an interrogator of both linguistic and social "truths" or norms. It is also a vehicle through which "everyday talk" enters the realm of aesthetics and politics. This use of poetry and component of the poetic aesthetic has characterized the tradition of afrodescendente literature especially because the denial of traditional political "say so" has been so much a part of its legacy.

4. I consider the possibility of how these twentieth-century manifestations might echo a more nuanced manifestation of this national "imagined communities" (which I discuss in more depth in chapters 2, 3, and 4) in the work of nineteenth-century poets of African descent. The *intra-* and *inter*textual analysis of this epilogue prefaces a more exhaustive analysis of three nineteenth-century poets—Ayala, Auta, and Harper—whose work gives us further insight into the textual manifestations of this transnational space during the period in which slavery was completely abolished in the Western Hemisphere and the ideological and political formulation of nation-states was under way. Ultimately, my reading aims to distill the implications of this transnational imaginary on the thematic, typological, structural, and lexical aspects of their work.

5. Kimberly Benston identifies this period in the literary history of African American literature as one that challenged the European philosophy that placed literary meaning strictly *outside* of the text as an expressive and performative act. Benston defines African American modernism as that which "designates that politico-aesthetic ferment arising with the black consciousness movement of the 1960s" (2000, 2). Benston challenges the simplistic opposition of "expression-as-structure" and "expression-as-event," dislodging such contingent binaries as assimilation and nationalism, language and self, form and content, oral and written, craft and politics. She suggests instead that criticism locate itself "at the challenging juncture of ideological and aesthetic concerns" (2000, 6).

6. During a trip to Cuba in 1978, Sonia Sanchez met Nancy Morejón and poet Nicolás Guillén.

7. Most probably derived from an African language, *balacobaco* is a popular colloquialism meaning something good or nice to look at, while at the same time carrying the connotation of mass confusion. The speaker suggests that her blackness is both aesthetically pleasing and something that will confuse old ways of thinking about identity.

8. *Enfim Nos/Finally Us* is an anthology of Afro-Brazilian women poets coedited by Miriam Alves and Carolyn Richardson Durham. With its publication, Durham and Alves aimed to document what they and Brazilian poets Esmerelda Ribeiro and Sônia Fátima da Conceção identified as the "atividade abundante creativa e teorica das mulheres afro-brasileiras" (the abundant creative and theoretical activity of Afro-Brazilian women). Such women were producing (and had been for over a decade in this context) work that was both aesthetically rich and political engaged, but also work that had been marginalized and virtually ignored on the national and international level.

9. Mieko Nishida suggests that in fact the use of "Negro" as a signifier for something other than poverty and powerlessness in the late twentieth century in Salvador, Brazil, was a political act that propelled various fleeting black movements throughout the twentieth century (2003, 165).

10. Nascimento's project fell in line with the aims of the sparse but definitive presence of black nationalist politics in modern Brazil. Founded in 1931, at the height of an ongoing effort to *whiten* Brazil through the governmentally subsidized emigration of Europeans to Brazil, the Frente Negra Brasileira (FNB; Black Brazilian Front), for instance, advocated racial solidarity among black Brazilians and active political movement against discriminatory practice in Brazil. FBN leaders urged black Brazilians to identify with their negro brothers, espousing a rhetoric of collective consciousness (Jones de Olivera 2003, 109). FNB members held rallies to protest the barring of black Brazilians from hotels, bars, schools, and other public spaces. It used its primary publication, *Voz da Raça* (Voice of the Race), to communicate its goal of inverting the prevailing racial ideology. The FNB fought against any form of integration that would suppress black Brazilian cultures and history. It challenged the terms of integration through an assertion of black nationalism.

11. The dictatorship of the Getúlio Vargas regime prohibited all coverage of Black Power activity in the United States and outlawed political parties, especially those with any hint of a race-based politics.

12. *Batuque* refers to a category of African-derived dances; *tocaia* is an ambush or trap.

13. Through the essay "El poeta Walt Whitman" (1887), Martí introduced Whitman to Latin America and demonstrated his knowledge of the poet (Grandin 2006, par. 6).

14. According to Doris Sommer,

> While white Cubans were negotiating their continued privilege under one empire or another, black and mullato countrymen were mounting a struggle for independence. Whites, including Villaverde and his stubbornly discreet narrator, tried

for a long time not to acknowledge that it was the only way to win freedom for Cuba. They told themselves a wishful story about annexation bringing gradual freedom. When that made no sense, some retrieved the equally unconvincing story about autonomy and Spanish reform. Neither of these stories was realistic, but both kept white privilege at the center. Meanwhile blacks were telling a counter-story (as they would in the novel): that the United States couldn't be trusted, which agreed with Saco and other reformists, and that Spain was a losing proposition too, which agreed with annexationists. Because both imperial partners were bad for Cuban independence was the only and obvious route. The only thing lost in this story was white privilege. Cubans of color argued and acted on this clarity; and the white leaders (along with Villaverde's narrator) continued to act as if they couldn't put the picture together. (1991, 200)

15. Brazilian intellectual and anthropologist Raimundo Nina Rodrigues (1862–1906) hailed the abolition of slavery in 1888 as "a maior e mas útil das reformes" (the best and most useful of reforms). In his ethnological work *Os Africanos no Brasil* (1905) he deemed the "problema Negro no Brasil" (the "Negro" problem in Brazil) the "esfigue do nosso futuro" (sphinx of our future) (1982, 1). He proudly proclaimed that the Brazilian "breed" of "Negro" was superior to that of the United States and that prejudice in Brazil simply did not exist. In the same breath, he went on to support the idea that the "raça negra" was in fact at an earlier, more primitive stage of intellectual and social development than its white counterpart and therefore inherently inferior (1982, 5).

16. See Euclides da Cunha's *Os Sertões* (1902) for instance, in which he examines "o sertanejo" in an effort to determine an authentically Brazilian type and a Brazilian culture undiluted by Western influence.

BIBLIOGRAPHY

Adorno, Theodor W. *Aesthetic Theory*: Newly translated, edited, and with a translator's introduction by Robert Hullot-Kentor. Minneapolis: University of Minnesota Press, 1997.
Almeida Pereira, Edimilson de. "Pulsações de Poesia Brasileira Contemporânea: o Grupo Quilombhoje e a Vertente Afro-Brazileira." In Niyi Alfolabi [et al.], eds. *The Afro-Brazilian Mind: Contemporary Literature and Cultural Criticism*. Trenton: Africa World, 2007. 165–90.
———. "Survey of African-Brazilian Literature." Trans. Phyllis Press. *Callaloo* 18, no. 4 (African Brazilian Literature: a Special Issue) (Autumn 1995): 875–80.
Altunaga, Eliseo. "The Dead Come at Midnight: Scripting the White Aesthetic/Black Ethic." In Cynthia Nelson and Jean Stubbs, eds. *Afro-Cuban Voices: On Race and Identity in Contemporary Cuba*. Gainesville: University Press of Florida, 2000. 87–96.
Alves, Miriam. "Enfim . . . Nós: Por Quê?" In Miriam Alves and Carolyn Richardson Durham, eds. *Enfim . . . Nós/Finally Us: Escritoras Negras Brasileiras Contemporâneas/Contemporary Black Brazilian Women Writers*. Colorado Springs: Three Continents, 1994. 5–15.
Alves, Miriam, and Carolyn Richardson Durham, Eds. *Enfim . . . Nós/Finally Us: Escritoras Negras BrasileirasContemporâneas/Contemporary Black Brazilian Women Writers*. Colorado Springs: Three Continents, 1994.
Anderson, Benedict R. O. *Imagined Communities: Reflections on the Origin and Spread of Nationalism*. London: Verso, 1991.
Assis Duarte, Eduardo de. "Literatura Afro-Brasileira: Um Conceito em Construção." In Niyi Alfolabi [et al.], eds. *The Afro-Brazilian Mind: Contemporary Literature and Cultural Criticism*. Trenton: Africa World, 2007: 103–12.
Atherton, Catherine. "Introduction." In Catherine Atherton, ed. *Form and Content in Didactic Poetry*. Bario: Levanti Editori, 1997.
Augusto dos Santos, Sales, and Laurence Hallewell. "Historical Roots of Whitening in Brazil." *Latin American Perspectives*. 29, no. 1 (January 2002): 61–82.

Ayala, Cristina. *Ofrendas Mayabequinas*. Güines: Tosco Heraldo, 1926.

———. "Me adhiero." *Minerva* Año II, Núm. 7 (26 de Enero de 1889): 2–3.

Azevedo, Celia Maria Marinho de. *Onda negra, medo branco: O negro no imaginário das elites, sexulo XIX*. Rio de Janeiro: Paz e Terra, 1987.

Azougarh, Abdeslam, Ed. *Juan Francisco Manzano: Esclavo Poeta el la Isla de Cuba*. Valencia: Episteme, 2000.

Bambara, Toni Cade. "Language and the Writer." In Toni Morrison, ed. *Deep Sightings and Rescue Missions: Fiction, Essays, and Conversations*. New York: Pantheon, 1996. 139–45.

Baraka, Amiri. "Cuba Libre." *The Leroi Jones/Amiri Baraka Reader*. New York: Thunder's Mouth, 1991. 125–60.

———. *Funk Lore: New Poems (1984–1995)*. Ed. Paul Vangelisti. Los Angeles: Littoral, 1996.

———. "Notes on History of African/Afro-American Culture." *Daggers and Javelins: Essays, 1974–1979*. New York: Morrow, 1984, 209–33.

———. "The Myth of 'Negro' Literature." In Angelyn Mitchell, ed. *Within the Circle*. Durham, N.C.: Duke University Press, 1994. 165–71.

Barbosa, José Carlos. *Negro Não Entra na Igreja: Espia da banda de fora Protestantismo e Escravidão no Brasil Império*. Piracicaba: Editora UNIMEP, 2002.

Barman, Roderick J. *Princess Isabel of Brazil: Gender and Power in the Nineteenth Century*. Wilmington, Del.: Scholarly Resources, 2002.

Barnstone, Willis *The Poetics of Translation: History, Theory, Practice*. New Haven, Conn.: Yale University Press, 1993.

Bastide, Roger. *Poesia afro-brasileira*. São Paulo: Martins, 1943.

Beckles, Hilary M. "Female Enslavement in the Caribbean and Gender Ideologies." In Paul Lovejoy, ed. *Identity in the Shadow of Slavery*, 2nd ed. London: Continuum, 2000. 163–82.

Bell, James Madison. *Poetical Works of James Madison Bell*. Lansing, Mich.: Wynkoop, 1994.

Benston, Kimberly. *Performing Blackness: Enactments of African-American Modernism*. London: Routledge, 2000.

Bercovitch, Sacvan. "The Typology of America's Mission." *American Quarterly* 30, no. 2 (summer 1978): 135–55.

Bernd, Zilá, Org. *Poesia Negra Brasileira: Antología*. Porto Alegre: Age, 1992.

Bhabha, Homi K. "Dissemination: Time, Narrative and the Margins of the Modern Nation." *The Location of Culture*. London: Routledge, 2004. 199–244.

———. "Narrating the Nation." In Homi K. Bhabha, ed. *Nation and Narration*. London: Routledge, 1990. 1–22.

Birth of a Nation. Dir. D. W. Griffith. 1915. (DVD, Image Entertainment, 1995).

Boggs, Colleen Glenney. *Transnationalism and American Literature: Literary Translation 1773–1892*. New York: Routledge, 2007.

Boyd, Melba Joyce. *Discarded Legacy: Politics and Poetics in the Life of Frances E. W. Harper 1825–1911*. Detroit: Wayne State University Press, 1994.

Brickhouse, Anna. *Transamerican Literary Relations and the Nineteenth-Century Public Sphere*. Cambridge: Cambridge University Press, 2004.

Brock, Lisa, and Digna Castañeda Fuertes, eds. *Between Race and Empire: African-Americas and Cubans before the Cuban Revolution*. Philadelphia: Temple University Press, 1998.

Brown-Marshall, Gloria J. *Race, Law and American Society: 1607 to Present*. New York: Routledge, 2007.

Calamari, Barbara, and Sandra DiPasqua. *Visions of Mary*. New York: Abrams, 2004.

Callahan, Allen. *The Talking Book: African Americans and the Bible*. New Haven, Conn.: Yale University Press, 2006.
Carreras, Julio Ángel. *Esclavitud, Abolición y Racismo*. Havana: Ediciones Jurídicas, 1985.
Carpentier, Alejo. *Visión de América*. Barcelona: Seix Barral, 1999.
Casas, Juan Bautista. *Estudios acerca del régimen y administración de España en Ultramar*. Madrid: San Francisco de Sales, 1896.
Cascudo, Luís da Câmara. *Vida Breve de Auta de Souza*. Recife: Imprensa Oficial, 1961.
Castellón, Manuel García. "Luiz Silva (Cuti): Afro-Brasileño, Paladin de Dignidad Étnica y Poeta de Liberación." In Niyi Alfolabi [et al.], ed. *The Afro-Brazilian Mind: Contemporary Literature and Cultural Criticism*. Trenton: Africa World, 2007.
Castillo, Debra A. *Talking Back: Toward a Latin American Feminist Literary Criticism*. Ithaca, N.Y.: Cornell University Press, 1992.
Castillo Téllez, Calixto. *La Iglesia Protestante en las luchas por la independencia de Cuba (1898–1898)*. Havana: Editorial de Ciencias Sociales, 2003.
Cespedes, Africa. "A Cuba" *Minerva* Año II, Num. 11 (16 Marzo 1889): 3.
Clark, Kathleen Ann. *Defining Moments: African American Commemoration and Political Culture in the South, 1863–1913*. Chapel Hill: University of North Carolina Press, 2005.
Coneição, Sônia Fátima da. "Branca Historia." *Cadernos Negros: Poemas*, no. 9. (1986).
Conceição da Silva, Jônatas. *Vozes Quilombolas: uma poética brasileira*. Salvador: EDUFBA, 2004.
Conrad, Robert Edgar. *The Destruction of Brazilian Slavery, 1850–1888*. Berkeley: University of California Press, 1972.
Cooper, Anna Julia. *A Voice from the South*. New York: Oxford University Press, 1990.
Cortez, Jayne. "The Guitars I Used to Know." *Jazz Fan Looks Back*. Brooklyn: Hanging Loose, 2002. 79–81.
Crook, Larry. *Brazilian Music: Northeastern Traditions and the Heartbeat of a Modern Nation*. Santa Barbara, Calif.: ABC-CLIO, 2005.
Cruz e Sousa, João da. "Cárcere das Almas." *Últimos Sonetos*. Rio de Janeiro: UFSC/Fundação, 1984. 12.
Cunha, Euclides da. *Os Sertões*. 1902.
Daibert Junior, Robert. *Isabel, a "redentora" dos escravos: uma história da princesa entre olhares negros e brancos, 1846–1988*. Bauru: EDUSC, 2004.
Davies, Carole Boyce. *Black Women, Writing and Identity: Migrations of the Subject*. London: Routledge, 1994.
DeCosta Willis, Miriam. *Daughters of the Diaspora: Afra-Hispanic Writers*. Kingston: Ian Randle, 2003.
Degler, Carl N. *Neither Black nor White: Slavery and Race Relationships in Brazil in the United States*. New York: Macmillan, 1971.
Diniz Barreto, José. "Patria Livre." In Leonardo Dantas Silva, ed. *A Imprensa e a Abolição*. Recife: FUNDAJ, 1988. 2.
Diop, Christiane Yandé. "Présence Africaine: Foreword." In V. Y. Mudimbe, ed. *The Surreptitious Speech: Présence Africaine and the Politics of Otherness 1947–1987*. Chicago: University of Chicago Press, 1992. xiii–xvi.
Dodson, Jualynne E. "Encounters in the African Atlantic World: The African Methodist Episcopal Church in Cuba." In Lisa Brock and Digna Castañeda Fuertes, eds. *Between Race and Empire: African-Americans and Cubans before the Cuban Revolution*. Philadelphia: Temple University Press, 1998. 85–103.
Douglass, Frederick. "Lynch Law in the South." In Susan Harris Smith and Melanie Dawson, eds. *The American 1890s*. Durham, N.C.: Duke University Press, 2000. 220–25.

———. *Narrative of the Life of Frederick Douglass an American Slave; Written by Himself.* Benjamin Quarles, Ed. Cambridge, Mass.: Belknap Press, 1960.

Du Bois, W. E. B. "The Conservation of the Races, 1897." In Jacqueline M. Moore, *Booker T. Washington, W. E. B. Du Bois and the Struggle for Racial Uplift.* Wilmington, Del.: SR Books, 2003.

———. *The Souls of Black Folk: Essays and Sketches.* Chicago: McClurg, 1907.

Duke, Dawn. "How She Strikes Back: Images of Female Strength in Esmeralda Ribeiro's Writing." In Niyi Alfolabi [et al.] ed. *The Afro-Brazilian Mind: Contemporary Literature and Cultural Criticism.* Trenton: Africa World, 2007. 99–120.

Durham, Carolyn Richardson. "Space and Time: Afro-Brazilian History in the Poetry of Miriam Alves." *CLA Journal* 16, no. 2 (1997): 185–96.

Eagleton, Terry. *Literary Theory: An Introduction.* Cambridge, Mass.: Blackwell, 1996.

Easton, David. *The Political System: An Inquiry into the State of Political Science.* Chicago: University of Chicago Press, 1981.

Estuch, Leopoldo Horrego. *Martín Morúa Delgado Vida y Mensaje.* Havana: Sánchez, 1957.

Fanon, Frantz. *The Wretched of the Earth.* New York: Grove, 1963.

Ferreira Gomes, Ana Laudelina. "Introdução Para um Estudo da Vida e Obra de Auta de Souza." In *Auta de Souza, Horto*, 5th ed. Natal: Editora da UFRN, 2001.

Ferrer, Ada. *Insurgent Cuba: Race, Nation, and Revolution, 1868–1898.* Chapel Hill: University of North Carolina Press, 1999.

Fireside, Harvey. *Separate and Unequal: Homer Plessy and the Supreme Court Decision that Legalized Racism.* New York: Carroll and Graf, 2004.

Foner, Philip Sheldon. *Antonio Maceo: the "Bronze Titan" of Cuba's Struggle for Independence.* New York: Monthly Review, 1977.

———. *A History of Cuba and Its Relations with the United States, Vol. II, 1845–1895.* New York: International Publishers, 1963.

Font, América. "Mis Opiniones," *Minerva* Año I, núm. 4 (30 de Diciembre de 1888): 3.

Foster, Frances Smith, ed. *A Brighter Coming Day: A Frances Ellen Watkins Harper Reader.* New York: Feminist Press, 1990.

———. "Changing Concepts of the Black Woman." *Journal of Black Studies* 3, no. 4 (June 1973): 433–54.

Friedman, Lawrence J. *Inventors of the Promised Land.* New York: Knopf, 1975.

Fuente, Alejandro de la. *A Nation for All: Race, Inequality, and Politics in Twentieth-Century Cuba.* Chapel Hill: University of North Carolina Press, 2001.

Garnet, Henry Highland. "Excerpt of the Speech of Rev. Henry Highland Garnet." *Slavery in Cuba: A Report of the Proceedings of the Meeting Held at Cooper Institute, New York City, December 13, 1872.* New York: Office of the Cuban Anti-Slavery Committee, 1872.

Gates, Henry Louis Jr. *The Signifying Monkey: A Theory of Afro-American Literary Criticism.* Oxford: Oxford University Press, 1988.

Gentzler, Edwin. *Translation and Identity in the Americas: New Directions in Translation Theory.* London: Routledge, 2008.

Giacomini, Sonia Maria. *Mulher e escrava: Uma introdoção histórica ao estudo da mulher negra no Brasil.* Petrópolis: Vozes, 1988.

Gilroy, Paul. *The Black Atlantic: Modernity and Double Consciousness.* Cambridge: Harvard University Press, 1993.

Gomes, Flávio. *Palmares: Escravidão e liberdade no Atlântico sul.* São Paulo: Contexto, 2005.

González Mandri, Flora María. *Guarding Cultural Memory: Afro-Cuban Women in Literature and the Arts.* Charlottesville: University of Virginia Press, 2006.

Graham, Richard, ed. *The Idea of Race in Latin America, 1870–1940*. Austin: University of Texas Press, 1990.

Grandin, Greg. "AHR Forum: Your Americanism and Mine: Americanism and Anti-Americanism in the Americas." *American Historical Review* 111, no. 4 (2006): 45 pars. Accessed July 31, 2008, from http://www.historycooperative.org/journals/ahr/111.4/grandin.html.

Griggs, William C. "Settling: Migration of the McMullan Colonists and Evolution of the Colonies in Brazil." In Cyrus B. Dawsey and James M. Dawsey, eds. *The Confederados: Old South Immigrants in Brazil*. Tuscaloosa: University of Alabama Press, 1995. 50–65.

Grosby, Steven. *Biblical Ideas of Nationality: Ancient and Modern*. Winona Lake: Eisenbrauns, 2002.

Gualberto Gómez, Juan. "La cuestión de Cuba." *Por Cuba Libre*. Havana: Oficina del Historiador, 1954a. 153–214.

———. "Programa del Diario 'La Fraternidad:' Nuestros Propósitos." *Por Cuba Libre*. Havana: Oficina del Historiador, 1954b. 215–41.

Gussi, Alcides Fernando. *Os Norte-Americanos (Confederados) do Brasil: Identidades no contexto transnacional*. Campinas: CMU/Unicamp, 1997.

Hahn, Steven. *A Nation under Our Feet: Black Political Struggles in the Rural South from Slavery to the Great Migration*. Cambridge, Mass.: Harvard University Press, 2003.

Hahner, June E. *Emancipating the Female Sex: The Struggle for Women's Right's in Brazil, 1850–1940*. Durham, N.C.: Duke University Press, 1990.

Hanchard, Michael George. "Black Transnationalism, Africana Studies, and the 21st Century." *Journal of Black Studies* 35, no. 2 (Special Issue: Back to the Future of Civilization: Celebrating 30 Years of African American Studies) (November 2004): 139–53.

Handley, George B. *Postslavery Literatures in the Americas: Family Portraits in Black and White*. Charlottesville: University Press of Virginia, 2000.

Harper, Frances Ellen Watkins. "A Factor in Human Progress." In Frances Smith Foster, ed. *A Brighter Coming Day: A Frances Ellen Watkins Harper Reader*. New York: Feminist Press, 1990a: 275–80.

———. "A Private Meeting with the Women." In Frances Smith Foster, ed. *A Brighter Coming Day: A Frances Ellen Watkins Harper Reader*. New York: Feminist Press, 1990b: 127–28.

———. "Could We Trace the Record of Every Human Heart" *National Anti-Slavery Standard*, May 23, 1857a: 3.

———. *Poems*. Philadelphia: Merrihew, 1857b.

———. "The Great Problem to Be Solved." In Frances Smith Foster, ed. *A Brighter Coming Day: A Frances Ellen Watkins Harper Reader*. New York: Feminist Press, 1990c. 219–22.

———. "The Women's Christian Temperance Union and the Colored Woman." In Frances Smith Foster, ed. *A Brighter Coming Day: A Frances Ellen Watkins Harper Reader*. New York: Feminist Press, 1990d. 281.

Harper, Phillip Brian. "Nationalism and Social Division in Black Arts Poetry of the 1960s." *Critical Inquiry* 19 (winter 1993): 234–55.

Harris, Marvin D. "Racial Identity in Brazil." *Luso-Brazilian Review* 1, no. 2 (wwinter 1964): 21–28.

Harter, Eugene C. *The Lost Colony of the Confederacy*. Jackson: University Press of Mississippi, 1985.

Hartman, Saidiya V. *Scenes of Subjugation: Terror, Slavery, and Self-Making in Nineteenth Century America*. New York: Oxford University Press, 1997.

Hegel, Georg Wilhelm Friedrich. *Lectures on the Philosophy of World History Introduction: Reason in History*. Trans. H. B. Nisbet. Cambridge: Cambridge University Press, 1975.

Helg, Aline. *Our Rightful Share: The Afro-Cuban Struggle for Equality, 1886–1912*. Chapel Hill: University of North Carolina Press, 1995.

Hewitt, Nancy A. *Southern Discomfort: Women's Activism in Tampa, Florida, 1880s–1920s*. Urbana: University Press of Illinois, 2001.

Higginbotham, Evelyn Brooks. "African-American Women's History and the Metalanguage of Race." *Signs* 27, no. 2 (winter 1992): 252–74.

Hill, Patricia L. "'Let Me Make the Songs for the People': A Study of Frances Watkins Harper's Poetry." *Black American Literature Forum* 15, no. 2 (1981): 60–65.

Hofstadter, Richard. *America at 1750: A Social Portrait*. New York: Knopf, 1971.

hooks, bell. *Ain't I a Woman: Black Women and Feminism*. Boston: South End, 1981.

Howard, Philip A. *Changing History: Afro Cuban Cabildos and Societies of Color in the Nineteenth Century*. Baton Rouge: Louisiana State University Press, 1998.

Johnson, James Weldon. *The Book of American Negro Poetry*. 1922; New York: Harcourt, 1958.

Johnson, Walter. "Time and Revolution in African America: Temporality and the History of Atlantic Slavery." In Thomas Bender, ed. *Rethinking American History in a Global Age*. Berkeley: University of California Press, 2002. 148–67.

Jones de Olivera, Kimberly F. "The Politics of Culture of the Culture of Politics: Afro-Brazilian Mobilization, 1920–1968." *Journal of Third World Studies* 20, no. 1 (2003): 103–20.

Kaplan, Amy. *The Anarchy of Empire in the Making of U.S. Culture*. Cambridge, Mass.: Harvard University Press, 2002.

Kelley, Robin D. G. "'But a Local Phase of a World Problem': Black History's Global Vision, 1998–1950." *Journal of American History* (The Nation and Beyond: Transnational Perspectives on United States History: A Special Issue) 86, no. 3 (December 1999): 1045–77.

King, Joyce E. "Perceiving Reality in a New Way: Rethinking the Black White Duality of Our Time." In Anthony Bogues, ed. *After Man Towards the Human: Critical Essays on Sylvia Wynter*. Kingston: Ian Randle, 2006. 25–56.

Kirkpatrick, Gwen. "Romantic Poetry in Latin America." In Angela Esterhammer, ed. *Romantic Poetry*. Amsterdam: John Benjamins, 2002. 401–16.

Kittleson, Roger A. "Women and Notions of Womanhood in Brazilian Abolitionism." In Pamela Scully and Diane Paton, eds. *Gender and Slave Emancipation in the Atlantic World*. Durham, N.C.: Duke University Press, 2005. 99–120.

Knies, Kenneth Danziger. "Idea of Post-European Science: An Essay on Phenomenology and Africana Studies" In Lewis Gordon and Jane Anna Gordon, eds. *Not Only the Master's Tools: African-American Studies in Theory and Practice*. Boulder, Colo.: Paradigm, 2006. 85–106.

Kutzinski, Vera. "Fearful Asymmetries: Langston Hughes, Nicolás Guillén, and Cuba Libre." *Diacritics* 34, no. 3/4 (fall–winter 2004): 112–42.

Lane, Jill. *Blackface Cuba 1840–1895*. Philadelphia: University of Pennsylvania Press, 2005.

Levander, Caroline F., and Robert S. Levine. "Introduction: Hemispheric American Literary History." *American Literary History* 18, no. 3 (2006): 397–405.

Lucinda, Elisa. *O semelhante*, 6th ed. Rio de Janeiro: Record, 2007. 86.

Luis, William, ed. *Juan Francisco Manzano: Autobiografía del esclavo poeta y otros escritos*. Madrid: Iberoamericana, 2007.

Maceo, Antonio. "A Los Cubanos de Color." In Isabel Monal and Olivia Miranda, eds. *Pensamiento cubano: Siglo XIX*. Havana: Ciencias Sociales, 2002a. 50.

———. "Carta al General José Lamothe." In Isabel Monal and Olivia Miranda, eds. *Pensamiento cubano: Siglo XIX*. Havana: Ciencias Sociales, 2002b: 48–49.

———. "Proclama ¡Viva Cuba Independiente! [1879]." In Isabel Monal and Olivia Miranda, eds. *Pensamiento cubano: Siglo XIX*. Havana: Ciencias Sociales, 2002c. 46–47.

Madhubuti, Haki. "Toward a Definition: Black Poetry of the Sixties (After LeRoi Jones)." *Within the Circle: An Anthology of African American Literary Criticism from the Harlem Renaissance to the Present*. Durham, N.C.: Duke University Press, 1994. 213–23.

Mansbridge, Jane. "Everyday Talk in the Deliberative System." In Stephen Macedo, ed. *Deliberative Politics: Essays on Democracy and Disagreement*. Oxford: Oxford University Press, 1999. 211–42.

Martí, José. "Nuestra América." In María Cristina Eduardo, ed. *Nuestra América*. Havana: Abril, 2001. 17–28.

Martínez-Echazabal, Lourdes. "Mestizaje and the Discourse of National/Cultural Identity in Latin America, 1845–1959." *Latin American Perspectives. Race and National Identity in the Americas* 25, no. 3 (May 1998): 21–42.

Marx, Anthony W. *Making Race and Nation: A Comparison of South Africa, the United States, and Brazil*. Cambridge: Cambridge University Press, 1998.

Mason, Julian D, ed. *The Poems of Phillis Wheatley*. Chapel Hill: University of North Carolina Press, 1989.

Matamoros, Mercedes. "Esclavitud." In Cira Romero, ed. *Mi desposado, el Viento: Antología poética*. Havana: Letras Cubanas, 2006. 80–81.

Matory, J. Lorand. *Black Atlantic Religion: Tradition, Transnationalism and Matriarchy in the Afro-Brazilian Candomblé*. Princeton, N.J.: Princeton University Press, 2005.

———. "Free to Be a Slave: Slavery as Metaphor in the Afro-Atlantic Religions." *Journal of Religion in Africa* 37 (2007): 398–425.

Maultsby, Portia K. "The Use and Performance of Hymnody, Spirituals, and Gospels in the Black Church." In James Abbington, ed. *Readings in African American Church Music and Worship*. Chicago: GIA, 2001. 77–98.

Mays, Benjamin E. *The Negro's God: As Reflected in His Literature*. New York: Negro University Press, 1938.

M'Baye, Babacar. *The Trickster Comes West: Pan-African Influence in Early Black Diasporan Narratives*. Jackson: University Press of Mississippi, 2009.

Méndez Ródenas, Adriana. *Gender and Nationalism in Colonial Cuba: The Travels of Santa Cruz y Montalvo, Condensa de Merlin*. Nashville: Vanderbilt University Press, 1998.

Mirabal, Nancy Raquel. "Telling Silences and Making Community: Afro-Cubans and African-Americans in Ybor City and Tampa, 1899–1915." In Lisa Brock and Digna Castañeda Fuertes, eds. *Between Race and Empire: African-Americans and Cubans before the Cuban Revolution*. Philadelphia: Temple University Press, 1998. 49–69.

Montejo Arrechea, Carmen. "*Minerva*: A Magazine for Women (and Men) of Color." In Lisa Brock and Digna Castañeda Fuertes, eds. *Between Race and Empire: African-Americans and Cubans before the Cuban Revolution*. Philadelphia: Temple University Press, 1998: 33–48.

Montenegro, Abelardo F. *Cruz e Sousa e o Movimento Simbolista no Brasil*. Fortaleza: UFC, 1998.

Morán, Francisco, ed. *Island of My Hunger: Cuban Poetry Today*. San Francisco: City Lights, 2007.

Morejón, Nancy. "La Belleza en Todas Partes." *Cuerda Veloz: Antología Poética 1962–1992*. Havana: Letras Cubanas, 2002a.

———. *Cuerda Veloz: Antología Poética 1962–1992*. La Habana: Editorial, 2002b.

———. "Prólogo." In Excilia Saldaña. *In the Vortex of the Cyclone: Selected Poems by Excilia Saldaña*. Ed. Flora M. González Mandri and Rosamond Rosenmeier. Gainesville: University Press of Florida, 2002c. ix–xiii.

———. "Race and Nation." In Pedro Pérez Sarduy and Jean Stubbs, eds. *AfroCuba: An Anthology of Cuban Writing on Race, Politics and Culture*. Melbourne: Ocean Press, 1993. 227–37.

Morrison, Toni. *Playing in the Dark: Whiteness and the Literary Imagination*. New York: Vintage, 1993.

Morúa Delgado, Martín. "Ideario de Morúa." Leopoldo Horrego Estuch. *Martín Morúa Delgado Vida y Mensaje*. Habava: Sánchez, 1957.

Mouralis, Bernard. "*Présence Africaine*: Geography of an 'Ideology.'" In V. Y. Mudimbe, ed. *The Surreptitious Speech: Présence Africaine and the Politics of Otherness 1947–1987*. Chicago: University of Chicago Press, 1992. 3–13.

Mullen, Edward J. *Afro-Cuban Literature: Critical Junctures*. Westport, Conn.: Greenwood, 1998.

Muzart, Zahidé. "Entre quadrinhas e santinhos: A poesia de Auta de Souza." *Revista Travessia*, Florianópolis, UFSC, no. 23, segundo semestre, 1991. 149–53.

Nabuco, Joaquim. *O Abolicionismo*, 5th ed. Petrópolis: Vozes, 1988.

Nascimento, Abdias do. "Quilombismo: An Afro-Brazilian Political Alternative." *Journal of Black Studies* 2, no. 2 (1980): 141–78.

Nascimento, Elisa Larkin. *The Sorcery of Color: Identity, Race and Gender in Brazil*. Philadelphia: Temple University Press, 2007.

Neal, Larry. "The Black Arts Movement." *Drama Review*. Black Theatre. 12, no. 4 (summer 1968): 29–39.

Nishida, Meiko. *Slavery and Identity: Ethnicity, Gender, and Race in Salvador, Brazil, 1808–1888*. Bloomington: Indiana University Press, 2003.

O'Grady de Paiva, Jorge. *Auta de Souza e o Lirismo Romântico e Cristão de Sua Poesia*. Rio de Janeiro: Companhia Brasileira de Artes Gráficas, 1972.

Ojaide, Tanure. *Poetic Imagination in Black Africa: Essays on African Poetry*. Durham, N.C.: Carolina Academic Press, 1996.

Oliveira Gonçalves, Luiz Alberto. "De Preto a Afro-descendente: Da Cor da Pele â Categoria Científica." In Lúcia Maria de Assunção Barbosa [et al.], ed. *De Preto a Afro-descendente: Trajetos de pesquisa sobre o negro, cultura negra e relações étnico-racias no Brasil*. São Carlos: EdUFSCar, 2003.

Ortiz, Fernando. *Contrapunto cubano del tabaco y el azúcar*. Caracas: Biblioteca Ayacucho, 1987.

———. *Martí y las razas*. Havana: Monumento de Martí, 1953.

Orwell, George. "Why I Write." *Why I Write*. New York: Penguin, 1984. 1–10.

Painter, Nell. "Voices of Suffrage Sojourner Truth, Frances Watkins Harper, and the Struggle for Woman Suffrage." In Jean H. Baker, ed. *Votes for Women: The Struggle for Suffrage Revisited*. Oxford: Oxford University Press, 2002. 42–55.

Patrocínio, José do. *Campanha abolicionista: Coletânea de artigos*. Rio de Janeiro: Fundación Biblioteca Nacional, 1996.

Patterson, Orlando. *Freedom in the Making of Western Culture*. London: Basic Books, 1991.

Pérez Cano, Tania, ed. *Alejo Carpentier*. Havana: Fondo Editorial Casa de las Américas, 2004.

Pérez Sarduy, Pedro, and Jean Stubbs, eds. *Afro-Cuban Voices: On Race and Identity in Contemporary Cuba*. Gainesville: University Press of Florida, 2000.

Pisarz-Ramírez, Gabriel. "Precursors of Hemispheric Writing." In Kevin Concannon [etal.], ed. *Imagined Transnationalism: U.S. Latino/a Literature, Culture, and Identity*. New York: Palgrave Macmillan, 2009. 95–115.

Pool, Rosey E. *Beyond the Blues: New Poems by American Negroes*. Kent: Hand and Flower, 1962.

Prados-Torreira, Teresa. *Mambisas: Rebel Women in 19th Century Cuba*. Gainesville: University Press of Florida, 2005.
Price, Richard, ed. *Maroon Societies: Rebel Slave Communities in the Americas*, 3rd ed. Baltimore, Md.: Johns Hopkins University Press, 1996.
Queirós Mattosso, Katia M. de. *To Be a Slave in Brazil: 1550–1888*. Trans. Arthur Goldhammer. New Brunswick, N.J.: Rutgers University Press, 1986.
Quilombhoje. *Cadernos Negros: Os Melhores Poemas*. São Paulo: Quilombhoje, 1998.
Raboteau, Albert J. *Slave Religion: the "Invisible Institution" in the Antebellum South*. New York: Oxford University Press, 1978.
Ribeiro, Esmeralda. *Cadernos Negros. No. 9 Poemas*. São Paulo, 1986.
Rodrigues, Raimundo Nina. *Os africanos no Brasil*. São Paulo: Companhia Editora Nacional; Brasília: Universidade de Brasília, 1982.
Rojas, Rafael. *Essays in Cuban Intellectual History*. New York: Palgrave Macmillan, 2008.
Said, Edward W. "Introduction to Orientalism." In Moustafa Bayoumi and Andrew Rubin, eds. *The Edward Said Reader*. New York: Vintage, 2000. 67–113.
———. *Orientalism*. New York: Vintage, 1978.
Saldaña, Excilia. "Mi Fiel." In Flora M. González Mandri and Rosamond Rosenmeier, eds. *In the Vortex of the Cyclone: Selected Poems by Excilia Saldaña*. Gainesville: University Press of Florida, 2002. 58–78.
Sanchez, Sonia, *I've Been a Woman: New and Selected Poems*. Chicago: Third World, 1985.
Santos, Thereza. "Criar." *Cadenos Negros* 4 (1981): 5–6.
Sarup, Madan. *Introductory Guide to Poststructuralism and Postmodernism*. Athens: University of Georgia Press, 1993.
Saussure, Ferdinand de. *Course in General Linguistics*. Trans. Wade Baskin. Fontana: Collins, 1974.
Scott, Rebecca J. *Slave Emancipation in Cuba: The Transition to Free Labor, 1860–1899*. Princeton, N.J.: Princeton University Press, 1985.
Scully, Pamela, and Diane Paton, eds. *Gender and Slave Emancipation in the Atlantic World*. Durham, N.C.: Duke University Press, 2005.
Silva, Luiz. "Introdução." *Cadernos Negros: Os melhores poemas*. São Paulo: Quilombhoje, 1998. 19–21.
Silva Souza, Florentina da. *Afro-descendência em Cadernos negros e Jornal do MNU*. Belo Horizonte: Autêntica, 2005.
Sizer, Lyde Cullen. *The Political Work of Northern Women Writers and the Civil War, 1850–1872*. Chapel Hill: University of North Carolina Press, 2000.
Smethurst, James Edward. *The Black Arts Movement: Literary Nationalism in the 1960s and 1970s*. Chapel Hill: University of North Carolina Press, 2005.
Smith, David Lionel. "The Black Arts Movement and Its Critics." *American Literary History* 3, no. 1 (spring 1991): 93–110.
Smith, Susan Harris, and Melanie Dawson, eds. *The American 1890s: A Cultural Reader*. Durham, N.C.: Duke University Press, 2000.
Sollors, Werner. *Beyond Ethnicity: Consent and Descent in American Culture*. New York: Oxford University Press, 1986.
———. *Neither Black nor White yet Both*. New York: Oxford University Press, 1997.
Sommer, Doris. *Foundational Fictions: the Nacional Romances of Latin America*. Berkeley: University of California Press, 1991.
Souza, Auta de. *Horto*. Natal: UFRN, 2001.
Sterling, Cheryl. "Blackness Re-Visited and Re-Visioned in the Works of the Black Arts Movement and Quilombhoje." In Niyi Alfolabi [et al.], ed. *The Afro-Brazilian Mind: Contemporary Literature and Cultural Criticism*. Trenton: Africa World, 2007. 45–66.

Still, William. *The Underground Rail Road*. Philadelphia: Porters, 1872.
Stoner, K. Lynn. *From the House to the Streets: The Cuban Woman's Movement for Legal Reform, 1898–1940*. Durham, N.C.: Duke Univerisiy Press, 1991.
Stowe, Harriet Beecher. *Uncle Tom's Cabin*. Cambridge: Riverside, 1851.
Strickrodt, Silke. "'Afro-Brazilians' of the Western Slave Coast in the Nineteenth Century." In José C. Curto and Paul E. Lovejoy, eds. *Enslaving Connections; Changing Cultures of Africa and Brazil during the Era of Slavery*. Amherst, Mass.: Humanity, 2004. 213–44.
Takaki, Ronald. *Iron Cages: Race and Culture in 19th-Century America*. New York: Oxford University Press, 1990.
Tannenbaum, Frank. *Slave and Citizen; the Negro in the Americas*. New York: Random House, [1963?]1946.
Tarragó, Rafael E. *La Libertad de Escoger: Poetas Afrocubanos*. Madrid: Orto, 2006.
Telles, Edward E. *Race in Another America: The Significance of Skin Color in Brazil*. Princeton, N.J.: Princeton University Press, 2004.
Tocqueville, Alexis de. *Democracy in America*. Trans. Stephen D. Grant. Indianapolis: Hackett, 2000.
Villaverde, Cirilio. *Cecilia Valdés; novela de costumbres cubanas*. Mexico: Porrúa, 1995.
Wade, Peter. "Rethinking Mestizaje: Ideology and Lived Experience." *Journal of Latin American Studies* 37 (2005): 239–57.
Walcott, Derek. "The Muse of History." In Alison Donnell and Sarah Lawson Welsh, eds. *The Routledge Reader in Caribbean Literature*. London: Routledge, 1996. 354–58.
Walzer, Michael. *Exodus and Revolution*. New York: Basic Books, 1985.
Wynter, Sylvia. "On How We Mistook the Map for the Territory, and Re-Imprisoned Ourselves in our Unbearable Wrongness of Being, of Désêtre: Black Studies toward the Human Project." In Lewis Gordon and Jane Anna Gordon, eds. *Not Only the Master's Tools: African-American Studies in Theory and Practice*. Boulder, Colo.: Paradigm, 2006. 107–20.

INDEX

abolition of slavery, 13–14, 118, 123–24
   in the Americas, 39, 105
   in Brazil, 104, 110–13, 116
   in Cuba, 15, 31–32, 70–71, 120
   feminization of, 111
   postabolition, 25–29, 72, 76–77, 81, 104–6, 113, 116
   as symbolic event, 80
   transtextual critique of, 23
Adorno, Theodor W., 10
African American literature. *See* black literature
African Americans, 125
   Americanizing, 73
   congregational participation of, 81
   exodus as a metaphor, 62, 64–66
   identity of, 43–44, 125
   modernism, 162*n*5
   racial violence and disenfranchisement of, 50
   relationship with afrodescendentes, 58
   spirituality of, 60
   struggle for freedom and equal rights, 43, 51
      during post-Reconstruction era, 56
Afro-Atlantic dialogue, 121

Afro-Brazilian literature, 35, 98, 99, 113, 116, 120–21, 139–40, 142, 143
"Afro-Cuban," 9
Afro-Cuban Independentista army, 49
Afrocubanismo, 32
afrodescendente literature, 5, 7, 9, 11, 12–13, 25, 39, 114, 117, 121–47
   political work of women's writing, 127–31
   territorial transgressions in, 144–47
   transnational movements in, 114, 131–44
afrodescendentes, 12–13, 43
   relationship with African Americans, 58
Afro-Latin view of slavery, 125 (*see also* slavery)
alcatraz, 133
allegory, 4, 24, 60, 62, 67, 75, 86, 88, 91, 93, 117
Allen, Bishop Richard, 81
alterity, 11
Altunaga, Eliseo, 9
Alves, Castro, 160*n*4
Alves, Miriam, 35, 96–97, 112, 162*n*8
American Civil War, 55, 66, 124
American Revolution, 66, 68

Americas, the, 11 (*see also* United States)
  abolition in, 39, 105
  black resistance in, 45
  pan-American space of, 137
  poetic representation, history of, 11–12
  transhemispheric space of, 136–37
  translation and identity in, 6
  transnational interchanges, existence of, 121
  transnational movements in afrodescendente poetry of, 131–44
"Américas negras" (black Americas), 134
ancestry, 12, 98, 116, 121, 128 (*see also* descent)
  African, 35, 58, 99, 129
  -based symbology, 115
  European, 159*n*9
  racial, 10
Anderson, Benedict, 150*n*5
Anglo-African American view of slavery, 125 (*see also* slavery)
apólogo, 89
aracialism, 145
Arrechea, Carmen Montejo, 154*n*2
Ayala, Cristina, 3, 4, 10, 13, 20, 25–33, 115–17, 120, 121, 125–28, 132, 159*n*13
  "A la Santísima Virgen María" (To the Most Holy Virgin Mary), 31
  "A Las Víctimas de Andalucía" (To the Victims of Andalucía), 33
  "A mi raza" (To My Race), 33, 75–80, 94, 117, 130
  "Al Culto Periodista Ramon Vasconcelos," 29
  "Al valle de Güines" (To the Valley of Güines), 26
  "Antonio Maceo, 118–19
  "Canto a la Raza Española" (Song to the Spanish Race), 32–33
  "Contestación," 151*n*12
  "Corona al Genio," 32
  "El arroyuelo y la flor" (The Stream and the Flower), 87–94, 117, 130
  "En la Pasión y Muerte de Nuestro Señor Jesucristo" (In the Passion and Death of Our Lord Jesus Christ), 30
  "En la Pasión" (In the Passion), 30
  "Fifteenth Amendment," 83–84
  "Himno a María al Pie de la Cruz" (Hymn to Mary at the Foot of the Cross), 31
  "La Escuela" (School), 29
  "La Fatalidad" (Fate), 27
  "Lamento del Alma" (Lament of the Soul), 28
  "Me adhiero" (I Believe), 119
  "Mi Flor" (My Flower), 28–29
  Morejón, Nancy and, 60
  Ofrendas Mayabequinas, 26, 152*n*23
  "Nuestra América" (Our America), 79
  "Pensamientos" (Thoughts), 27
  "Plegaria ante Cristo crucificado" (Prayer before the Crucified Christ), 30–31, 155*n*10
  "Redención" (Redemption), 25, 33, 60, 61, 67–72, 116, 117, 130
  "Una Rosa después del baile" (A Rose after the Dance), 27–28

balacobaco, 162*n*7
Baldwin, James, 141
Bambara, Toni Cade, 3
baptism, 101, 102, 158
Baraka, Amiri, 44–45, 136–37
  "Cuba Libre," 137
  "Myth of 'Negro Literature, The," 136–37
Barbosa, Domingos Caldas, 160*n*4
Barnstone, Willis, 7, 10
Bastide, Roger, 152*n*19
Beckles, Hilary M., 128–29
Bell, James Madison
  "Triumph of Liberty, The," 78–79
Benston, Kimberly, 162*n*5
Bercovitch, Sacvan, 155*n*7
Bernd, Zilá, 34–35
Bhahba, Homi, 6, 125, 144
  Nation and Narration, 144
Biblical exodus, victory over slavery through, 18, 39, 60–65, 68, 115–16
black(ness), 9, 58, 78, 113, 122, 134, 136, 162*n*7
  ancestry, 99
  intellectualism, 120
  internationalism, 124
  resistance, mythology of, 44–49
Black Arts Movement (BAM), 44–45, 135–37
Black Brazilian Front, 162*n*10
"black codes," 154*n*1

black literature, 4–5, 9–10, 35, 42, 58, 60, 116, 119, 120, 132, 153n4, 162n5
Black Power movement, 135, 136
blank wilderness, 118
Boggs, Colleen Glennes, 6
bondage and freedom, 101, 103, 109, 113
Boucicault, Dion, 78
  Octoroon, The, 78
"Brasil livre," 104, 109
Brazil, 4, 43, 44–49, 58, 97, 123–24, 125, 139, 147
  abolitionism, 104, 110, 158nn1, 5, 159n10
  africanization of, 123, 138
  Black Brazilian Front, 162n10
  black literature in, 35
  black resistance in, 44–49
  flight in, 99
  Frente Negra Brasileira (FNB), 160n4, 162n10
  gender discourse in, 110–12
  identity of, 109
  Movimento Negro in, 139, 160n4
  postabolition, 116
  Quilombhoje in, 135, 139, 140–43
  racial democracy in, 8
  sexual corruption in, 129
  vs. United States, nation concept, 146
  womanhood in, 113
Brickhouse, Anna, 126, 152n22
"Bronze Muse," 49–57
"Bronze Titan," 49–57
Brooks, Gwendolyn, 132
Brown, James, 136
Byron, Lord, 120

Callahan, Allen Dwight, 54, 65, 153n4
call-and-response, 83
Candomblé, 160n6
Carpentier, Alejo, 3, 149–50n3
  perspective of African slavery, 5–6
Cascudo, Luis da Camara
  on de Souza, Auta, 35
Castellón, Manuel, 141
Castillo, Debra, 129
Catholicism, 31, 116
Cecilia (*Cecilia Valdés*), 92, 146
Cespedes, Africa
  on Cuban independence, 94–95
Chole, Aunt (*Uncle Tom's Cabin*), 22–23, 24

Christianity, 22, 31
  freedom and, 53–54
Clark, Kathleen Ann, 50
community(ies)
  imagined racial, 33, 40, 66, 76, 77, 117, 143–44
comparative literature, 3–6, 10
Conspiración de la Escalera (Ladder Conspiracy), 15, 17
Cooper, Anna Julia, 128
Cortez, Jayne, 139
  "Guitars I Used to Know, The," 139
Crummell, Alexander, 75
Cruz e Sousa, João da, 103, 160n4
  "Cárcere das Almas" (Prison of Souls), 103, 104
Cuba, 4, 43, 49–57, 60–61, 67–72, 73, 75–80, 87–94, 145–46
  Jim Crow system in, 50
  post -and pre-slavery, 76
  postabolitionism in, 145
  race in, 8–10, 31, 157n2
  religious support for slavery, 71
  struggle for independence, 71, 72, 73, 92–94, 116, 123, 145, 146, 155n11, 157n2
Cuba Libre, 51, 56, 58, 92
cubanidad, 9, 145
Cuban Revolution, 137
"Cuba y su gente" (Cuba and Its People), 75
Cult of the Virgin Mary, 158n8
culture, 124, 132
  mixing, 8–9, 138
Cunard, Nancy
  Negro, 5

Davies, Carole Boyce, 75, 160n4
Dawson, Melanie, 66
de Assis, Machado, 152n20, 153n2
death and freedom, 44–49, 54, 97, 100, 102, 105, 116, 118
de Azevedo, Celia Maria Marinho, 147
décimas, 17–18
Degler, Carl, 8
de Gobineau, Authur, 147
Delany, Martin, 75, 124
  Blake; or, The Huts of America, 124
Delazaria, Benedita, 140–41
  "Homenagem ao 'Quilombhoje'" (Homage to "Quilombhoje"), 140–41

Delgado, Morúa, 79–80, 157*n*4
de Paiva, Jorge O'Grady, 152*n*20
de Saussure, Ferdinand, 153*n*5
descent, 12, 20, 25, 33, 115, 116, 121 (*see also* ancestry)
de Sílva, Jônatas Conceição, 140
de Souza, Auta, 3, 4, 10, 13, 20, 34–39, 115, 116, 118, 121, 122, 125–28, 130, 132, 152*n*20, 159*n*13
  "Agnus Dei," 37
  "Fio Partido" (Broken Thread), 97, 99–105, 116, 118
  freedom and the literary reimagining of, 98–99
  "Melancolia" (Melancholy), 36
  "Minh'alma e o Verso," 98, 99, 105–13, 130
  "No Horto" (In the Garden), 37
  "Oraçáço da Noite" (Night Prayer), 38
  "Saudade" (Longing), 37
de Tocqueville, Alexis, 54
  on American nationalism, 54
Dias, Gonçalves, 152*n*20
diaspora, 11, 12, 25, 39, 40, 58, 120, 122, 126
didacticism, 152*n*23
Diop, Alioune, 132
Dodson, Jualynne E., 154*n*2
Douglass, Frederick, 83, 154*n*6
  on American nationalism, 54
Dred Scott v. Sandford (1857), 25, 46
Duarte, Eduardo de Assis, 35
Du Bois, W. E. B., 74, 75, 132
Duke, Dawn, 124
Dunbar, Paul Laurence, 152*n*2
Durham, Carolyn Richardson, 162*n*8

Eagleton, Terry, 149*n*1
Easton, David
  on political life, 127
education, 29, 157*n*4
emancipation, 21, 26, 40, 61, 65–67, 69, 70, 72, 74, 81, 116
empathy, 151*n*14
escape, modes of, in poetics of freedom, 94–113
Escobar, Ángel
  "Paráfrasis sencilla," 117–18
Evarista, Conceição, 97

Exodus, 59, 72, 73, 115, 117, 155*n*7
  in "Deliverance," 61–67

face-to-face dialogue, 121
fate, 27
femininity, 40, 111, 113 (*see also* women)
Ferrer, Ada, 92
flight and freedom, 94–113
Foster, Frances S., 128
Fragas, Maria Cristina. *See* Ayala, Cristina
Frederick Douglass' Paper, 124
freedom, 96
  bondage and, 101, 103, 109, 113
  as by-product of slavery's abolition, 48, 60–61, 75, 81–87, 92
  in death, 44–49, 54, 97, 100, 102, 105, 116, 118
  economic, 79
  flight and, 99–113
  hemispheric discourse of, 44, 98–99, 101
  national, 17, 43–44, 53, 55, 95
  as poetic process, 41, 79
  political, 44, 53
  postabolition, 25–29, 72, 104, 116
  postindependence, 25–29
  racial, 17, 52, 53, 68
  racial uplift and redemptive, 63–64
  social, 53
  through active resistance, 44–49, 54
  through self-sacrifice, 56
Free Womb Law, 158*n*6
French Symbolism, 98, 152*n*19
Frente Negra Brasileira (FNB), 160*n*4, 162*n*10
Freyre, Gilberto, 8, 139
Fugitive Slave Act, 25, 43

Gama, Luís, 160*n*4
Garnet, Henry Highland, 51, 75
Gates, Henry Louis, Jr., 126
gender, 5, 20, 87–94, 95, 110–12, 113, 127–31, 159*n*9
  -based symbology, 115
  identity, 41, 124, 125, 127, 129, 138 (*see also* identity(ies))
  role in nation-building, 74–95, 117
Gentzler, Edwin, 6, 7
  Translation and Identity in the Americas: New Directions in Translation Theory, 6

Gilroy, Paul, 44, 124
   Black Atlantic, The, 124
Gomes, Ana Laudelina Ferreira, 35–36, 96, 97–98
   Horto, 152*n*21
Gómez, Juan Gualberto, 31–32, 70, 79, 80
   "La Cuestión de Cuba en 1884," 79
   "Programa," 157*n*3
Gonçalves, Luiz Alberto Oliveira, 8
Great Awakening, 66
Griffith, D. W., 146
   Birth of a Nation, The, 146
Grosby, Steve, 66

Haitian Revolution of 1791, 52, 124, 161*n*1
Hanchard, Michael, 42, 125, 152*n*1
Handley, George B., 120
Harper, Frances, 3, 4, 10, 13, 20–25, 98, 99, 113, 115–18, 120, 121, 125–28, 132, 159*n*13
   "Bible Defense of Slavery," 24
   "Christ's Entry into Jerusalem," 24
   "Colored People in America, The`," 22
   "Death of Zombi," 24, 25, 43, 44–49, 54, 117
   "Deliverance," 60, 61–67, 72, 73, 116, 117, 130
   "'Do Not Cheer, Men Are Dying,' Said Capt. Phillip, in the Spanish American War," 24
   "Eliza Harris," 84–87, 94, 130
   "Learning to Read," 23
   "Maceo," 24, 43, 44, 49, 50, 118, 119
   "Moses: A Story of the Nile," 23
   "Our English Friends," 24
   Palmares, 45–47
   "Resurrection of Christ, The," 24
   "Room to Myself Is a Luxury, A," 21
   "Simon's Countrymen," 23–24
   "Slave Mother, The," 21–22
   "We Are Rising," 80–84, 94
Harper, Phillip Brian, 137
Harris, Eliza (*Uncle Tom's Cabin*), 84–87, 116
Harris, Marvin, 8
Hartman, Saidiya, 11, 105, 124
Hegel, Georg Wilhelm Friedrich
   Lectures on the Philosophy of World History, 150–51*n*9
Hewitt, Nancy, 154*n*2

Higginbotham, Evelyn Brooks, 127
   "African-American Women's History and the Metalan-guage of Race," 127
Higginbotham, Evelyn Brooks, 75
hispanophone, 13, 15
"historical impulse," 10, 122
Hofstadter, Richard, 66
Howard, Philip A., 156*n*15
Howe, Julia Ward, 82
   "Battle Hymn of the Republic, The," 82
hymns, 81, 82, 83

iconography, 4, 101, 105, 129
identity(ies), 39, 43–44
   cultural, 9
   gender, 41, 124, 125, 127, 129, 138
   group or collective, 9, 10, 94
   historical, 66
   individual, 9
   language, 109, 135, 139
   marker, 63
   national, 24, 29, 40, 44, 50, 58, 61, 66, 84, 145
   racial, 12, 29, 43–44, 58, 61, 129, 138
   and text, relationship between, 23
   in translation, 6, 24, 142–43
imagination, 13–14
imagined communities, 4, 5, 12, 45, 61, 63, 80, 144, 150*n*5 (*see also* community(ies))
Infante, Joaquín, 71
international laws, about slavery, 25
Isabel, Princess, 110–12
Israelites
   victory over slavery through biblical exodus, 18, 39, 60–65, 68, 116

Jakobson, Roman, 149*n*1

Jim Crow system, 50
Johnson, James Weldon, 5, 42–43, 152*n*2, 153*n*2
   Book of American Negro Poetry, 5, 42–43
Johnson, Walter, 11
Juana Inés de la Cruz, Sor, 120
Junior, Robert Daibert, 112

Kaplan, Amy, 50, 126
Kelley, Robin D. G., 120
Kesteloot, Lilyan
   Anthologie Négro-Africaine, 5

King, Joyce, 11
King, Martin Luther, Jr., 141
Kittleson, Roger A., 110, 159*n*10
knowledge, 23, 27
  nonpolitical, 127
Kutzinski, Vera, 9

Lamothe, José, 51, 146
language, 11, 12, 17, 66, 80, 83, 88, 114, 115, 122, 135, 147
  and identity, 137, 138–39
  poetic use of, 4, 149*n*1
  and political work, 128
La Verdad, 51
Levander, Caroline F., 42, 126
Levine, Robert S., 42
liberty, 51, 52, 69, 87, 92
  law of, 57
  life and, 66
  triumph of, 78–79
liminality, 11, 40, 85–87, 92
"literatura negra," 121, 160*n*4
Lucinda, Elisa, 142–43
  "Constatação" (Proof), 142–43

Maceo, Antonio, 4, 24, 43, 49–57, 70, 80, 116, 145, 154*n*1
  "A Los Cubanos de Color" (To Cubans of Color), 52
  death of, 53–56
Madhubuti, Haki, 137
Malcolm X, 141
mambisa, 93
Mansbridge, Jane
  on political life, 127, 161*n*3
Manzano, Juan Francisco, 13, 15–17, 153*n*2
  "La Esclava Ausente," 16–17
  "La Visión del Poeta. Compuesto en un Ingenio de fabricar azúcar" (Vision of the Poet Composed in a Sugar Factory), 15–16
  "Una hora de tristeza" (A Time of Sadness), 17
Marley, Bob, 59
Martí, José, 74, 145–46, 154*n*1, 157*n*2
martyrdom, 19, 28
Marx, Anthony W., 10, 125, 146–47
masculinity, 40, 89
Matamoros, Mercedes, 70
  "Esclavitud" (Slavery), 70

Matory, J. Lorand, 121, 160*n*6
  "Free to be a Slave," 125
Mattosso, Katia M. de Queirós, 104, 150*n*7
Mays, Benjamin E., 60
McKay, Claude, 132
  "Negro's Tragedy, The," 131
mestizaje, 8, 138
Michael Walzer, 155*n*7
Minerva: revista quincenal dedicada a la mujer de color (Minerva: The Bi-weekly Magazine for the Woman of Color), 26, 33, 118, 119, 120, 154*n*2, 159–60*n*3
Mirabal, Nancy Raquel, 154*n*2
miscegenation, 8, 9, 147 (*see also* transculturation)
modinhas, 34
Montenegro, Abelardo F., 105
Morán, Francisco
  on Escobar, Ángel, 117
Morejón, Nancy, 9, 132
  Ayala, Cristina and, 60
  In the Vortex of the Cyclone, 134
  "Mujer Negra" (Black Woman), 132–33
Morrison, Toni, 7, 114
  Beloved, 7
Moses, 63, 68
mother, 159*n*9
  slave, 21, 84–87
Movimento Negro Unificado, 160*n*4
mulatez. *See* mestizaje
Mullen, Edward J., 32
myth, 13, 78, 112
  of black resistance, 44–49
  of colonial discovery, 5–6
  messianic, 117
  of the nation, 144–47
  of women, 128

Nabuco, Joaquim, 123
  O Abolicionismo, 123, 158*n*1
Nascimento, Abdias do, 139
Nascimento, Elisa Larkin, 30, 113, 162*n*10
  on identity, 39
nation, the, 6, 42, 144, 150*n*5 (*see also* transnation)
  imperial power of, 43
  myth of, 144–47, 150*n*6
  race and, 9, 34
national freedom, 103

national identity, 145
nation-building, 115
   gender and, 87–94, 117
   role of women in, 24, 25, 31
nation-state, 5, 20
   racism and, 40, 73, 146
Neal, Larry, 135
   "Black Arts Movement, The," 135
negro, 131, 139
"Negro republic," 52, 145
Negro spirituals, 54, 60
New World, 4–6, 11–14, 25, 38, 41, 61, 63, 67, 72, 78, 114, 115, 120, 125–27, 129, 131–33, 150n3
   black consciousness, 58
   forced migration of Africans into, 42
   poetic imagining of freedom in, during abolition eras, 4, 13–14
   poetry of, 4
   transatlantic slavery in, 4
Nishida, Mieko, 162n8
nonpolitical knowledge, 127
North Star, The, 124

Old Testament, 62
O Philartista, 104
oppression, 18, 22, 28, 43, 49, 50, 52, 53, 57, 69, 72, 112, 118
Ortiz, Fernando, 8–9, 155n11, 156n14, 157n2
   Contrapunto cubano del tobaco y el azúcar (Cuban Counterpoint of Tobacco and Sugar), 155n11
Orwell, George, 10, 122
   "Why I Write," 127
"other" concept, 11
Our Lady of Lourdes, 105

Palmares, 45–47, 57, 139
Paton, Diane, 113
patriotism, 28–29
Patrocínio, José, 110
Patterson, Orlando
   on freedom, 74
Pereira, Edimilson de Almeida, 99, 143
   "Survey of African-Brazilian Literature," 99
Pernambuco, 45, 139
Pisarz-Ramírez, Gabriel, 145

Plácido, 13, 17–20, 28
   "Décima," 18–19
   "Despedida" (Farewell), 19–20
   "El Juramento" (The Vow), 19
   "En la Muerte de Jesucristo" (In the Death of Jesus Christ), 18
   "La Resurrección" (The Resurrection), 18
   "Plegaria a Dios" (Prayer to God), 17, 18
Plessy v. Ferguson (1896), 153–54n1
Poesia Negra Brasileira (Black Brazilian Poetry), 34–35
poetry
   didactic, 25, 40, 55, 80, 88, 95, 117, 130, 152n23
   lyric, 32, 34, 37, 81, 101, 107
   narrative, 60–67, 72, 73, 81, 83, 85, 87, 88, 93, 107–8, 115, 117, 134
   redemption songs and, 59–73
"political impulse," 10
political life, 127, 161n3
Pool, Rosey, 132
   Beyond the Blues: New Poems by American Negros, 132
Prados-Torreira, Teresa, 95
Présence Africaine, 131–32
promised land, 65, 66, 67, 73, 155n7
Pushkin, Alexander, 120

Quilombhoje, 135, 139, 140–43
Quilombismo, 139–40
   Cadernos Negros (Black Notebooks), 140, 141
quilombo, 45

Raboteau, Albert, 66
race(ism), 7, 8, 73, 77–78, 116, 117, 125, 159n13
   in Brazil, 8
   in Cuba, 9–10, 31, 157n2
   and gender, 80, 127, 128, 153n1
   nation-state and, 40, 73, 146
racial absolutism, 9
racial ancestry, 10 (*see also* ancestry)
racial community, 33, 40, 66, 76, 77, 117, 143–44 (*see also* community(ies))
racial demarcation, 127
racial democracy, 8, 9, 139
racial equality, 50
racial identity, 12, 29, 43–44, 58, 61, 129, 138 (*see also* identity(ies))

racial miscegenation, 147
racial ordering, 125
racial politics, 9, 121, 135
racial segregation or discrimination, 70, 147
racial slavery, 9, 39, 45, 51–52, 68, 117, 128
 (*see also* slavery)
racial solidarity, 79, 162*n*10
racial unity, 80
racial uplift, 25, 40, 60, 62, 75, 78–80, 84, 95, 117, 119, 120, 157*n*5
 in the Americas, 39, 105
 postabolition, 26, 81
 redemptive freedom and, 63–64
racial violence, 50, 57, 83
reading as translation, 7
redemption, 18, 30–31, 53, 55, 67, 72, 111, 118, 155*n*7
redentora, 112
religion, 54, 66
remembering, act of, 64–65
revolution, 52–53, 137
 American Revolution, 66
 Cuban Revolution, 137
 Haitian Revolution of 1791, 52, 124, 161*n*1
Ribeiro, Esmerelda, 134–35
Ródenas, Adriana Méndez, 129
Rodrigues, Raimundo Nina, 129–30, 147, 163*n*15
Rufino, Alzira, 137–39
 "Resgate" (Ransom), 137–39

Said, Edward, 127
 Orientalism, 127
Saldaña, Excilia, 133–34
salvation, 112
Sanchez, Sonia, 135–36
Santos, Thereza, 141–42
Sarduy, Pedro Pérez, 9
Scott, Dred, 45, 49
Scott, Rebecca J., 70
Scrotton, S. R., 51
Scully, Pamela, 113
self, 11, 40, 139, 144
 free, 14
semiotic–literary relationship, between slavery and freedom, 5
Silva, Luiz ("Cuti"), 141
Sizer, Lyde
 on women's political work, 127

slavery, 5–6
 abolition of (*see* abolition of slavery)
 Afro-Latin view of, 125
 Anglo-African American view of, 125
 definition of, 4
 freedom and, 48, 60–61, 75, 81–87, 92
 international laws related to, 25
 oppression of, 18, 22, 28, 43, 50, 52, 57, 69, 72, 112
 racial, 9, 39, 45, 51–52, 68, 117, 128
 stain of, 69, 79, 85, 87, 157*n*5
 transatlantic, 4, 6, 11, 12, 50, 58, 126, 132
 transhemispheric, 11, 12
 victory over, through biblical exodus, 18, 39, 60–65, 68, 115–16
slavery-to-freedom narrative, of American history, 11–12
Smethurst, James Edward, 137
Smith, David Lionel, 137
Smith, Susan Harris, 66
Sollors, Werner, 78, 155*n*7
Sommer, Doris, 162–63*n*14
Sonia Fátima da Conceição
 "Branca História" (White History), 135
Souza, Florentina da Silva, 120
sovereignty, 43, 70, 73, 93
Soyinka, Wole, 141
Spanish-American War, 24, 50, 145–46
speech, 83, 127
stain of slavery, 69, 79, 85, 87, 157*n*5 (*see also* slavery)
Sterling, Cheryl, 135, 139
Stevens, Wallace, 3
Stowe, Harriet Beecher, 22, 84, 151*n*14
Stubbs, Jean, 9
symbolic freedom, 103
symbolism, 98–99

Tannenbaum, Frank, 8
 Slave and Citizen, 8
Teixeira e Sousa, Antônio Gonçalves, 152*n*19
Telles, Edward E., 8
Téllez, Calixto Castillo, 156*n*13
textuality, 114–15
"thrill of sorrow," 49–50
trafficking, 12, 25
transatlantic slavery, 4, 11, 12, 50, 114, 132, 133
transcendent dream, 16–17

transculturation, 8–9 (*see also* miscegenation)
transgression
   of physical body, 102
   territorial, 144–47
trans-hemispheric, 24, 33, 132
   of the Americas, 136–37
   slavery, 11, 12
   space, imagined, 46, 126, 135
   trafficking, 25
translation, 6–7, 11, 44
   reading as, 7
transnation, 6–12 (*see also* nation, the)
transnational imaginary, 132
transnationalism, 6–12, 33, 39, 43, 56, 114, 121, 124, 160*n*6
   afrodescendente literature, 131–44
Tribuna, A, 104
Turner, Henry McNeal, 75

Uncle Tom's Cabin, 22–23, 84, 151*n*14
United States, 50, 73, 120, 125
   abolitionism in, 23
   Black Arts Movement, 44–45, 135–37
   black codes in, 154*n*1
   black literature in, 4–5, 43, 132
   vs. Brazil, nation concept, 146
   racial democracy in, 8
   racial mixing in, 8
   racial uplift in, 75, 80
   during Reconstruction era, 124, 154*n*2
   slavery-to-freedom narrative history, 11–12
   whitening, 8, 36

Valdés, Gabriel de la Concepción. *See* Plácido
Vargas, Getúlio, 162*n*11

Vasconcelos, Ramon, 29
   "Palpitaciones de la raza" (Pulse of the Race of Color), 29
Ventura, Adão
   "Desencontro," 143
Villaverde, Cirilio
   Cecilia Valdés, 92, 146
Virgin Mary, 105, 116

Wade, Peter, 138
Walcott, Derek, 4, 5, 59
War of Independence, 94
Webster, Noah, 6
Wheatley, Phillis, 6, 13–15
   "America," 14–15
   "On Imagination," 13–14
   "On Recollection," 14
white female domesticity, 128
whitening, 8, 36, 71
white supremacy, 50
Whitman, Walt, 145
womanhood, 92–93, 113, 129, 159*n*9
   white woman as, 128
women, 28, 66, 95, 87–94, 95, 113, 159*nn*9, 10 (*see also* femininity)
   and abolitionism in Brazil, 110, 159*n*10
   afrodescendente writing, political work of, 127–31
   in Brazilian abolitionist movements, 110–12
   and Brazilian nationhood, 109
   myths about, 128–29
   and racial uplift, relationship, 75, 77–78
   role of, in nation, 24, 25, 31, 92–94, 130
writing, 29
Wynter, Sylvia, 57

Zumbi, 4, 24, 43, 44–49, 58, 149*n*2